Multicultural
Children's Literature

To the storytellers and story listeners in my life . . .
Thank you for passing on your love of literature.
A.G.

Multicultural A Critical Issues Approach
Children's Literature

Ambika Gopalakrishnan

California State University, Los Angeles

Los Angeles | London | New Delhi
Singapore | Washington DC

For information:

SAGE Publications, Inc.
2455 Teller Road
Thousand Oaks, California 91320
E-mail: order@sagepub.com

SAGE Publications Ltd.
1 Oliver's Yard
55 City Road
London EC1Y 1SP
United Kingdom

SAGE Publications India Pvt. Ltd.
B 1/I 1 Mohan Cooperative Industrial Area
Mathura Road, New Delhi 110 044
India

SAGE Publications Asia-Pacific
Pte. Ltd.
33 Pekin Street #02-01
Far East Square
Singapore 048763

Printed in the United States of America

Library of Congress Cataloging-in-Publication Data

Gopalakrishnan, Ambika.
Multicultural children's literature : a critical issues approach/Ambika Gopalakrishnan; with contributions by Kimberly Persiani-Becker.
    p. cm.
Includes bibliographical references and index.
ISBN 978-1-4129-5522-5 (pbk.)
    1. Children's literature—History and criticism. 2. Multicultural education—United States. 3. Children's literature—Study and teaching—United States. 4. Young adult literature—History and criticism. 5. Multiculturalism in literature. I. Persiani-Becker, Kimberly. II. Title.

PN1009.5.M84G67 2011
809'.89282—dc22   2009043896

This book is printed on acid-free paper.

10 11 12 13 14   10 9 8 7 6 5 4 3 2 1

Acquisitions Editor:	Diane McDaniel
Editorial Assistant:	Ashley Conlon
Production Editor:	Carla Freeman
Typesetter:	C&M Digitals (P) Ltd.
Indexer:	Wendy Allex
Cover Designer:	Gail Buschman
Marketing Manager:	Carmel Schrire

Brief Contents

Detailed Contents

Preface

For the last few decades, children's literature has increasingly gained acceptance as a means to promote reading and literacy activities. Many teacher preparation programs across the country also have some components of children's literature in them, if not specially designed courses on multicultural children's literature. In response to these needs, in recent years there has been an explosion of textbooks on how to teach children's literature. For the most part, these texts follow an approach that either introduces teachers to children's books and genres or lightly touches on issues in relation to literacy and language arts activities. Although exemplary teachers in many fields have always used children's literature to address social issues, this has yet to become a trend in teacher preparation programs.

This book grew out of the need for a comprehensive book to prepare teachers to address social, cultural, and critical issues, through the use of multicultural children's books. Each chapter is based on practical discussions and activities that have been used in teaching such courses at our institution. The rich exchange that we have had between the very diverse groups of preservice and inservice teachers and college professors in our classes around issues and trends in children's literature informs this book.

Purpose

A critical issues approach is relevant and necessary for the politically charged times in which we live. Life situations that children across the country and the world face are no longer limited to differences in cultural aspects and understanding. Today's children face the same issues and conflicts that we as adults struggle to deal with: terrorism, violence, war, sexuality, politics, censorship, child labor, death, and so on. The goal of this book is to address these issues that concern children through literature that is written for them. Hence the main purpose of this book is to provide preservice and in-service teachers various methods to address difficult issues in their classrooms through the safety of multicultural children's literature.

Intended Audience

This text is specifically aimed at preservice and inservice teachers who may use it to initiate conversations around critical issues such as those mentioned earlier. It is also aimed at teacher-preparation programs in college classrooms, where it may be used as a core book in children's literature courses or as a supplemental text for literacy, reading, social studies, or multicultural education courses. Finally, librarians and parents may also find it useful in considering children's books for their collections.

Key Features

There are several key features of this book that distinguish it from other texts in the field.

A Critical Issues Approach

Multicultural educators have been iterating the need for more than just a *contributions approach* for some time now. A contributions approach focuses on holidays, food, festivals, and special months that are set aside to learn about occasions like Black History Month and so on (Au, 1993; Banks, 1999). However, authentic literature can be used for so much more than merely learning about genres, cultural differences, cultural aspects, and so on. As Fox and Short (2003) suggested, there are strong connections between multicultural children's literature and multicultural education in general. Authentic literature deals with similar issues that multicultural education deals with: power, race, class, authentic representation, and cultural authenticity, to name a few. In taking a critical issues approach, this book brings those topics into the classroom and helps teachers choose books for children that discuss difficult issues through a critical perspective.

A Sociocultural Approach to Multicultural Children's Literature

Most popular children's literature texts usually take one of two approaches to children's literature. One is a genre approach that introduces various genres like poetry, historical, realistic fiction, traditional literature, picture books, science fiction, and so on, in which multicultural children's literature is a separate chapter that looks at books across genres that have characters, events, and situations that pertain to race or ethnic differences. A second approach is when multicultural children's literature is included in a chapter on international and world literature that also looks at traditional tales from these ethnicities or nationalities. In this book, a broader view is taken that not only looks at race and ethnicity but also sociocultural elements that are inclusive. Although, this book has a separate chapter on multicultural children's literature, this chapter concentrates on the development of multicultural literature over the decades, drawing from a variety of educators and theorists of children's literature in order to situate the sociocultural aspects that are emphasized.

Sample Response Lessons

In order to help teachers (both novice and experienced) bring critical issues into the classroom, every chapter of this book has a detailed lesson plan that is geared to two different age ranges: primary and secondary. These sample response lessons are very detailed, giving teachers the freedom to either follow them exactly or tailor them to suit their classroom. The lessons are deliberately long so as to allow enough time for students to discuss and critically analyze the issue at hand. Teachers may choose to use parts of these lessons over 40- or 60-minute periods or use them as a week-long or longer theme. All of these lessons have been tried and tested in actual classrooms and some actual responses and discussions are also reported after the lessons, to show the depth of these response lessons.

Selective Annotated Bibliography

At the end of each chapter, there is a selective annotated bibliography that is organized by and pertains to each chapter's issue. This annotated bibliography is not exhaustive; rather it is a sample of exemplary books that deal with the issue. Following these examples, readers may choose books that pertain to the issue that is discussed in the chapter.

Engaging and Easy to Read Style

This book is written in a very conversational and engaging style rather than in an instructional tone. Every chapter has the following parts:

- A brief overview of the chapter issue
- A discussion of why the issue is important
- Current and updated research on the issue
- The uses of the issue for discussion with children
- The various stereotypes surrounding the issue
- Current trends surrounding children's literature in that issue

Reflective Questions for Teachers

In addition to the aforementioned elements of each chapter, every chapter also has a short reflective section specifically for teachers. Based on the premise that it is important to approach critical issues through a reflective practice, this section is fashioned as a list of questions that teachers may ask themselves before introducing the topic to their students. By engaging in a reflection of what they feel about the issues discussed, these questions may help teachers reflect on their own choices and practices in the classroom. These questions may also help college instructors who teach preservice and in-service teachers in designing a course that looks at issues in depth.

Organization of the Text

This text is organized into three broad parts and each part has three or four chapters that deal with various issues. These parts and their corresponding chapters are as follows.

Part I: Taking a Critical Issues Approach

This part serves as an introduction to the rest of the book and contains three chapters: an introductory chapter on approaching multicultural children's literature through a critical issues approach, a chapter describing and discussing the essentials and foundations of multicultural children's literature, and a chapter on choosing books and reading critically. The introductory chapter sets the tone for the rest of the chapters by looking at the role of children's literature in schools today and by describing what critical literacy is in the context of its use in this book. This first chapter also gives a brief description of how to plan lessons across the curriculum with a critical issues approach. The second chapter goes into the details of multicultural children's literature in the context of this book and provides a broad discussion of issues that relate to multicultural children's literature, such as cultural authenticity, validation, representation, and so on. The third chapter provides a detailed description of transactional theory that is useful and fundamental to reader responses and a critical issues approach. This chapter has a very detailed section on questioning, which is fundamental to critical issues.

Part II: Exploring Issues in Multicultural Children's Literature

This part picks issues that are not immediately apparent in relation to multicultural children's literature, yet most books that relate to these issues may be considered multicultural. In keeping with a sociocultural approach to multicultural children's literature, the chapters in this part explore issues such as censorship, gender, and violence. Chapter 4 provides an in-depth discussion of censorship, its effects and legalities, and gives several examples of books that were censored for not being from a mainstream culture. This chapter also gives teachers many tools and samples to deal with censorship in their own classrooms. Chapter 5 discusses gender issues, sexuality, and equity related to multicultural children's literature. Chapter 6 looks at violence and discusses the difficulties in understanding or justifying violence.

Part III: Realities in Life and Multicultural Children's Literature

The four chapters in this part are based on the realities that many children in the world face on a daily basis but that may not always be discussed in relation to multicultural children's literature. Chapter 7 discusses war, terrorism, justice, and freedom, topics that are difficult and sometimes abstract to many children and adults who live within the safety of North America. However, recent events have brought these topics into school and college classrooms, making it necessary to be prepared to not only discuss but also teach tolerance and sensitivity in relation to these. Chapter 8 discusses issues that are more personal in nature but nevertheless as devastating for children, like prejudice, bullying, abuse, and so on. Chapter 9 discusses disabilities and the special child, and Chapter 10 discusses digital literature. Although most would not consider a topic like digital age literature to relate in any way to multicultural children's literature, it is one of the foremost ways in which we can relate to international materials and books. Further, in today's world, one cannot afford to be lacking in digital knowledge, especially given the impact it has on books and reading.

REFERENCES

Au, K. (1993). *Literacy instruction in multicultural settings.* Forth Worth, TX: Harcourt Brace College Publishers.

Banks, J. (1999). *An introduction to multicultural education.* Boston: Allyn & Bacon.

Fox, D., & Short, K. (2003). (Eds.). *Stories matter: The complexity of cultural authenticity in children's literature.* Urbana, IL: National Council of Teachers of English.

Acknowledgments

Foremost, I would like to acknowledge and thank my colleague, Dr. Kimberly Persiani-Becker, who has contributed considerably to the development of this book. Dr. Persiani-Becker has not only researched and written early drafts of five of the chapters in this book, she also developed the template for the sample response lessons. The five chapters that she contributed to are listed in the brief contents section, and within the book, her name appears at the beginning of each chapter that she contributed to.

I would also like to thank my editor, Diane McDaniel, and her assistant, Ashley Conlon, from SAGE Publications, for their patience and comments in this sometimes laborious process. Further, I would like to thank Carla Freeman for her involvement during the production process.

I also want to thank the following reviewers who provided feedback on the prospectus and the draft reviews: Joyce Armstrong, King's College; Gina Boldman, Eastern Michigan University and Washtenaw Community College; Gayles Evans, Chicago State University; Kathy Fox, University of North Carolina at Wilmington; Marcella Kehus, University of Toledo; Cathy Kim, Muhlenberg College; Gail Taylor, Old Dominion University; Gayle Luck, Cornell University; Kathy Phillips, University of Nebraska, Lincoln; Lynda Robinson, Cameron University; Leah van Belle, The University of Michigan, Ann Arbor; Joy L. Wiggins, University of Texas at Arlington.

Finally, I would like to thank my husband and toddler son, away from whom I spent countless hours researching and redoing many drafts of the chapters. Without your smiles, kisses, and hugs at the end of each day, I would not have been able to complete this book.

PART I

TAKING A CRITICAL ISSUES APPROACH

Chapter 1

Introduction to Multicultural Children's Literature

A Critical Issues Approach

M any of our fondest memories of grade school are of those moments when we had fun while learning, the moments where we uncovered a certain concept or understood something suddenly or discovered that we could do something well. Especially selections from works written for children, called *children's literature*, afford us those moments, and they are quickly becoming an invaluable part of the curriculum of not only grade schools but also university classrooms that prepare teachers to teach. But what distinguishes children's literature for this unique job? While it is written for children and usually reflects children's experiences, in recent years this body of literature spans a range of topics that includes almost everything, even those previously considered unsuitable for children. This body of literature also aims to reach out to a developmental span that is gigantic and has grown into a category of multiple proportions that provides avenues of learning that are atten-tion grabbing and motivating. But what is children's literature and what is its role in today's schools? What distinguishes this body of literature from literature in gen-eral? How can this body of literature be inclusive of many diverse perspectives and reflect the stories, experiences, and voices of all children? In this introductory chapter, these questions are unpacked with a brief historical overview of children's literature.

A definition of **multicultural children's literature** is given and its role in schools today is explored. In this text, the importance of critical literacy is emphasized along with an issues approach to multicultural children's literature. A critical approach is imperative in these times when schools and classrooms in the United States have a population that is more and more diverse.

CHILDREN'S LITERATURE DEFINED

Ask the average person what children's literature is and you may get answers like "They are books with bright pictures," "They encourage children to read," "They are fairy tales and folk tales or animal tales,"· and so on. But few realize that there are over 10,000 trade books published each year in the United States alone in a variety of genres, topics, and formats, and that many of these books are so sophisticated in their plots, stories, and designs that they are enjoyed by adults and children alike. While experts would define children's literature in many ways, ultimately it is literature that is written with children as its main audience. A look at some experts' definitions of children's literature gives us an idea of not only how complicated it is to define this body of literature, but also how difficult it is to pinpoint what makes a children's book, except to say that it is for and about children.

Temple, Martinez, Yokota, and Naylor (2002) said, "Children's literature is the collection of books that are read to and by children . . . from birth to about age fifteen" (p. 6). They also acknowledged that "it is surprisingly hard to define a children's book" (p. 5).

Norton, Norton, and McClure (2003), rather than directly defining children's literature, simply talked about the qualities of good literature for children and the development of literature for children in recent times: "When students of children's literature look at the beautiful books published to meet children's needs, interests and reading levels, many are amazed to learn that not long ago books were not written specifically for children" (p. 42). They continued: "When childhood began to be viewed as a special part of the human life cycle, literature written specifically for children became very important" (p. 42).

Charlotte Huck, long considered one of the original theorists of children's literature, said, "Children's books are books that have the child's eye at the center" (Huck, Kiefer, Hepler, & Hickman, 2004, p. 5). These educators also discussed how "children have become more sophisticated and knowledgeable about certain life experiences than children of any previous generation" (p. 4), acknowledging that the topics of this body of literature are therefore very hard to distinguish from adult literature in many cases. Death, war, starvation, terror, violence—everything is part of children's literature now, as it is, unfortunately, a part of some children's lives. As Huck et al. mentioned, children no longer are spared any emotions; the evening news brings them everything vicariously, and in fact, "today's children are exposed to violence purely in the name of entertainment" (p. 4).

One could argue that distinguishing children's literature from other types of literature is unnecessary, because what was once thought of as material written for adults may now be termed children's literature. For example, *To Kill a Mockingbird*, by Harper Lee, was not originally written with children in mind, although the main character is 8-year-old Scout and the whole story, which spans a period of 2 years, is told through her voice and eyes. Publishing houses have further muddied the definitions by the demands that certain books have commanded in the market. For example, with the *Harry Potter* series, by J. K. Rowling, although it started off as writing aimed at children, it is clearly debatable as to who more enjoys these books, especially when taking into account the sheer vastness of its reading audience. In all of these definitions, however, the most important point that distinguishes children's literature from other types of literature is that it *validates* all children's experiences.

MULTICULTURAL CHILDREN'S LITERATURE

Validation for all children's experiences needs to include the diversity present in our society today, therefore, throughout this text, the emphasis is on multicultural children's literature, rather than simply naming this body of literature as children's literature. Simply put, multicultural children's literature is literature that is not of the mainstream in the United States. Rather, it is about groups who have been previously underrepresented and often marginalized by society as a whole, especially in depictions in children's literature in the United States. Although it is difficult to exactly define this body of literature in rigid terms, the following definition may serve to clarify the ideas represented in this text: "Multicultural children's literature is about the sociocultural experiences of previously underrepresented groups. It validates these groups' experiences, including those occurring because of differences in language, race, gender, class, ethnicity, identity, and sexual orientation." Although the term *multicultural children's literature* is explored in detail in Chapter 2, one of the main purposes of children's literature is to be inclusive of and provide validation for all children's experiences, hence books that are from many different sociocultural backgrounds are included in this text. This text takes a broad view of the term *multicultural* to include all sociocultural aspects and not just those aspects that are apparent because of ethnicity and race culture. Please see Chapter 2 for more on this.

A BRIEF HISTORICAL OVERVIEW

Just as defining children's literature is murky, historically, it is hard to pinpoint when books began to be written for a primarily child audience. However, most educators agree that children's books reflect the historical times in which they were published, particularly the perspectives of what makes up a child. Largely didactic tales with mainly moralistic and religious overtones were popular during the 16th and 17th centuries. Books such as *Pilgrim's Progress,* by John Bunyan; Horn books with moral verses; and stories of Gods and apostles, mythological tales and legends, flourished. Even in many Asian cultures, the precursors to children's literature today were moralistic tales with animal characters that were specifically created to teach short didactic lessons. One such example from India is the short animal tales from the collection called the *Panchatantra* or "Five Principles" of life. These kinds of stories reflected the perspective of a child who was thought of as a young adult, someone who needed to be instructed on the ways of society, on the rights and wrongs and "dos" and "don'ts." As people's attitudes on children changed, so did books for children.

The 18th and 19th centuries saw travel and adventure stories as people began to discover new lands, foray into new fields, and communicate with new cultures and peoples. Hence this era saw books for children such as *Gulliver's Travels* and the *Grimms' Fairy Tales,* collected and written by the brothers Grimm, two German brothers, Jacob and Wilhelm Grimm, whose collection is largely about central Europe and life during that time. Anyone reading the original tales as written down by the Grimm brothers will agree that these stories were more cautionary and violent, meant to scare children and adults alike into correct behavior. Other didactic books include those published by John Newbery's publishing house, including titles that he wrote himself. Newbery's publishing house was the first known to cater to a child audience. He published such titles as *Little Goody Two Shoes* and wrote one of the first books for children, called *A Little Pretty Pocket Book,* an alphabet book. Today, the Newbery Medal for children's books, which started in 1922, is given annually to an author of children's books in his remembrance.

The 19th century also saw the advent of magazines for children, the most famous of which is the *St. Nicholas Magazine,* which started in 1872 and was in publication well into the 20th century. This magazine is reputed to have given many authors and illustrators of those times an avenue to showcase their talents. Stories of faraway lands, folk tales, historical fiction, and adventure and discovery, interpreted by a mainly White authorship, were the staple content of these magazines. In fact, it is believed that many of the folk and fairy tales as we know them today, including their illustrations, were the result of authors' and illustrators' interpretations in the *St. Nicholas Magazine.* For example, Reginald Birch, a well-known illustrator of that time, gave us the character of the potbellied jolly Santa Claus, with the white beard and red suit, carrying a huge sack of presents, that most children identify as the icon of Christmas today.

In the early 20th century, as a result of the gross stereotypes and misrepresentations of people from other ethnicities and races like Black, Asian, and Latino/a, the *Brownies' Book* magazine was also started. Although the focus of this magazine was a Black or African American audience, its stories and representations tried to reach out to all children. Please see Chapter 2 for an in-depth description of the *Brownies' Book* magazine.

Although these books and magazines began to be produced with a child audience in mind, it was not until the late 20th century that children's books really began coming into their own. While the previous decades saw mainly traditional literature, including folk and fairy tales, as the mainstay of children's books, the later part of the 20th century saw distinctions of genres of children's literature as we know them today, including **realistic fiction, historical fiction, poetry, picture books, modern fantasy, science fiction,** and so on. In fact, books began to be written specifically as teaching aids for children, to motivate them to read and learn about the world. In other words, from just entertainment, children's literature began to play a leading role in schools and classrooms.

ROLE OF MULTICULTURAL CHILDREN'S LITERATURE IN TODAY'S SCHOOLS

A quick look at the curriculum of any school district in reading and literacy or language arts shows us that it includes literature selections in some form or other. Usually, this is where children's stories or literature specifically written for children is used to enhance vocabulary, reading, writing, listening, speaking, language, and the like. Further, college classrooms that prepare teachers have recognized the importance of this category of literature and many have specific courses and seminars specialized in children's literature. For example, the California Department of Education has an extended recommended literature list that has annotations of over 1,000 books in it. This list spans an age range of K–12 (see http://www.cde.ca.gov) and is used by many college preparatory programs in California. The Language and Literacy Standards of the California Department of Education also include children's literature in some form or other, especially in terms of language and reading abilities that include phonemic awareness and phonics. However, many classrooms use only children's books that are written specifically to teach certain lessons, such as identify the plot of stories, predict from pictures what may happen, be able to answer questions about the story, learn new words used in context in the story, recognize parts of a story, and so on. Some of these books are written solely to engage in these simple classroom activities and are widely used in classrooms, like the "Dick and Jane" books of the early 20th century or the more recent themed readers published specifically to address simple language arts lessons. Multicultural children's literature in such classrooms is mainly used for children's free choice of reading, for entertainment purposes, or for specific preassigned times like Black History Month or Asian Appreciation Month.

This book, however, advocates for an approach that integrates multicultural children's literature throughout the day, throughout the school year, and at all times, for all types of lessons. By using the wonderful, creative, complex, and rich literature that encompasses multicultural children's literature to its fullest extent in all lessons, across the curriculum, it is hoped that a child's ability to fully participate and function in the world will be enhanced. In fact, in order to truly appreciate and understand the richness and depth of the available multicultural literature written especially for children, to engage with multicultural authors and their endeavor to contribute to the expanse of children's experiences, and to acknowledge the social and cultural relevance of multicultural children's literature today, a critical issues approach to reading multicultural children's literature is more useful. In other words, the use of multicultural children's literature in schools and classrooms may be intricately linked to **critical literacy.**

CRITICAL LITERACY AND MULTICULTURAL CHILDREN'S LITERATURE

Changing demographics in the United States and abroad, in conjunction with an increased focus on technology today more than ever before, brings the spotlight on literacy, which continues to make a greater demand on children and adults. In many places, literacy divides the population in terms of who gets to go to the best schools, who gets the best jobs, and who is the most successful, in general. In fact, the ways in which we speak and act within the literate world often helps to determine who we are and the world in which we interact (Shor, 1999).

Students and teachers today are called on to be literate in more complex ways than ever before. In such a world, *literacy* is not just knowing how to read and write; it is much broader. It is making apparent and revealing the inner workings of a particular group or society and the ways in which the group or society defines itself in different contexts. In order to "be literate," therefore, one needs to know enough information to be able to participate and function fully within various contexts in that society or group. So a simplistic example would be when one is "computer literate," one knows the ins and outs of using a computer, one knows and understands the language that computer professionals use, and so on. In other words, a computer literate person knows enough about the inner workings of computers and people associated with computers in order to fully participate in that society. Another example would be texting. The children and youth of today are more "literate" in their text messaging world, which includes various short forms for commonly used phrases, to the point where literature in Japan is being redefined. Novels are written and published and distributed only on text messages on cell phones. Books are no longer published in the regular sense (Day, 2008). In order to read and comprehend one of these "cell novels," one would need to be "text literate," as the language used in these would be amusingly abbreviated words that have meaning only to those that are *literate* in that context.

Critical literacy is an extension of the aforementioned definition of literacy and grew out of a critical approach to education. A critical approach teaches students to question, inquire into, and reveal the power relations that exist in the workings of a society or a group. It encourages students and teachers to take an active role in their learning, to take action and be doers rather than merely passive listeners. It is a methodology that teaches students that they can be independent agents of a change for the better; rather, they *should* be agents of change, creating opportunities and choices for themselves. The scope of critical literacy goes beyond a two-dimensional transaction of knowing how to function in a group to creating possibilities for multidimensional understandings between the individual and the group or society. *Critical literacy* may be defined as the process of becoming literate about a society or group through questioning, through seeing things from various viewpoints, through uncovering biases and reading "between the lines," and through critically analyzing the workings of a society historically and culturally, in order to thrive in it.

Educators and theorists such as Anderson and Irvine (1993) described critical literacy as follows: "Learning to read and write as part of the process of becoming conscious of one's experience as historically constructed within specific power relations" (p. 82). In their interpretation then, reading and writing are a means to becoming conscious of our experiences as historically constructed and not just as situated within a particular time and space. In such a definition, reading and writing are not isolated literacy events; rather they are situated within the contexts of history, of all that has happened before this point in time and what that means and how that weighs on how we interact now. Not only is literacy not viewed as merely basic skills in reading and writing, but critical literacy requires students to "question the assumptions of institutionalized knowledge and to use knowledge to take action" (Banks, 2003, p. 18).

In this text, critical literacy is related to multicultural children's literature through an issues approach. By teaching children the relationships between the texts they are reading and their lives, we help them "read the world through the word" (Shor, 1999, p. 1). For example, take a well-loved picture book such as *The Rainbow Fish,* by Marcus Pfister. In it, there is a beautiful rainbow fish that has rainbow colored scales but has no friends. However, the wise octopus advices the fish to share his rainbow scales by giving one to each of the other fish. The rainbow fish does so and gains friends. A simple read of this text tells us a sweet story of sharing. A more critical read of this story, however, tells us something different.

In this world of fishes, when one "reads the world through the words" of this text, one learns that sometimes one has to compromise in order to be part of a larger group. One learns that sometimes conformity is better than uniqueness or standing out of the group and that sometimes in order be assimilated, one has to make some tough choices. One could combine this book along with *Swimmy,* by Leo Lionni (a book about a fish that teaches its friends to swim in formation so they can escape the big tuna fish that will eat them), to teach a lesson that there is strength in numbers, that when a group works together, conforming to the larger good of the group, everyone gains.

Exemplary literature has that power to help children see themselves in the curriculum. Reading about children like themselves has the power to motivate them to participate more in the curriculum. Reading about children around the world in a variety of different situations has the power to expand their worldviews, creating opportunities for understanding. Further, helping children read through a lens of critical literacy gives them the power to see the value of their readings and to help them believe that they can succeed and change the world to be a better place for themselves, in other words, to own the curriculum.

FORMING ISSUES INTO AND THROUGH CRITICAL LITERACY LESSONS

In an issues approach to multicultural children's literature, one can have multiple transactions with a text, allowing for a multitude of understandings. Rather than merely reading children's books, we can begin to situate these books and what they are saying historically. We can interpret these from multiple perspectives, gaining a critical vantage point from which to understand them. For example, take the topic of immigration. There are numerous books that describe the various nuances of immigration: the journey, the separation from one's homeland, the feelings of loneliness, the feelings of joy as one starts a new life, and so on. When we read these books, we gain an insight into the lives of immigrants. When we read them from a critical literacy point of view, we are able to gain multiple understandings into the complex situations that make up immigrants. We are able to place them historically, and we are able to make attempts to relate to them and step into their shoes for a minute. Such readings help foster tolerance and cooperation amongst students because they lay bare the processes of curriculum. Further, an issues approach with a critical literacy goal helps students see themselves in the curriculum. It helps them shape and ask questions of the curriculum, and it helps them read themselves into the curriculum.

As mentioned before, there are children's books that have been written about a vast range of topics and stories. Integrating exemplary children's books throughout the curriculum is not only possible but necessary in today's classrooms, given the sociocultural and socioeconomical range of students in schools today. Topics may be chosen by a two-pronged process: seeing what interests students and what needs to be covered in the classroom in terms of content. A commonly used technique is a simple and well-known webbing technique to connect the two processes of students' wanting to know and needing to learn. Webbing also helps bring out ideas for the range of the topic or issue in terms of connections, subject matter, curriculum areas, and other related topics. Although webbing is a good place to begin, a technique that lays bare the curriculum for the students is much more effective in motivating students to participate and form the curriculum. For example, take students into confidence by letting them know why they need to learn and know certain topics. Show students, through creating a *web of significance,* what they need to learn for school to succeed in school. Show them the state standards, and connect these standards to real-life issues or real-life processes that they will use. This process allows students to see that what they learn in school is not just for school but actually useful for life skills, giving them the opportunity to participate in their curriculum and understand that they will use these skills in their real lives in the future. In fact, teachers of gifted students are taught many such techniques to keep students engaged fully. Fun learning activities such as drama are commonly used with gifted students. However, in an approach that has critical literacy and issues, *all* students can be motivated to engage fully.

Creating a "Web of Significance"

A web of significance may look like the concentric circles of a ripple effect in water, beginning in the middle and radiating out into larger and more inclusive circles. Put down the main topic that they will be learning for school, making sure that this topic is broad enough for them to approach through multiple perspectives. Next, put down how this topic connects with their real lives in the future or in the current times or in the past, laying bare the significance of this topic. Showing this connection or significance will show students why they need to learn about this topic now, creating a motive. Ask students what they would like to learn and know for themselves as related to this topic and as related to their individual interests and needs, showing them that they have choices in what they learn. Have plenty of resources about the topic ready for students to use, for research and inquiry. Books on all genres on this topic are usually a very good place to start for resources. Once the class has gone through an exercise of building a web of significance, put this up in a prominent place in the classroom for all to see and consult with, throughout the time that this topic will be focused on. Here is a snapshot of the process:

- Choose a very broad main topic to learn for school.
- Show the significance of this topic. How does it connect to students' real lives?
- Create a motive. Show them why they need to learn about this topic.
- Give them choices. What do they want to learn about this topic? What interests them?
- Have a variety of multimedia resources available. Students can choose what interests them.
- Display the web of significance so the class can consult with it.

Once this web of significance has been created with the students as participants, the teacher could begin with a regular curricular activity such as a read-aloud with carefully chosen multicultural children's books that may be read to the whole group or read by themselves in small groups. Allow enough time for students to inquire into this topic, including any personal interests about the topic that they may want to explore. Lead students with carefully chosen open-ended questions around the topic that furthers their inquiry into it. Next, help them connect the topic to their lives by bringing in an actual past, current, or imminent future event. Help students connect with the lives of characters in the multicultural children's books chosen for the topic through a creative medium such as writing in role or writing to a character or as a character. In making these connections, students get a chance to interact with the curriculum, putting themselves into it.

As can be seen, any topic may be turned into a critical literacy lesson by following these simple steps, given here using the topic of immigration as an example:

- Create a web of significance to see in which direction the lessons could go.
- Begin the lesson with a familiar curricular activity, such as a read-aloud.
- Let students browse through carefully chosen books, in small groups.
- Guide students' thinking with carefully chosen questions and provide information to their queries about immigrants and their experiences.
- Ask them to connect their lives and experiences through various creative avenues to the lives of immigrants in the books.
- Transform these connections into something they can actually put into action, such as writing letters, forming a group to help, and so on.
- Help students critically associate with immigrant experiences in the real world through writing, depicting a scene, discussing, and so on.
- Mediate a whole-class discussion to transform their knowledge to the real world and for reflection and closure of the lesson.

Following these same principles, the chapters in this book are also divided into an issues approach, highlighting various topics in multicultural children's literature that are imperative to explore today.

REFLECTION QUESTIONS FOR THE TEACHER

Any topic may be turned into a critical literacy angle by asking ourselves a few simple questions:

1. What real-life issue does this school or curriculum topic relate to?

2. What real-life event has happened, will happen, or is happening that can be connected to this school or curriculum topic?

3. If I were a professional working or living within this real-life context, event, or issue, how would I deal with it? What historical references can I draw and learn from that has happened before?

4. What can I do to change and learn from the event, problem, or issue?

5. How can I connect this curriculum topic or school topic to my current situation to make it better?

6. What steps (however small or large) can I take to make a change?

7. How will my actions affect others now, later, and in the future?

SAMPLE RESPONSE LESSON 1.1
Forming a Critical Literacy Lesson Using Educational Drama

Elementary Grades (2nd to 5th): In the Classroom, by Teachers, Parents, or Tutors

Duration: 1 Day or 1 Week

Overview

The teacher chooses a broad critical topic that may be from the curriculum standards or a current topic that is relevant to the class such as immigration that can be viewed from many

(Continued)

(Continued)

different angles. The teacher brainstorms along with students on what possibilities and avenues of learning this topic offers. This may be done using well-known techniques such as a K-W-L chart (what I *know,* what I *want* to know, and what I *learned*) or a webbing technique.

The teacher picks several carefully chosen picture books on immigration that show various aspects of the topic and has students read them in small groups of four or five. Students may read books such as the following: *The Tangerine Tree,* by Regina Hanson; *The Keeping Quilt,* by Patricia Polacco; *Lights for Gita,* by Rachna Gilmore; *American Too,* by Elisa Bartone; and *Grandfather's Journey,* by Allen Say.

After the students have read the stories, the teacher uses a simple drama technique such as still image or tableau to help students connect with the characters in the story. Through carefully worded questions, the teacher guides students into some of the possible points of view of the characters in the story. Finally, the teacher has students rewrite the stories creatively as a screenplay for a possible movie.

Materials

Various books on immigration such as the ones mentioned earlier, poster paper, markers, journals for screenplays, butcher paper for a whole-group activity

Key Vocabulary and Terms

Immigrants, Perspective, Screenplay, Tableau, Journey, Leaving

Anticipatory Set

1. *Focus:* Students will learn to view a topic from within a perspective. They learn about immigrants and what they may have felt when they were about to leave their homes. Students inquire critically into immigrants' possible lives and depict creatively what it might have been like to be in the immigrant characters' shoes.

2. *Objective:* By the end of the lesson, students learn about different immigrants' possible motives to move homes and what it may feel like to be an immigrant. Students creatively interpret immigrants' lives by writing a short scene in a screenplay or a play.

3. *Transfer:* As students depict still images with their bodies and discuss each others' still image pictures, they begin to gain insights into some of the complexities of immigrant lives. Students will also gain practice in writing and interpreting stories from books. As they will do this in a group, stronger writers can help the others, and students learn structures of plot, story, and so on.

Instructions

1. The teacher divides the class into groups of four or five students and distributes one book to each group. Each group is asked to read the book and understand the story.

2. The teacher explains what a still image or a tableau is: "It is a moment in time like a still picture that you will depict with your bodies. There is no movement and no dialogue." The teacher then instructs the groups to pick the moment when the characters in their respective books first arrived in the new country. Students will be given about 10 minutes to discuss amongst themselves how they will depict the pictures with their bodies as a still image or tableau.

3. The teacher calls on each group one after another to depict their still image. As the group freezes into position, the teacher will ask the rest of the class to interpret what is going on in the image depicted. Carefully chosen questions will be asked, such as the following: "What do you think might be happening in this picture?" "Where do you think these people are?" "What are they doing?" "What is going on in this person's mind?" "What can we tell about this family from looking at this picture?" (This technique is very similar to asking students to "predict" from a picture walk by showing a picture book, except that it is far more interactive and allows for students' active participation.)

4. The teacher will also instruct the groups responding that there are no right or wrong answers, that these are our own interpretations or "readings" of what we feel is depicted. After all the groups have had a turn, discuss with the whole class what they understood from this exercise on immigrants' experiences.

Independent Practice

After the whole-group discussions, tell the students that they are "expert filmmakers" (usually students know what filmmakers do; if not, explain that filmmakers work from a script). Ask the group to pick a scene in their respective books and rewrite it as a scene with dialogue. Model for students how you can take one short scene and rewrite it with possible dialogue. (At the end of this lesson, you will find some actual examples of this, done in a fourth-grade classroom.)

Closure

Have students share their scripts and enact them in class.

Extension

The teacher or school may have a guest speaker or a fellow classmate share an experience of being an immigrant and give students a chance to connect their classroom experience with that of a real person in real life.

(Continued)

(Continued)

Modifications: Secondary Grades

The same lesson may be followed with books that also concentrate on other aspects of immigration, such as being a refugee or an illegal immigrant. You can use books such as *The Circuit* and *Breaking Through*, by Francisco Jimenez, two sequel books that follow the autobiographical life of Dr. Jimenez, whose early life in this country was that of an illegal migrant farmworker. High school students may also read *Grapes of Wrath*, by John Steinbeck, that talks about the Joad family's journey west. Although this is not about immigration, the aspects of leaving home and looking for a better life are wonderfully depicted in this book.

EXAMPLES OF RESPONSES TO LESSON 1.1

Here are some examples of first scenes from screenplays created by a fourth-grade class.

Students' response to *Lights for Gita,* by Rachna Gilmore:

Gita: Did you get the matches?

Father: Yes! I did.

Gita: Let's go then, Dad.

Mother: Ok, Put on your coats. Let's get them out.

Students' response to *The Tangerine Tree,* by Regina Hanson:

Rosa: Is that snow in your hands?

Miguel: Yeah, can you believe it?

Mom: Before you go outside put on your coats.

Miguel: I can't believe that there's snow outside, can you? I mean in Jamaica we never get any snow and when we came all of a sudden there is snow!

Students' response to *The Keeping Quilt,* by Patricia Polacco:

Wilma: Grampa, who are these people? *(Looking at a photograph)*

Grampa: You don't know them, but that's me and my brother before I came to America.

Wilma:	Why isn't he in America now?
Grampa:	Because he did not want to leave his country
Wilma:	Why, Grampa?
Grampa:	Well, I tell him, Hershel, I am going to America, do you want to come? And he says, No, I am scared. So I came alone to America. *(Phone rings)*
Wilma:	I'll get it. . . . Hello?
Grampa:	Who is it?
Wilma:	Grampa, it's Uncle Hershel. . . .

SELECTED ANNOTATED BIBLIOGRAPHY

Bartone, E. (1996). *American too* (T. Lewin, Ill.). New York: HarperCollins.

Rosina thinks she must shed her Italian ways to be really American. She insists that her parents call her Rosie, and she changes her doll's name from Allesandra to the good "American" name of Meghan O'Hara. Although her family speaks Italian, waving their hands around, Rosie sits on her hands and answers in English. And when Papa tells her that she'll be the queen of the feast of San Gennaro, she storms, "Why do we always have to do Italian things? This is America, not Italy!" While gazing at the Statue of Liberty, she has a wonderful idea, a way to be American and Italian, too, a way to have the best of both worlds. Recommended age 3 years and up.

Bunting, E. (1998). *Going home* (D. Diaz, Ill.). New York: HarperCollins.

A family goes back to their village in Mexico on a car trip. Told through the eyes of second-generation American children, it brings out the nostalgia felt by the parents and gives the children a unique peek into the lives of their parents. Beautifully illustrated by Diaz, the colors and flow of the pictures will grab even the youngest of babies. Recommended age 0 to 10 years.

Bunting, E. (1997). *A day's work* (R. Himler, Ill.). Boston: Sandpiper Books.

A grandfather and his 7-year-old grandson wait for work as day laborers. Everyone around them gets picked up but the grandfather as he seems too old to do any work. Finally a man comes asking for a gardener. The grandson, who is there to help translate for the grandfather, tired of waiting, hastily says his grandfather can do the job. Not knowing the difference between weeds and new samplings, they pull out the wrong plants in the man's yard. Upon confrontation, the grandfather apologizes and says he will return the next day to fix the problem without pay. The grandson learns a lesson in commitment and honesty from his grandfather. Recommended age 4 years and up.

Fleischman, P. (2004). *Seedfolks.* New York: Harper Teen.

Originally published in 1997, this inspiring story is told in the first person through a series of short vignettes, introducing us to the trials and tribulations of each person who lives in this community. A vacant, deserted, and littered lot in the middle of a cosmopolitan street in Cleveland becomes the grounds for a community garden when Kim, a young Vietnamese girl, plants some lima beans. People from various cultures and ethnicities come together, working to make this garden successful. The garden, in turn, reflects the hope and inspiration that these immigrants gain from this community effort. Recommended age 6 years and up.

Gilmore, R. (2000). *Lights for Gita* (A. Priestley, Ill.). Gardiner, ME: Tilbury House.

In a picture book first published in Canada, an immigrant child from India celebrates the Hindu holiday of *Divali* for the first time in her new home. *Divali* is a holiday celebrated at the end of October and the beginning of November with lights, fireworks, street theater, sweets, and parties. Many consider it the beginning of a new year. In the November gloom of her new apartment, Gita longs for her extended family in New Delhi and the warmth she's left behind. She cries when an ice storm knocks out the power in all the buildings on her street; but with her parents and her best friend, she lights the *diyas* (lamps) for the festival, and she comes to see that the lights of *Divali* can beat the darkness outside and the sadness within. Recommended age 3 years and up.

Hanson, R. (1995). *The tangerine tree.* Boston: Clarion Books.

This picture book about a small child in Jamaica dramatizes the anguish of families separated by migrant labor. Ida's papa must leave to go and work in New York City. We feel the family's heartbreak as the time for Papa's leaving gets closer and the bus finally takes him away from them. Before he goes, he gives Ida a gift, a book of Greek myths, and he tells her that by the time she can read it by herself, he'll be back. The expressive acrylic paintings in bright tropical colors express the family's love and loneliness. Recommended age 4 years and up.

Polacco, P. (2001). *The keeping quilt.* New York: Simon & Schuster Books for Young Readers.

"We will make a quilt to help us always remember home," Anna's mother said. "It will be like having the family in backhome Russia dance around us at night." And so it was. From a basket of old clothes, Anna's babushka, Uncle Vladimir's shirt, Aunt Havalah's nightdress, and an apron of Aunt Natasha's become *The Keeping Quilt,* passed along from mother to daughter for almost a century. For four generations the quilt is a Sabbath tablecloth, a wedding canopy, and a blanket that welcomes babies warmly into the world. In strongly moving pictures that are as heartwarming as they are real, Patricia Polacco tells the story of her own family and the quilt that remains a symbol of their enduring love and faith. Recommended age 4 years and up.

Say, A. (1993). *Grandfather's journey.* Boston: Houghton Mifflin.

Home becomes elusive in this story about immigration and acculturation, pieced together through old pictures and salvaged family tales. Both the narrator and his grandfather long to return to Japan, but when they do, they feel anonymous and confused: "The funny thing is, the moment I am in one country, I am homesick for the other." Allen Say's prose is succinct and controlled, to the effect of surprise when monumental events are scaled down to a few words: "The young woman fell in love, married, and sometime later I was born." The book also has large, formal paintings in delicate, faded colors that portray a cherished and well-preserved family album. Recommended age 2 years and up.

Winter, J. (1992). *Klara's new world.* New York: Random House.

When a drought brings tough times to her Swedish family, Klara, not yet 8, fears she'll be hired out to work on the manor. Then a letter arrives from a friend in America, urging them to sell out and join him. Hesitantly, they decide to do so, leaving home, friends, and grandfather forever. Crossing the Atlantic in a sailing ship, they continue by train and steamboat to their Minnesota destination, where Papa's friend Bertil helps them establish a new home. Recommended age 4 years and up.

REFERENCES

Anderson, G. L., & Irvine, P. (1993). Informing critical literacy with ethnography. In C. Lankshear & P. L. McLaren (Eds.), *Critical literacy: Politics, praxis, and the postmodern* (pp. 81–104). Albany: SUNY.

Banks, J. (2003). Teaching literacy for social justice and global citizenship. *Language Arts, 81*(1), 18–19.

California Department of Education. (2001). *Recommended literature: Kindergarten through grade twelve.* Available from http://www.cde.ca.gov/ci/rl/11

Day, L. (2008, January 9). Tone language. *TIME Magazine,* p. 28.

Huck, C. H., Kiefer, B. Z., Hepler, S., & Hickman, J. (2004). *Children's literature in the elementary school* (8th ed.) New York: McGraw-Hill.

Norton, D. E., Norton, S. E., & McClure, A. (2003). *Through the eyes of a child: An introduction to children's literature* (6th ed.) Upper Saddle River, NJ: Prentice Hall.

Shor, I. (1999). What is critical literacy? In I. Shor & C. Pari (Eds.), *Critical literacy in action: Writing words, changing worlds* (pp. 1–24). Portsmouth, NH: Boynton/Cook.

Temple, C., Martinez, M., Yokota, J., & Naylor, A. (2002). *Children's books in children's hands: An introduction to their literature* (2nd ed.). Boston: Allyn & Bacon.

Chapter 2 The Essentials and Foundations of Multicultural Children's Literature

The term *multicultural* evokes strong feelings in people. Signifying different things to different people, this term has generated considerable controversy ever since it has been in use. In fact, the term multicultural, when used in conjunction with children's literature, has, in recent years, generated much debate amongst educators and multicultural theorists around topics that go deeper into cultural, sociopolitical issues and political correctness. Fifty years ago, a book such as Ezra Jack Keats's *The Snowy Day* (1962), about a young boy enjoying a day out in the snow, was welcomed as it depicted a Black character in a positive light, where there were none. Today, the same book may bring up questions of tokenism. Across fields, theorists are asking who has the right to write about certain issues or ethnicities. Who has the experience to authentically depict certain topics? What may or may not be included in these stories and based on whose experiences?

Multicultural children's literature can be situated in multiculturalism, the result of the civil rights movement, which touched many fields in an effort to give voice and equal rights to previously underrepresented people. In an interesting article, Taxel (1995) went so far as to say that there are intricate connections between political correctness and multiculturalism in relation to children's literature. He cited convincing data to show how most attacks on political correctness are about the meanings, connotations, and applications of multiculturalism.

Although multicultural children's literature is the main focus of this chapter, the meanings and connotations of multiculturalism are also traced in order to provide a basis to understand the issues around multicultural children's literature. Possibly, one could think of multicultural children's literature in terms of degrees, that in today's climate of being politically correct, of being inclusive and of being **culturally** conscious, there are degrees to which a literary piece may be multicultural. This degree depends upon various factors such as issues of representation, issues of cultural authenticity, range of experiences depicted, and so on. Although these factors may fill a book themselves, in this chapter they are discussed as they pertain to children's literature, beginning with a brief historical overview of multiculturalism followed by a discussion specifically of multicultural children's literature as it evolved and is understood today.

TRACING A BRIEF HISTORY OF MULTICULTURALISM

Multiculturalism began with a motive toward **cultural pluralism**, a way to recognize cultures and ethnicities not of the mainstream, beginning with ethnic studies (Banks & Banks, 2001). The term multicultural has been used as a qualifier for many things in an effort to show inclusivity in some form. Therefore, this word prefaces many words, such as multicultural issues, multicultural education, multicultural books, multicultural marketing, multicultural vision, multicultural experiences, and multicultural literature, to name a few. It has also been used as an action term, a beginning point to fight for one's rights, to be recognized as a person; in other words, multiculturalism has been used as a means to social justice.

The term as it is used today has its roots in the civil rights movement. Banks and Banks (2001) traced four phases of multiculturalism. The first phase began with educators incorporating the "history and cultures of ethnic minority groups," that is, ethnic studies, into school curriculum (p. 10). The second phase began when these same educators realized that merely inserting ethnic histories and cultures into the curriculum was not sufficient in changing attitudes toward ethnic minorities. In this phase, a push for equality and equity in education came about. The third phase emerged when groups who viewed themselves as previously disadvantaged by the system demanded that their histories and cultures also be included in multicultural education. In this phase, experiences of disabled people, experiences of gays and lesbians, experiences unique to women, and so on, began to be included. Finally, the current and fourth phase of multiculturalism is the "development of theory, research and practice that interrelate variables connected to race, class and gender" (p. 11). See Figure 2.1 for a visual representation of these phases.

As the meanings associated with the word multiculturalism were used across fields, so also in children's literature, we began to see a consciousness that multiculturalism in children's books needed to be depicted in terms of books for and about different ethnicities, for and about different experiences and histories.

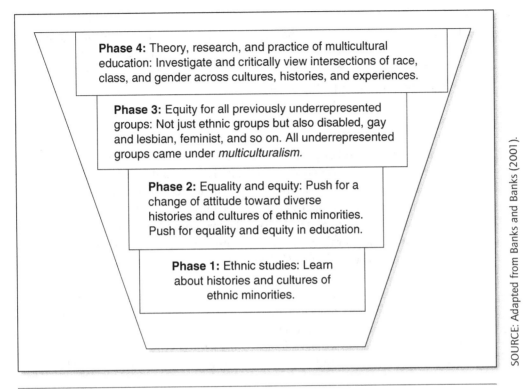

Phase 4: Theory, research, and practice of multicultural education: Investigate and critically view intersections of race, class, and gender across cultures, histories, and experiences.

Phase 3: Equity for all previously underrepresented groups: Not just ethnic groups but also disabled, gay and lesbian, feminist, and so on. All underrepresented groups came under *multiculturalism.*

Phase 2: Equality and equity: Push for a change of attitude toward diverse histories and cultures of ethnic minorities. Push for equality and equity in education.

Phase 1: Ethnic studies: Learn about histories and cultures of ethnic minorities.

SOURCE: Adapted from Banks and Banks (2001).

Figure 2.1   The Four Phases of Multiculturalism as They Formed Over the Years

MULTICULTURALISM TO MULTICULTURAL CHILDREN'S LITERATURE

Sims Bishop (2007) called the advent of multiculturalism and the multicultural education movement "one of the most hopeful developments in children's literature" (p. xiv). In terms of children's literature, the term multicultural has come to signify the inclusion of literature of underrepresented groups in classrooms "with a view to promoting appreciation and respect for diversity" (Sims Bishop, 2007, p. xiv) and an affirmation for children who may not have seen themselves in positive depictions in books for children.

Following the phases of multicultural education through the years, some of the first books that could be considered multicultural children's literature depicted different cultures and ethnicities in the illustrations and the content, simply for the sake of bringing ethnically and racially underrepresented characters into books. For example, the stories may be folktales of Native American tribes or they may depict an African American child having a fun day out or an Asian folktale and so on. Subsequently, some educators characterize children's literature according to race and ethnicity, dividing it according to the five major ethnic groups present in the United States (i.e., African American, American Indian or Native American, Asian and Asian American, Hispanic or Latino/a, and Middle Eastern). This characterization may leave out biracial or multilingual children and children of different classes and gender, and more importantly, it does not recognize the diversity in each of these major groups. For example, Hispanic is an umbrella term for Latino/a, Chicano/a, and many other groups whose experiences are distinctly different. And in fact, *Hispanic* is a term created in the United States to depict people from a large and diverse group of peoples (Spring, 2008). Therefore, over the years it has become important to take a more inclusive view not only because of the complexities of defining a race or ethnicity and its historical experiences, but also because one of the major aims of multicultural children's literature is to depict the lives of all previously underrepresented groups. As Cai (1998) noted,

> Multiculturalism is about diversity and inclusion, but what is more important, it is also about power structures and struggle. Its goal is not just to understand, accept, and appreciate cultural differences but also to ultimately transform the existing social order to ensure greater voice and authority to the marginalized cultures, and to achieve social equality and justice. (p. 313)

As such, multicultural children's literature needs to be viewed and analyzed from a sociohistorical point of view, as arising from the social, historical, and cultural contexts of the 20th century and all the controversies and struggles of that time. Although multicultural children's literature began in the 20th century, in the 21st century, it is also imperative to note that it affects everyone regardless of race, class, and gender, as conceptually the stories are located in the struggles of the people.

Evolution of Multicultural Children's Literature

There is little evidence and much difference of opinion as to when multicultural children's literature first began to make its appearance in classrooms and in the vast field of children's literature. Although some ascribe books published in the 16th century as multicultural literature (Norton & Norton, 2003), others acknowledge only those published in the last couple of decades (Au, 1993). As with any widely discussed topic that affects large groups of people, there are bound to be differences of opinion, as the naming process reveals the underlying perspective on which it is defined. As Cai (1998) rightly put it, trying to define multicultural literature is not simply "bickering over terminology in the ivory tower of academia" as "we should not underestimate the power of naming" (p. 311). Similarly, there are differences of opinion in terms of content too; while some would include only those books that are published by and about different ethnicities living within the United States, others include international literature or literature about children in other countries or experiences written only by authors of that culture or ethnicity. There are also considerable differences of opinion within ethnic groups themselves as to the beginning of multicultural children's literature.

As mentioned before, it is important to couch this evolution in a historical perspective, keeping in mind the social and cultural times in which multicultural children's literature first began to appear. Some literary works gained importance because of the purpose they served in particular historical time periods in relation to particular ethnic and cultural groups and their struggles to gain equality and recognition, although ultimately, these stories affect everyone. For example, Sims Bishop (2007) located the beginning of African American children's literature in the "Black people's struggles for liberation, literacy and survival" (p. 1) well before the 1900s in slave songs and oral tales, particularly mentioning Frederick Douglass, a man born into slavery and later freed, who wrote his autobiography, *Narrative of the Life of Frederick Douglass: An American Slave* (1845). Flor Ada (2003) traced the beginning of Latino literature to the late 19th century with Cuban writer Jose Marti and to a journal called *Le Edad de Oro* (The Golden Age, also cited in Kiefer, Hepler, & Hickman, 2007). However, it would be approximately another 75 years before more literature about the experiences of these ethnic groups began to appear and be validated with recognition like the Pura Belpré Awards.

Before and After the Civil Rights Movement

Although many educators and theorists credit the civil rights movement in the midpart of the 20th century as the beginning of an awareness that multiple perspectives need to be depicted in children's books, in reality there were many people who had already felt the need for these and had made huge strides in this direction. For example, in the 1920s, African American poets, storytellers, and artists, like Langston Hughes, Arna Bontemps, and Zora Neale Hurston, published exemplary works for children and adults alike (Kiefer et al., 2007; Sims Bishop, 2007). However, it was not until a widely publicized article in *The Saturday Review of Books* specifically on this topic written in 1965 that really sparked people's attention to the extent of the lack of multicultural children's literature. Cited in most texts and works on multicultural literature, Nancy Larrick's "The All White World of Children's Books" (1965) has become an iconic piece of writing that sparked a flurry of activity in the years immediately following it. Of special mention are two significant groups that formed, which helped to further bring multicultural children's literature to the fore: the Council on Interracial Books for Children, founded in 1965 (as cited in Kiefer et al., 2007, although Temple, Martinez, Yokota, & Naylor, 2006, say it started in 1966), and the Coretta Scott King Award, established for authors and illustrators of African American and Black descent in 1972. The Council on Interracial Books for Children, although no longer in service, has produced some excellent guidelines on multicultural children's literature, including the pamphlet "10 Quick Ways to Analyze Children's Books for Racism and Sexism" (although the original brochure is not available, see an adaptation at http://www.chil-es.org/10ways.pdf). The organization also has worked with many government bodies to create awareness about multiculturalism specifically in books and texts that children read.

Although the 1960s and 1970s saw some progress in creating awareness and encouraging more authors to write books about different ethnicities and experiences, there was a lull again until the 1990s in terms of quality multicultural children's literature. During the lull, although books were being published about children from diverse backgrounds and of people from different experiences, these seemed to reiterate many of the stereotypical depictions, giving rise to unrest about the authenticity of these stories and experiences. The 1990s saw a number of criticism works that questioned issues of cultural authenticity in children's books being published. In particular, Native American groups and tribes began to not only question the cultural authenticity of these works, but they also protested against the "stealing of their stories" that began to be depicted from a mainstream perspective. In this regard, in 1990, an organization called Oyate was formed of people from various native tribes and groups. It began its operation to "see that our lives and histories are portrayed honestly, and so that all people will know our stories belong to us" (see "About Us" at http://www.oyate.org/). An exemplary resource, this Web site offers commentary, resources, workshops, booklists, and much more. Self-professed as a very small organization of a lot of friends, this group has brought out two very influential works in the last two decades: *Through Indian Eyes: The Native Experience in Books for Children* (Seale & Slapin, 2006) and *A Broken Flute: The Native Experience in Books for Children* (Seale & Slapin, 2005), both exhaustive edited book reviews and essays by native people of many tribes.

MULTICULTURAL CHILDREN'S LITERATURE AND LEVELS OF MULTICULTURALISM

As the word multicultural began with the multicultural education movement, many of the meanings and connotations of this category of literature go hand in hand with its applicability and usability in classrooms today. Going from the basic premise that this body of literature should be reflective of the diverse experiences and histories of children in schools and classrooms all over the United States, it would be useful to also mention the level to which multiculturalism needs to permeate school curriculum.

Earlier, in the introduction to this chapter, it was mentioned that multicultural children's literature is defined in terms of degrees of multiculturalism. This definition has evolved from the four levels of multicultural education that James Banks so efficiently described in the late 1980s. A brief recap of these levels will help to clarify and couch the definition. In the following section, each level is explained according to multiculturalism and then related to multicultural children's literature.

Level 1: In the first and lowest level of approaching curricular reform in multicultural education is the *contributions* approach (Banks, 1999). In terms of multicultural children's literature, it may also be called the *tourist approach* or a *food and festivals approach,* where books of different cultures are introduced on certain holidays and months, giving a sense of visiting different cultures and ethnicities. In this approach, one is least committed and a superficial effort is made to include literature about heroes, holidays, celebrations, and festivals representative of the culture depicted. The literature itself may not have been evaluated for authenticity and representation. Although this approach is an excellent way to introduce a body of literature to a class that is unaware of this group, it may not suffice. Some examples are cooking salsa and eating tortillas when reading Gary Paulsen's, *The Tortilla Factory* (1995). *The Tortilla Factory* is a picture book written in simple evocative poetry and narrates the cycle of how a kernel of corn becomes a tortilla.

Level 2: The next level is the *additive* approach, where content is added without changing or evaluating the basic structure. In terms of multicultural children's literature, it may involve reading folktales from around the world that are representative of a class's demographic, bringing in guest speakers or authors representative of certain cultures to talk about certain practices, and so on. Although slightly better, no interaction as to questioning historical facts or critically engaging with literature may be possible as there are no structural changes that have been made. For example, students might read *Lights for Gita* (2000), by Rachna Gilmore, a story of a young girl celebrating Diwali, the Indian festival of lights, as a new immigrant to the United States, and then watch a guest demonstrate wearing a sari and eat some Indian sweets. Although this demonstration gives students a nice introduction, a first-person account of what Diwali is like, and allows for interaction with a person of the culture, it remains a "visit" to an exotic land.

In the busy lives of many teachers, these two approaches may be the easiest to begin with, as they don't need much planning or structural or curricular changes. Many classrooms still follow these approaches, which is evident in the monthly celebrations of "Black History Month," when everyone reads about Dr. Martin Luther King, Jr., or "Asian Appreciation Month," when stories and folktales of Asian origin are read.

Level 3: The third level or the *transformation* approach turns the fundamental curriculum around in that it helps "students view concepts, issues, events and themes from the perspective of diverse ethnic and cultural groups" (Banks, 1999, p. 31). From a multicultural children's literature point of view, in such an approach, students are given literature that is "against the grain," that gives a point of view of historical events not only from the mainstream perspective but also from the perspective of the affected parties. In such an approach, children are given the opportunity to see different perspectives of many parties involved toward an attempt at an Anti-Bias and equitable education.

For example, *1621: A New Look at Thanksgiving* (2001), by Margaret Bruchac and Catherine O'Neill Grace, gives a perspective of thanksgiving from the native point of view. *Harvesting Hope: The Story of Cesar Chavez* (2003), by Kathleen Krull, gives a brief biography of the farmworkers' union leader Chavez, who worked tirelessly to pave the way for migrant and farmworkers' rights. *Voices From the Fields: Children of Migrant Farmworkers Tell Their Stories* (2000), by Beth Atkin, are firsthand accounts of children who have lead the hard life of migrant workers,. *The Circuit* and *Breaking Through,* by Francisco Jimenez, are autobiographical tales of Dr. Jimenez, who is now professor of Modern Languages and Literature at Santa Clara University. These give authentic and appropriate accounts from an insider's perspective, creating opportunities for rich discussions.

Level 4: The fourth and most desirable level of multiculturalism is the *social action* approach or an approach that involves students in not only the curriculum but also in social action, in speaking out against injustice, in engaging with power structures to take active action to modify and transform society toward a more equitable and just life. Although these seem like tall orders for young classrooms, this approach is more than ever before necessary at all levels of society if we as teachers want our students to become responsible and critically aware people of tomorrow.

In terms of multicultural children's literature, this may be accomplished by reading real accounts of famous historical events and applying the knowledge to current events by taking action through the media, the Internet, and in the community, or to connect an everyday occurrence to issues in the real world. For example, when we buy a soft toy and see the "made in China" label on it, we hardly think about child labor laws. But a book such as Sally Grindley's, *Spilled Water* (2004), gives us an account in the first person about the extreme conditions and unimaginable hardships that Lu Si-Yan, a 11-year-old Chinese girl, faces as she is sold down the river by her uncle after her father's death. For the next 3 years, Lu Si-Yan is alone, fending for herself finding work in the big cities until she comes to a factory that makes toys for export. She is hired at first to stitch eyes on cute soft bears and later to be a "runner," delivering parts of toy trucks that are completed to the next person in the assembly line. Enduring extremely long hours with no rest, Lu Si-Yan manages to "race, race, race" (p. 194) for 3 months, working from dawn to midnight until she completely collapses one day. Are there relationships between this poignant tale of poverty and helplessness and the demands for cheap toys in Western countries? What can children do in helping other children across the world? Perhaps children can do something small, like writing letters to corporations who inadvertently support child labor in poorer countries. These may be some questions that could be raised and discussed in classrooms along with taking deliberate action through a class project.

To recap, the four levels of multiculturalism starting from the lowest level are a contributions approach, an additive approach, a transformative approach, and the social action approach. See Figure 2.2 for a visual representation of these.

DEFINING MULTICULTURAL CHILDREN'S LITERATURE

Multicultural children's literature is defined in this book as literature that is by and about diverse populations and includes different perspectives. This definition has evolved from the aforementioned approaches and many other interpretations and connotations of the word multicultural. Specifically, multicultural children's literature validates all sociocultural experiences, including those occurring because of language, race, gender, class, ethnicity, and ability. Although this is a broad view of multicultural children's literature, I qualify this definition and further explain it with an extension of Sims Bishop's (1982) definitions of socially conscious, culturally conscious, and melting pot books, by extending them to all multicultural children's literature. Although there are no hard and fast rules to signify these terms, a useful construction may be to look at what these terms meant in the past and then adapt and apply them when analyzing books written for children today.

Melting Pot Books

Generally speaking, the term *melting pot* has come to signify a fusion of many cultures, ethnicities, and experiences. In reaction to the multicultural movement in the late 1960s and early 1970s, this term was most commonly used to connote the cultural assimilation of the various peoples into one country. Similarly, books about diverse cultures and experiences were based on showing fusion or cultural assimilation, showing that all people are the same eventually, that we must not discriminate based on cultural and ethnic differences. The idea here is that everyone has similar experiences at some levels. It is a way to show the "normalcy" that existed in all people despite their color and cultural differences. Such books have been variously called *culturally generic* (Temple et al., 2006) or *universally themed* (Thompson,

LEVEL 4: The Social Action Approach

Students are empowered to change and own the curriculum.
Students discuss social issues and take positive action. Children's
books on real historical and social events told from authentic and
diverse perspectives are read and compared to current events.
Students may put themselves "in the shoes of the characters" through
educational drama. Students take action through the media, letters,
the Internet, the community in striving for social action, justice, and
equal rights.

LEVEL 3: The Transformative Approach

Structural changes as well are made to help students view concepts,
events, and themes from diverse perspectives. Children's books of
authentic historical accounts from different perspectives are read,
and culturally authentic depictions are discussed and contrasted with
current ones. Books are read that advocate an Anti-Bias Education
and an equitable approach.

LEVEL 2: The Additive Approach

Content, concepts, themes, and perspectives are added, but there
are no structural changes. Children's books with folktales and stories
from different cultures are read, and authors of different ethnicities
are added to the class library.

LEVEL 1: A Contributions Approach

There is a designated time for certain holidays, food, festivals, and
other cultural elements. Children's books that show costumes, food
recipes, and holiday celebrations of different cultures are read.

SOURCE: Adapted from Banks and Banks (2001).

Figure 2.2   Levels of Multiculturalism Relating to Multicultural Children's Books

1995) and come from the stance of defining multicultural as multiple + cultures (Cai, 1998). For example, on the cover of Eve Bunting's *The Flower Garden* (1994) is a small girl's smiling face, shown among tulips and other flowers. It is very hard to make out the race or ethnicity of the girl, although on the cover and in the illustrations inside she is shown as brown skinned. The content of the story does not give us any clues, either, as it shows her living in an apartment in an urban city, traveling by bus, and buying potted flowers as a birthday surprise for her mother. Illustrated vibrantly by Kathryn Hewitt, this book is a good example of what could be termed melting pot or marginally multicultural. It is multicultural only because it talks about the universal experience (getting a surprise birthday present) of a girl living in an urban apartment complex who does not have a car but travels by public transportation. In fact, one could go so far as to say that except for the token color of the picture showing the girl as brown skinned, one cannot distinguish this book from any other mainstream books; in other words, it shows the universality of the human condition, thereby fitting into a melting pot category. So what warrants this book's inclusion (however marginal) under multicultural children's literature? The only reason is that it shows a child in an urban locality with an urban lifestyle. Going back to the aforementioned definition, all sociocultural experiences are validated, including those of class. Most books in many classrooms would fall into this category of melting pot books, showing the universality and being marginally multicultural, taking a contributions or additive approach. As mentioned before, these books are easy to come by as they do not create controversy or need much preplanning to introduce to a classroom, and they can easily be incorporated as a beginning to a larger unit. Many of Eve Bunting's books fall into this category and make great beginning books to larger units. For example, *A Day's Work* is a good introductory book about the hard-working day laborers who are forced to find menial work in a new country. This is the story of a 7-year-old boy who helps his grandfather find work as a day laborer in California by translating for him. In the process, he learns a valuable lesson of honesty from his grandfather.

Socially Conscious Books

Socially conscious books, according to Sims Bishop (2007), are about introducing one cultural group and its unique experiences to the mainstream in a way to educate or make "socially conscious" the trials and tribulations of that group to the larger group. Their main purpose "seemed to engender empathy and sympathy . . . to promote tolerance for racial desegregation or integration" (Sims Bishop, 2007, p. 61). This seems to be a unique characterization which I would like to change slightly to encompass all groups; in other words, I would like to say that socially conscious books may be those books that depict a social issue that makes us more "empathetic and sympathetic" toward a group that has come together as a people on the grounds of having a common social experience such as poverty, war, urban experiences, and so on. As such, socially conscious books are also culturally generic in the sense that they may include or be about people from any background, color, race, or ethnicity, but by experiencing similar social occurrences or events that are unique to their groups, they become multicultural. Some examples are as follows: *Allison* (1997), by Allen Say, is about a Japanese girl adopted by a White family who discovers that she doesn't look like her parents and learns about adoption. *The Wall* (1992), by Eve Bunting, is about a father and son searching for his grandfather's name on the Vietnam War Memorial in Washington, D.C. *Fly Away Home* (1993), also by Eve Bunting, is about a homeless family struggling to make ends meet and living in an airport. These books still fall into the additive approach; however, the experiences of this group of people help us empathize with and therefore transform our ideas about them. These would loosely correspond with Levels 2 and 3 of multiculturalism.

Culturally Conscious Books

Culturally conscious books, according to Sims Bishop (1982), are those that depict the cultural traditions, languages, and ethnicities of certain groups' experiences in an authentic voice, most often from an insider's perspective. Also termed *culturally specific* (Temple et al., 2006), books under this category talk about specific nuances and experiences that may not appear universally. At first glance, one may say that these are the books that are the most multicultural, in that they talk specifically about cultural aspects that are unique to certain groups, thereby giving us a glimpse into the lives of people who are from this group. Some examples include *Grandfather's Journey (1993), Tea with Milk (1999)*, and *Tree of Cranes (1991)*, all by Allen Say, a series of biographical tales about his grandfather, mother, and himself, respectively. *Grandfather's Journey* is a poignant tale of Say's grandfather's journey to California, where he settles to have a family. After a time he misses his land back in Japan and goes back for a visit, but when he wants to come back to California, World War II starts and "scattered our lives like leaves in a storm." Say's grandfather never comes back, but his daughter, Say's mother, was born and raised in San Francisco, and *Tea with Milk* is her story of growing up in Japan. *Tree of Cranes* depicts how Say's mother shows him the tradition of making and decorating a Christmas tree when he was growing up in Japan. These three books show the unique perspective of immigrants comfortable in two countries; in fact, "when I am in one country I miss the other," wrote Say, capturing aptly the feelings of many immigrants.

Neeny Coming, Neeny Going (1997), by Karen English, a Coretta Scott King Honor book, is a tale of changing times on Daufuskie Island off the coast of South Carolina. Told in the melodic language that follows the island dialect, it is the story of Essie, whose cousin Neeny comes to visit from the mainland. Although it may not have been a conscious choice, uniquely, nowhere in the book do we see the color White even as a backdrop for words on the page; rather the book is illustrated with vibrant colors of reds, yellows, browns, and blues. Other examples include *Roll of Thunder, Hear My Cry,* by Mildred D. Taylor. This is one of a series of riveting historical fiction books about four African American siblings caught in the tumultuous times of the Depression Era. *Esparanza Rising,* by Pam Muñoz Ryan, is loosely based on her grandmother's experiences and is told through the voice of Esparanza Ortega, a rich Mexican girl who moves to California as a migrant farmworker after losing everything due to her father's murder by bandits. *Baseball Saved Us* (1995), by Ken Mochizuki, is a heartwarming tale of survival from the point of view of a young boy who is of Japanese descent interned during World War II and how his father began a baseball team at the camp. As these are unique experiences, the stories give us specific insights from an insider's point of view that is not there in other books, helping us engage culturally with this group.

To reiterate the idea of "degrees of multiculturalness," books that may be put under the criteria of melting pot books are on the border of multicultural literature. They are only multicultural insofar as giving outsider, universalist perspectives that may show differences in class, personal experiences, and points of view in the content. The resolution of the story is often one that celebrates sameness as opposed to uniqueness. These books do not engage us in critical dialogue about the content. Books that may be put under the criteria of socially conscious are those that make us aware of social issues but may also be from an outsider's perspective and may not resolve the issue within the story. Although they may engage us in critical dialogue, these are more of a universal nature, for the larger good of the society. Culturally conscious books are insider perspectives that really teach us about specific nuances of cultural conflict that help us engage in critical dialogue in order to question larger power relations.

THE NEED FOR MULTICULTURAL CHILDREN'S LITERATURE

Other than the overwhelming statistics that show the need for multicultural children's literature, because of the diversity of students in classrooms today, which has been cited regularly in countless texts, magazines, and articles, there are deep connections between what happens inside the classrooms and what happens in the real world. In a time when the world is growing technologically smaller in terms of being accessible through the Internet, it is no longer a choice for classrooms to adopt a multicultural view, if there ever was a choice, because "the world outside the classroom transacts daily with the world inside the classroom and each reflects, shapes and is shaped by the other" (Fecho & Allen, 2003, p. 233). This means that racism, sexism, classism, and many other "isms" are apparent in the classrooms of today, but they "don't get discussed in complicated ways in many classrooms" (Fecho & Allen, 2003, p. 233). Multicultural children's literature, especially authentic accounts from an insider's perspective, offers multiple ways of intersecting with students' experiences and their learning. To borrow a sentence from Fecho and Allen (2003), although these authors are not writing about children's literature, "too few educators . . . have considered the ways students' experiences—e.g., cultural identity, socioeconomic circumstances, family language and culture, political issues, religion—transact with their efforts and opportunities to learn" (p. 233). It is because of this that there is an urgent need for multicultural children's literature to permeate the curriculum in schools, for genuine accounts that address many of these issues from an insider's point of view, to give children a way to validate their feelings and experiences; to create understanding, empathy, and tolerance; to break debilitating stereotypes; to give equal voice and representation. In this section, two important aspects of the need for multicultural children's literature are discussed in detail: equal representation and validation, and cultural authenticity.

Equal Representation and Validation

First and foremost, multicultural children's literature is important, as it gives equal representation and validation to countless voices that had either been silenced or did not have an opportunity to see themselves aptly represented in literature. Although the question of apt representation or cultural authenticity is still a sticky issue, there is at least hope that more works on diverse perspectives are becoming available to children of today. Educators and progressive thinkers of the early 20th century also felt the same and were some of the first to set the stage for equal representation. In the next few paragraphs, a brief history of the fight for equal representation and validation in books for children is traced.

As mentioned earlier in this chapter, under the section on tracing a brief history, it is not until the early part of the 20th century that nonmainstream works for children began to appear as a reaction to extreme stereotyping, gross misrepresentations, and skewed stories that were written from a White perspective. Some of these first works appeared from the African American community, which pioneered the pathways for those of other cultures to make their voices heard. One of the earliest is *The Brownies' Book* (1920–1921). A monthly magazine and the brainchild of W. E. B. Du Bois, it was the result of a number of "social and political circumstances" (Sims Bishop, 2007, p. 21). Its goal, as DuBois envisioned it, was to show Black children as normal and beautiful, to showcase their achievements and history from an authentic point of view, and foremost to help them see themselves in books as they were and not as someone else envisioned them. There were ample "poems, stories, biographical sketches, illustrations, photographs, and a number of featured columns" (Sims Bishop, 2007, p. 25). Along with Jessie Fauset and Augustus Dill, 24 issues of the *Brownies Book* magazine ran successfully to counter the debilitating stereotypes that were, until then (and later), rampant in stories such as *Little Black Sambo*. The *Brownies Book* magazine was published specifically for "The Children of the Sun . . . Designed for All Children, But Especially for *Ours*" (emphasis in text; January 1920, cover page; retrieved on May 12, 2008, from the Rare Books and Special Collections Division of the Library of Congress Digital Collections: http://www.loc.gov/library/libarch-digital.html). The cover page also says "it will seek to teach Universal Love and Brotherhood for all little folk, black and brown and yellow and white" (January 1920, cover page 2; also cited in Sims Bishop, 2007, p. 23). As can be seen by this quote, the aim was to reach out to all children, setting the stage for multicultural children's literature (Sims Bishop, 2007) and to validate children's experiences as they were. Until then, most children's books and magazines, like the *St. Nicholas Magazine* started in 1872, showed Black characters only as either comic relief or as less intelligent. As for other ethnicities, they were mostly nonexistent or shown as "uncivilized savages" that needed to be put on the right path.

With the help of the NAACP (National Association for the Advancement of Colored People) and the vision of DuBois, *The Brownies' Book* created a short but legendary respite for Black children. However, things were only getting worse for children from many Native American or American Indian tribes. Many schools around the United States and Canada, the most famous being The Carlisle Indian Industrial School started by Richard Henry Pratt, were rampantly forcing horrific changes on children ages 6 to 15. These children were systematically forced to be at these schools. They were sometimes kidnapped and forced to forget their languages, ways of living, eating, thinking, and so forth, in order to "become civilized." Validation had no meaning in these schools, with extreme corporal punishments for mere infractions of speaking their own language or even not knowing what was being said (Seale & Slapin, 2005). Authentic accounts of their stories were not even told until 70 or 80 years later, and most of these accounts have been found to be unauthentic, grossly underplaying or changing facts or fabricating points to give a watered-down version of their stories. Many of these are widely endorsed and circulated, reemphasizing many of the rampant stereotypes about native tribes. Examples include *My Heart Is on the Ground: The Diary of Nannie Little Rose, a Sioux Girl* (1999), by Ann Rinaldi, and *The Ledgerbook of Thomas Blue Eagle* (1994), by Grutman and Matthaei, titles that even those of us deeply concerned with multicultural issues are confused by because of the manner in which these stories are couched in "historical facts." These two books talk of the infamous schooling practices mentioned earlier. However, it is not to say that these should not be read;

rather these stories will serve as good beginning points and as books to compare to the authentic tales. Often the true and authentic tales are very difficult and shocking to read but the stories need to be told. Further, because of the graphic details in the authentic stories, they are not as widely publicized and as readily available. For example, *As Long as the Rivers Flow,* by Larry Loyie, a biographical tale of Loyie, who was forced to go to one of these schools, gives a first-person account that is heart-rending. *When the Rain Sings: Poems by Young Native Americans,* edited by Lee Francis (1999), is a compilation of poems by contemporary children from various native tribes. Similarly there is little written about other ethnicities that were settled in the United States like Chinese, Japanese, Mexican, and Cuban children during the early part of the 20th century. It is for these that we owe multicultural children's literature, to validate their experiences and to give equal representation.

Some works, although they are token, warrant a mention simply because there were no depictions until that point in time: Two books by Ezra Jack Keats are *The Snowy Day* (1963), which shows a Black child discovering that snow has fallen during the night, and *Pet Show* (1972), about a clever boy who takes a germ as his pet for the local pet show. Although Keats's books fall into the melting pot category, they at least began to appear in a climate where there were only White characters in books.

Cultural Authenticity

While works such as Keats's show universal themes and have a token representation of a different culture, the controversy comes about when authors tell stories about a different culture based on their imagination and perhaps only their experience and may make innocuous mistakes along the way. One has to wonder if these were innocuous mistakes or watering down or misrepresentation of the facts for motives such as authorial imagination, publishing choices, and demand. Cultural authenticity is an extremely complex issue that goes far deeper than the dichotomous insider–outsider perspectives. As Fox and Short (2003) discovered, there are as many controversies as points of view that range from the author to larger sociopolitical issues. In their excellent edited book called *Stories Matter: The Complexity of Cultural Authenticity in Children's Literature* (2003), devoted solely to this topic, they draw from authors, illustrators, educators, political theorists, to teachers in the field, covering such a wide range of topics from an author's social responsibility, authorial freedom, intentions and motivations, to the sociopolitical nature of multiculturalism, the politics of political correctness, and so on. As can be seen, this topic alone needs a book-length treatment, although in this chapter, only those aspects that are pertinent to evaluating and introducing multicultural children's literature are discussed.

So what is cultural authenticity in terms of multicultural children's literature and what does it entail? Simply, one could say that when you recognize certain aspects of your culture as described or portrayed in a book and you find those to be true, you may feel the book is culturally authentic (Fox & Short, 2003). However, this is a view from the reader's perspective, when you read a book and find yourself and your experiences in the book. But it may not have been *written* by an author who is from that culture, or a text could be construed as authentic when the plot and setting of a time period are authentic. In other words, defining cultural authenticity could produce as many theories as reader-response theories, depending on what position you are in: author, reader, or text.

For the purposes of this chapter, it will be useful to go to the crux of the issue, that is, multiculturalism and its goals to challenge racism, and affirm pluralism and equality. Sims Bishop said that cultural authenticity is "an elusive term that carries a number of different connotations . . . it has to do with the success with which an author is able to reflect the cultural perspectives of the people about whom he or she is writing and make readers from inside the group believe that the writer knows what's going on" (Sims Bishop, 2003, p. 29). She also contended that a "close critical examination of the work can reveal the distinctive features of the body of literature thereby provide [ing] some sense of [what] culturally authentic literature" could look like (Sims Bishop, 2003, p. 30). From these definitions, we can ascertain that authenticity is determined by how close the author's perspective is to the reader's perspective. A "close critical examination" is necessary in order to make sense of multicultural children's literature's cultural authenticity, and this is discussed in detail in the next section.

Cultural Authenticity: Whose Perspective?

In terms of representation, the danger comes about when a literary work is read and "given awards" and then is discovered to have historical misrepresentation or provides only a one-sided view. For example, Walach (2008) called for a close reading of books before they are taught in schools. He analyzed why *So Far From the Bamboo Grove* (1986), by Yoko Kawashima Watkins, a semiautobiographical tale of Watkins's escape from North Korea as a child to Japan during World War II, created a controversy, especially amongst the Korean descendants in a Massachusetts school district. He found that although the book talks about the atrocities of Korean communists against Japanese, it does not acknowledge or ignores the atrocities of Japanese against Koreans during that time. Walach, therefore, cautioned that teachers need to be especially careful in providing balanced accounts of historical facts, because "despite our lack of historical expertise, schools and parents expect teachers to choose appropriate books for children and in the process discern historical fiction from historical indifference or fabrication" (Walach, 2008, p. 17).

Amongst all the issues and controversy around multicultural children's literature, cultural authenticity is the most significant because it goes to the crux of multiculturalism itself. In other words, the whole reason why there was a movement for multicultural education was to give previously silenced groups a voice to be heard. However, when these voices are again usurped and used to distort through the stories and literature, it defeats the purpose.

Insider and Outsider Perspectives

There are clearly two sides to this issue: on the one hand are those that believe that only "cultural insiders" may write about a certain culture and its stories (see http://www.oyate.org), and on the other hand are those that believe that "cultural outsiders" may write about their stories because no one can be fully representative of an entire culture. One person's interpretation may not agree with others in the culture, and no culture's experience is so homogenous as to have one point of view (Gates, 2003, Taxel, 2003). However, the controversy comes in when one looks at larger issues of privilege and position about whose stories get published and publicized. For example, because of the decades of systematic suppression of peoples from most of the native tribes, very few children's authors have come out to tell their stories. Further, even those stories that have come out may be censored due to their horrific truthfulness. In such a situation, what can teachers do to authentically portray native tribes? This was the dilemma that Moreillon (2003) faced when she was looking for books that her students in the Sonoran Desert could read about where the Tohono O'odham American Indians live. She found no children's books that depicted them in an authentic manner and finally wrote one, against the advice of many people. A widely accepted author such as Paul Goble, who has told many Native American tales and has won many awards for his work, is another such example. However, Oyate, the group of Native American educators from various tribes, recommends that only cultural insiders or people who belong to their tribes are qualified to tell and represent their stories. They not only reject Goble as a storyteller but also declare him negligent in trying to understand these stories from an insider's point of view, even though he claims that he has done his research well, as noted by Seale (in Seale & Slapin, 2005). This brings us to yet another aspect of cultural authenticity, that of convincing insiders that their stories are interpreted well. Sims Bishop (2007) asked writers to understand the risks and difficulties in writing about a culture that they are only superficially familiar with and called it arrogance on the part of the writers. So who has the right to tell whose stories? There are no easy answers to this question. Celebrated author Julius Lester (2004) offered this:

> Multiculturalism is a two-way street. If the proponents want others to accept
> multiculturalism's challenge to Western cultural norms and relinquish power

and control, the proponents cannot move into what is now a power vacuum and usurp the same power they detest. (p. 122)

In other words, he said that we must be ready for others to make a story their own and tell it, and in being able to do so lies the "integrity" of multiculturalism, the "risk of living in a democracy" (Lester, 2004, p. 122). Although for the scope of this chapter suffice it to say that one needs to remember the larger principles of multicultural children's literature and draw upon criteria to evaluate children's literature so that one may not get caught up in the quagmire of these controversies, rather one can teach children to evaluate literature from a critical point of view.

Criteria for Evaluating Multicultural Children's Literature

Consider the following points in terms of the illustrations and the content of the text.

- *Author's and Illustrator's Perspective:* Evaluate the author's and illustrator's perspective; read the pictures and text closely. Is the author portraying characters and the story line from an "insider's" perspective? In other words, do the actions of the characters seem recognizable or agreeable by people of the culture that the book portrays? An insider's perspective is not only determined by an author or illustrator's birth and ethnicity but also by the meticulous research into the culture that comes through in the complete characterizations of the characters and plot line and resolution of the story.
- *Multidimensionality:* Evaluate multidimensionality in character, setting, and plot. Are characters multidimensional? Do they have a well-rounded personality? Are they stereotyped in illustrations? Are they recognizable as being from a particular cultural group? Is the setting multidimensional in terms of showing the culture's depth and breadth? For example, African Americans may live in urban areas or in apartments; they may be upper class, well educated, and so on. Similarly, Asian women may be illiterate, or Native Americans may live in houses in a city, and so on. Is the plot and setting multidimensional, making us believe that this story could be true and realistic? Is it recognizable and not superficial?
- *Stereotyping:* Check the illustration, characterization, and story resolution for possible stereotypes. Are illustrations token ones? Do they have recognizable real features of the culture or people depicted? Do the characters have unique characteristics that are not caricatures or stereotypes? Is the story resolved in a realistic manner?
- *Authentic Language:* Is the language spoken by the characters authentic? Is the language in which characters are depicted and the story line that is developed devoid of negative and derogatory connotations? Are words "loaded," that is, filled with negative or stereotypical connotations?

See also *10 Quick Ways to Analyze Children's Books for Racism and Sexism.* Adapted version available at http://www.chil-es.org/10ways.pdf.

CONCLUSION

The push for multiculturalism is perhaps the most important need of the times, especially in a country such as the United States of America, where there are people from practically every part of the globe (Lester, 2004). As we become smaller in terms of connectivity through the Internet, and we become bigger in terms of reach, our work as teachers becomes more complicated by the day. It is no longer a question of including materials reflecting a classroom's population; rather it has become imperative to learn about one another, to challenge ourselves, to question our assumptions, to relinquish power, to "see" history from many different points of view, and to become sensitized to the untold stories. Further, it is no consolation that we are doing this in a climate of uncertainty about what multiculturalism is. Renowned author Julius Lester (2004) rightly stated this:

> Let's be honest. None of us has a good idea what multiculturalism is. We in America are attempting something that has never been attempted in world history. We have created a nation that has a population that includes people from practically every country on the globe, and the grand adventure of the twenty-first century is figuring out how we can all live together while simultaneously cherishing and sharing the unique customs and ways of our particular groups.
>
> As we grapple with challenges humans have not grappled with before, it is all right to be confused . . . if we are agreed that what we want in our lives and thus our literature, is the inclusion of as wide a variety of the human experience as possible. (p. 122)

Lester's idea of including a wide variety of human experiences in order to represent as many people as possible seems easy enough, although as we discussed in this chapter, there are several nuances to this important topic, including striving for a level of multiculturalism that includes social action and justice, striving for cultural authenticity and equal representation, and evaluating books to fit into a curriculum that is culturally responsive.

It is heartening to know that there are already several teachers whose classrooms strive for a **culturally responsive approach** following an **anti-bias curriculum**, yet we have much work to do as the meanings and connotations of multiculturalism evolve in the 21st century.

REFLECTION QUESTIONS FOR THE TEACHER

1. What criteria can I use to define multicultural children's literature?

2. What criteria can I use to choose authentic and quality multicultural books in my classroom?

3. What do the terms melting pot, socially conscious, and culturally conscious mean in my classroom context?

4. What steps could I take to make my classroom and materials culturally conscious?

5. In what ways could I incorporate the four levels of multiculturalism into my classroom curriculum?

SAMPLE RESPONSE LESSON 2.1
Check for Authenticity

Primary Grades: In the Classroom, by Parents, Tutors, and Librarians

Duration: 1 Day

Overview

The teacher will read *The Keeping Quilt*, by Patricia Polacco, a family tale of a quilt that was passed from mother to daughter over four generations. Made from a basket of old clothes, Anna's babushka, Uncle Vladimir's shirt, Aunt Havalah's nightdress, and an apron of Aunt Natasha's become *The Keeping Quilt*, passed along from mother to daughter for almost a century. The quilt is a Sabbath tablecloth, a wedding canopy, and a blanket that welcomes babies warmly into the world told through strongly moving pictures. After the read-aloud, the teacher discusses family traditions that symbolize values and memories. The teacher will give information about Polacco's background and her immigrant story that is reflected in this book.

Or the teacher will read aloud *Grandfather's Journey*, by Allen Say, another family tale of Say's grandfather who moves to California from Japan. Eloquent yet succinct language, along with large, formal paintings in delicate, faded colors are portrayed to give the impression of a cherished and well-preserved family album. The teacher will give information about Allen Say's background and the immigrant story reflected in the book.

Materials

The Keeping Quilt by Patricia Polacco or *Grandfather's Journey* by Allen Say, poster paper, markers, colored pencils, chart paper for a compare and contrast chart, butcher paper for whole-group activity

Key Vocabulary and Terms

Traditions, Immigrant, Journeys, Perspective

(Continued)

(Continued)

Anticipatory Set

1. *Focus:* Students will discuss what they know about traditions, values, immigrants, and journeys. Perhaps they or their families are immigrants who have come on a long journey. Perhaps their grandfathers or grandmothers or aunts and uncles came as immigrants. Students discuss what traditions are. Students also learn about the authors and their backgrounds.

2. *Objective:* By the end of the lesson, students have learned about authors' perspectives. The teacher helps them come up with a list of queries to check the books for authenticity, including words, characterization, pictures, and historical information. With the help of the teacher, students may create a compare and contrast chart of the traditions in each book with those of their family members.

3. *Transfer:* As students learn about author's perspective and experiences, they will begin to recognize insider versus outsider perspectives. Students will also gain practice in reading pictures for authenticity through historical facts. This will help them gain an understanding of multidimensionality.

Instructions

1. After the read-aloud, the teacher will lead the students through a discussion of the authors' real lives and how they came to be immigrants. The teacher begins by asking students if they or their families or somebody they know may have moved here from a different country. If the teacher has an anecdotal tale, it may be nice for students to know about the teacher. The teacher needs to be open to stories and discussion, as often students may divert and talk about other journeys or vacations they have taken. A distinction should be made between vacations and an immigrant's journey.

2. The teacher could ask critical questions that lead the students to recognize insider perspectives. Have them look at the pictures in the books. Are they stereotyped or token? Are they recognizable and characteristic? The teacher may bring in actual pictures for the students to compare. Are the characters' clothes, features, and settings authentic? What kind of traditions do they recognize in the books? On a large chart, have students compare the authors' stories. The teacher should provide historical facts about the two authors and their respective stories.

3. On a poster paper, the teacher, along with the whole class, generates some guidelines on how to critically read picture books for authenticity and to determine whether they are multicultural. Suggestions include looking at the copyright date, pictures, story resolution, the author's background, and so on.

Independent Practice

After the whole-group discussion looking at the books, the teacher can have students pair together or work in small groups and look at other picture books with the guidelines that have been created as a whole class. Students could create a chart of their opinions on whether the books they looked at are multicultural and why they feel so.

Closure

The teacher could then share the opinions charts about the books that students chose and display them in the classroom.

Modifications: Secondary Grades

The same lesson may be followed but by using books such as the following: *Baseball Saved Us*, by Ken Mochizuki, which is the tale of a young Japanese boy interned along with his family during WWII and how baseball became a pastime to forget the tough times they were facing; or *Kite Runner*, by Khaled Hosseini, which is a multigenerational tale of a young boy's friendship and struggles in Afghanistan before, during, and after the Taliban rule. Older students will want to get historical facts and go deeper into the authenticity of the stories, using guidelines that are developed as a class.

SELECTED ANNOTATED BIBLIOGRAPHY

Melting Pot Books

Bunting, E. (1994). *The flower garden*. Orlando, FL: Voyager Books.

In this simple, vibrantly illustrated picture book, a young girl goes to the store to buy her mother a surprise birthday gift of a flowering garden. Kathryn Hewitt's beautiful illustrations show the girl as she travels by bus to the store and comes back to her apartment to plant the flowers in a window pot arrangement. The illustrations suggest a possible Manhattan setting. Recommended age 0 to 4 years.

Bunting, E. (1997). *A day's work*. Boston: Sandpiper Books.

Seven-year-old Francisco waits with his grandfather as they look for daily wage work along with many others at a street corner. As his grandfather does not speak English, Francisco is there to translate. In his rush to get his "Abuelo" a job, Francisco agrees to gardening, although they do not know anything about it. In the process, he learns a valuable lesson on honesty from his grandfather. Recommended age 4 years and up.

Keats, E. J. (1962). *The snowy day*. New York: Viking Children's Books, Penguin Group.

A young boy enjoys a day out in the snow. The illustrations are done using cut paper, watercolors, and striking collages, and they show Peter as he discovers that snow has fallen overnight. This book shows Peter as a Black boy enjoying a day out in the snow. Recommended age 0 to 4 years.

Paulsen, G. (1998). *The tortilla factory*. Orlando, FL: Voyager Books.

This is the story of how a kernel of corn becomes a tortilla. Told in beautiful yet simple poetic prose, the story takes a cycle of life approach. Illustrated by beautiful paintings by Ruth Paulsen, this book is sure to become a favorite for an early childhood audience. The story line is a little simplistic, although the book can be enjoyed for its colors. Recommended age 0 to 5 years.

Socially Conscious Books

Atkin, B. (2000). *Voices from the field: Children of migrant farmworkers tell their stories*. New York: Little, Brown Young Readers.

This photographic memoir of nine families of farmworkers is a moving depiction of the struggles and living conditions that many children of farmworkers endured. The interviews are rewritten sometimes in the first person and are compiled well with photographs to make an emotional yet sensitive impact for any reader. Recommended age 8 years and up.

Bunting, E. (1990). *The wall*. New York: Clarion Books.

In this story, a young boy and his father travel to Washington, D.C., to find his grandfather's name on the "the wall," or the Vietnam War memorial. Through sensitive and stirring language, Bunting captures the emotions of a father in search of his loved one and a child seeing his grandfather through his father's eyes. The moving language tries to convey the complex emotions of war. Recommended age 4 years and up.

Bunting, E. (1993). *Fly away home*. Boston: Sandpiper Books.

A boy and his father live in an airport along with another family. This revealing tale talks about the poverty that many people go through at certain points in their lives in spite of working hard. Told through the child's voice, Bunting voices the boy's wish to go to school and live in an apartment. Recommended age 4 years and up.

Grindley, S. (2004). *Spilled water*. New York: Bloomsbury Publishers USA.

This is the heart-rending story of 11-year-old Lu Si-Yan, a Chinese girl who grows up in a loving family until her father dies and her family becomes very poor. She is so poor that her uncle sells her so that her mother and her brother can have a better life. For the next 3 years,

Lu Si-Yan is alone fending for herself finding work in the big cities until she comes to a factory that makes toys for export. She is hired at first to stitch eyes on cute soft bears and later to be a "runner" delivering parts of toy trucks that are completed to the next person in the assembly line. Enduring extremely long hours with no rest, Lu Si-Yan manages to "race, race, race" (pg. 194) for 3 months, working from dawn to midnight, until she completely collapses one day. Recommended age 9 years and up.

Krull, K. (2003). *Harvesting hope: The story of Cesar Chavez*. San Diego, CA: Harcourt Children's Books.

This is the story of the man who mobilized the farmworkers to form a union in the 1960s. As a child, Chavez belonged to this group of people who were oppressed with poor wages, long and grueling work hours, and inhuman treatment. Krull relates this biography of Cesar Chavez through evocative language that is illustrated beautifully by Yuyi Morales. Although not complete in its details, it provides enough information for children to begin to understand the struggles of many in California. Recommended age 4 years and up.

Say, A. (1997). *Allison*. Boston: Sandpiper Books.

In this heartwarming tale, Say tells the story of a young Japanese girl who suddenly realizes that she is adopted when she goes to preschool. Her disappointment and grief at not looking like her parents melts away when she finds a stray cat that she wants to keep. The beautiful water color illustrations lend emotion to the valuable lesson that there are all kinds of families. Recommended age 4 years and up.

Culturally Conscious Books

Bruchac, M. M., & Grace, C. O. (2001). *1621: A new look at thanksgiving*. Washington, DC: National Geographic Society Children's Books.

This nonfiction book gives historical information about the supposed thanksgiving meal shared by the Wampanoag tribe and the Plymouth settlers. Bruchac and Grace break many myths in this book around the events surrounding the thanksgiving story and say that most of what has been passed down as legend is more fiction than fact. Through beautifully illustrated photographs recreated to imitate some of the original scenes, this book gives valuable information about the Wampanoag people. Recommended age 6 years and up.

Douglass, F. (2007). *The narrative of the life of Frederick Douglass: An American slave*. Boston: Book Jungle. (Original work published 1845)

Told in first-person voice, this is an evocative narrative of Frederick Douglass, a slave who, after gaining his freedom, educates himself to become a famous orator and writer. It begins with Douglass saying he does not know when he was born and shows through simple language the horrors of slavery. Recommended age middle to young adult.

English, K. (1997). *Neeny coming, Neeny going.* New York: Troll Communications.

A Coretta Scott King Honor book, this is a tale of changing times on Daufuskie Island off the coast of South Carolina, told through the eyes of Essie, whose cousin Neeny comes to visit from the mainland. It is told in the melodic language that follows the island dialect. Recommended age 3 years and up.

Gilmore, R. (2000). *Lights for Gita.* Gardiner, MN: Tilbury House.

In a picture book first published in Canada, an immigrant child from India, Gita celebrates the Hindu holiday of *Divali* for the first time in her new home. *Divali* is a holiday celebrated at the end of October and the beginning of November with lights, fireworks, street theater, sweets, and parties. Many consider it the beginning of a new year. In the November gloom of her new apartment, Gita longs for her extended family in New Delhi and the warmth she's left behind. She cries when an ice storm knocks out the power in all the buildings on her street; but with her parents and her best friend, she lights the *diyas (lamps)* for the festival, and she comes to see that the lights of *Divali* can beat the darkness outside and the sadness within. Recommended age 4 years and up.

Jimenez, F. (1999). *The circuit.* Orlando, FL: Houghton Mifflin Books for Children.

This is the first in the series of the autobiographical tale of Professor Francisco Jimenez, who came to the United States, along with his family, as a migrant farmworker. Through simple and direct language, Jimenez conveys the hardships, the sacrifices, and the fears of a migrant farmworker child. In this book, he relates how he and his brother have to change schools often, miss classes, or even run away from school, as *La Migra* or immigration officers come to deport them. Recommended age 8 years and up.

Jimenez, F. (2002). *Breaking through.* Boston: Sandpiper Books.

In this book, Jimenez continues his story from where he left off in the previous story and talks about how he successfully completes high school and goes on to college. At the end of the book are many photographs of him and his family that he has been able to gather.

Jimenez, F. (2008). *Reaching out.* Orlando, FL: Houghton Mifflin Books for Children.

This is the third in the series of fictionalized autobiographies of Jimenez and relates the struggles that he faces as he does odd jobs to put himself through college and graduate school. Jimenez relates the "double life" he leads as he does not let on to anyone that he is the child of a migrant farmworker, although he has great respect and love for his family. As the first in his entire family to go to college, he reflects the hopes of his people.

Say, A. (1991). *Tree of cranes.* Orlando, FL: Houghton Mifflin Books for Children.

This is the story of Allen Say's Christmas in Japan as a young boy when his mother decorates a pine tree with paper cranes and tells him about how trees are decorated in California. It is another autobiographical incident that Say turned into a poignant story. Recommended age 4 years and up.

Say, A. (1993). *Grandfather's journey.* Orlando, FL: Houghton Mifflin Books for Children.

This is the story of Allen Say's grandfather, who emigrates to the United States from Japan and settles in California. Illustrated by colorful panels that show the grandfather as a young, handsome man in Japan, traveling to the United States in a boat, wearing fashionable Western clothes, and later as an older man in Japan, the watercolor paintings capture each sentiment and each emotion beautifully as in a personal photo album. The words evoke every immigrant's feelings when he ends with "the funny thing is when I am in one country, I am homesick for the other." Recommended age 4 years and up.

Say, A. (1999). *Tea with milk.* Orlando, FL: Houghton Mifflin Books for Children.

This is the story of Allen Say's mother who was born in San Francisco but travels back to Japan with her parents as a young girl. The cultural shift she has to make is evident in her everyday existence as a Japanese American in Japan. She finally meets a Japanese business man who is able to help her bridge this gap. This is a heartwarming tale of East meets West. Recommended age 5 years and up.

REFERENCES

Au, K. H. (1993). *Literacy instruction in multicultural settings.* Fort Worth, TX: Harcourt Brace Jovanovich College Publishers.

Banks, J. A. (1999). *An introduction to multicultural education.* Upper Saddle River, NJ: Pearson Education.

Banks, J. A., & Banks, C. M. (2001). (Eds.). *Handbook of research on multicultural education.* San Francisco: Jossey-Bass.

Cai, M. (1998, Fall). Multiple definitions of multicultural literature: Is the debate really just "ivory tower" bickering? *The New Advocate, 11*(4), 311–324.

Fecho, B., & Allen, J. (2003). Teacher inquiry into literacy, social justice and power. In J. Flood, D. Lapp, J. R. Squire, & J. M. Jensen (Eds.), *Handbook of research on teaching the English language arts* (2nd ed., 232–246). Mahwah, NJ: Lawrence Erlbaum.

Fox, D., & Short, K. (Eds.). (2003). *Stories matter: The complexity of cultural authenticity in children's literature.* Urbana, IL: National Council of Teachers of English.

Gates, H. L. (2003). "Authenticity" or the lesson of Little Tree. In D. Fox & K. Short (Eds.), *Stories matter: The complexity of cultural authenticity in children's literature* (pp. 135–142). Urbana, IL: National Council of Teachers of English.

Kiefer, B., Hepler, S., & Hickman, J. (2007). *Charlotte Huck's children's literature* (9th ed.). New York: McGraw-Hill.

Larrick, N. (1965, September). The all white world of children's books. *The Saturday Review,* 63–65, 84–85.

Lester, J. (2004). Reflections. In L. M. Pavonetti (Ed.), *Children's literature remembered: Issues, trends and favorite books* (pp. 117–123). Westport, CT: Libraries Unlimited.

Moreillon, J. (2003). The candle and the mirror: One author's journey as an outsider. In D. Fox & K. Short (Eds.), *Stories matter: The complexity of cultural authenticity in children's literature* (pp. 61–77). Urbana, IL: National Council of Teachers of English.

Norton, D. E. (2009). *Multicultural children's literature: Through the eyes of many children* (3rd ed.). Upper Saddle River, NJ: Pearson Education.

Norton, E., & Norton, S. E. (with McClure, A.). (2003). *Through the eyes of a child: An introduction to children's literature.* Upper Saddle Fiver, NJ: Merrill/Prentice Hall.

Seale, D., & Slapin, B. (2005). *A broken flute: The native experience in books for children.* Lanham, MD: Altamira Press.

Seale, D., & Slapin, B. (2006). *Through Indian eyes: The native experience in books for children.* Philadelphia New Society Publishers.

Sims Bishop, R. (1982). *Shadow and substance: Afro-American experience in contemporary children's fiction.* Urbana, IL: National Council of Teachers of English.

Sims Bishop, R. (2003). Reframing the debate about cultural authenticity. In D. Fox & K. Short (Eds.), *Stories matter: The complexity of cultural authenticity in children's literature* (pp. 25–37). Urbana, IL: National Council of Teachers of English.

Sims Bishop, R. (2007). *Free within ourselves: The development of African American children's literature.* Portsmouth, NH: Heinemann.

Spring, J. (2008). *American education* (13th ed.). New York: McGraw-Hill.

Taxel, J. (1995). Cultural politics and writing for young people. In S. Lehr (Ed.), *Battling dragons: Issues and controversy in children's literature* (pp. 155–169). Portsmouth, NH: Heinemann.

Taxel, J. (2003). Multicultural literature and the politics of reaction. In D. Fox & K. Short (Eds.), *Stories matter: The complexity of cultural authenticity in children's literature* (pp. 143–164). Urbana, IL: National Council of Teachers of English.

Temple, C., Martinez, M., Yokota, J., & Naylor, A. (2006). *Children's books in children's hands: An introduction to their literature* (3rd ed.) Boston: Allyn & Bacon.

Thompson, D. (1995). Family values and kinship bonds: An examination of African American families in selected picture books 1974–1993. In S. Lehr (Ed.), *Battling dragons: Issues and controversy in children's literature* (pp. 87–104). Portsmouth, NH: Heinemann.

Walach, S. (2008, January). Speaking my mind: *So Far From the Bamboo Grove*: Multiculturalism, historical context, and close reading. *English Journal, 97*(3), 16–20.

Chapter 3

Choosing Books and Reading Critically

Many children are first introduced to reading and writing through stories that are read aloud to them by parents, teachers, caregivers, and others. It is believed that reading aloud to a child even 15 minutes a day makes a huge difference in that child later being able to read and write in school. Although reading stories aloud is largely a Western concept, the idea that more exposure to language and communication increases children's vocabulary has been proven perhaps all over the world. Even children who may not be exposed to reading aloud in the traditional sense but are exposed to oral tales, finger-plays, rhymes, and song begin to show their grasp of language. In fact, in this world of billboards, advertisements, televisions, the World Wide Web, and so on, one could argue that it is actually hard to get away from print in some form or other. So why is there the necessity to read aloud to a child? Why should parents and caregivers read to children? And what has prompted the large demand for children's books, especially early childhood products to encourage reading? The answer, simply, is that reading aloud is the single most effective way to engage and communicate with a child while at the same time teaching the child the conventions of printed language and communication. However, even in this world where one would have to try very hard to get away from print, a 2004 research report by the National Endowment for the Arts noted that there is a great decline in reading, that overall average reading scores continue to worsen especially among teenagers and young men. They also cautioned that this has serious civic, social, and economic implications (National Endowment for the Arts, 2004). In light of this, it has become even more imperative to teach children not only how to read, but to read critically, to engage with the world in which they live.

This chapter goes further than just touching upon the traditional read-aloud strategies such as predicting, plot recognition, and so on. This chapter concentrates on the concept of choosing critical books to read aloud in the belief that this is a powerful strategy that can be used throughout one's school years and beyond, to engage in and with connecting the curriculum to current events and students' lives.

Choosing Critical Children's Books

The role of particularly one kind of lesson that almost always uses a children's book stands foremost in language arts and literacy or reading classes: the read-aloud. A read-aloud is simply the reading of any book aloud to children, usually in an elementary or a primary classroom or to a group of children, followed by specific activities. In the average classroom, the primary purpose of a read-aloud is to help students learn vocabulary aspects of plot, make predictions, answer questions related to the story, and so on. Rather than using a read-aloud story only to teach reading strategies, it may also be used to expose children and young adults to rich and diverse literature. More importantly, reading aloud may be used to elicit critical dialogue about the story's social topic as a means to get children and young adults thinking on a deeper level about their own role in society and the responsibilities that go with it. In keeping with the theme of this book, this chapter emphasizes critical literacy and shows how multicultural children's literature, when used suitably, through read-alouds, can play an important role in creating a student and youth force of critical thinkers.

As mentioned in Chapter 1, there are more than 10,000 children's trade books published each year, and that number almost doubled to 17,500 in 2008 (Kiefer, 2010), all of which come under the broad category of children's literature. To weed out and choose meaningful and authentic children's books becomes a difficult task, given the variety and volume of books. Further, when choosing books, it is important to keep in mind the goals and objectives of the lesson. Two related principles on choosing books help immensely:

1. *Wide Audience Appeal:* Books that have wide audience appeal are those that can reach out to a wide variety of audiences in terms of comprehension and situations. Further, such books can be read and enjoyed equally by children of a wide age range, providing them with aspects to connect with at their comprehension levels and at their developmental level. In other words, there is something for everyone in these books. Although most multicultural children's books, when written by a master author, provide these opportunities, some books stand out more than the rest. In the following paragraphs more details are provided.

2. *Possibility for Critical Analysis:* Critical analysis is not simply critiquing a book and its content; rather, critical analysis may be understood as getting to

critical aspects of the content of the story and connecting it to real life and the curriculum to question, discuss, analyze, make inferences, and so on. Particularly, these books may offer revealing insights, change attitudes, and show diverse perspectives.

These principles are not new for a critical literacy curriculum; rather, here they are redefined in relation to reading aloud in a way to incorporate what reading educators have all along said are successful strategies in terms of teaching reading to students. A book for a read-aloud picked with these two principles is sure to elicit deeper conversations and comprehension from students. The following are specific things to look for when choosing books that have wide audience appeal and possibilities for critical analysis:

Language use:

- Simple and vivid, with word choices evoking visual aspects
- Brevity of words to evoke depth of meaning rather than long descriptions
- May have metaphorical, rhythmic, onomatopoeic, or symbolic language (but not required)
- May use a variety of dialects, ways of speaking, mannerisms, and/or code-switch to be culturally authentic

Illustrations (if any):

- Complement the text to create an equal union between text and illustrations
- Have vivid colors or colors that depict the mood, setting, emotional and cultural content of the text or story line
- Are multilayered and multidimensional to provide wide depth of meaning
- Are culturally authentic in their art form

Content:

- Culturally relevant and provides culturally and historically authentic information (if any)
- Connects to a current event, real-life incident, event, or fact
- Well researched, informative, and provides a new perspective
- Provides openings for questions, queries, wonderings, and "what ifs"

There are numerous examples of books that have wide audience appeal and possibilities of critical analysis. Some favorites are *Honey Baby Sugar Child,* a read-aloud book for preschool and kindergarten. With beautiful colors and realistic action pictures, the book shows a mother and her baby playing throughout the day. The words depict the African American language as the mother says, "I wanna kiss ya, squeeze ya till the sugar's gone. . . . Child I want to eat you up." Other books that show wonderful language use include Pat Mora's *Confetti Poems for Children* (1992) and *Agua, Agua, Agua* (1994). *Henry's Freedom Box* (2007), by Ellen Levine, is based on a true story first retold in an 1872 publication about the Underground Railroad. Excellently illustrated by Kadir Nelson, the book shows the beauty, dignity, and integrity of the Black people: "Do you see those leaves blowing in the wind? They are torn from the trees like slave children are torn from their families," says Henry's mother in the story. The same leaf motif is used by Allen Say in *Grandfather's Journey* (2008) to talk about the devastation of World War II: "Our lives were "scattered . . . like leaves in a storm."

Mildred D. Taylor's part autobiographical stories about the Logan family who owns some land in the early 1930s are all written with vivid language that puts us instantly into the times in which they were written. These short chapter books are perfect for reading aloud to a primary or elementary class. Most are less than 60 pages long. *Song of the Trees, The Friendship, Mississippi Bridge, The Well, The Gold Cadillac,* and others are told through the eyes of the Logan children, Cassie and her brothers Stacey, Little Man, and Christopher-John. These stories show the injustices in the lives of pre–civil rights African American families.

Clara Caterpillar tells the story of Clara, a caterpillar, and her friends, as they go from caterpillar to cocoon to butterfly. Clara turns into a plain cabbage butterfly while Connie turns into a beautiful red butterfly. As Connie shows off her colors, a bird chases her to eat her till Clara distracts the bird and then camouflages herself so that the bird loses interest. Vibrant colors and the use of many words starting with the letter *c* give us a wonderful text to read aloud for primary age children. Other books for this age group include Leo Lionni's *Frederick, Swimmy,* and *Little Blue and Little Yellow*. More examples of books that have wide audience appeal and possibilities for critical analysis are given in the annotated bibliography at the end of this chapter. A read-aloud with a book chosen along these lines makes for a deeper reading engagement for students.

The Traditional Read-Aloud

In the traditional classroom, a read-aloud is generally done for one of two purposes: to teach specific reading lessons and for entertainment or transition times. The traditional classroom read-aloud usually follows a pattern such as this:

- The teacher picks a book to read, usually a picture book and usually to an elementary or younger age class.

- The teacher does a "picture walk" or a similar version of this by asking questions for "predictions," such as, "What do you think this book is about?" "Can you tell me what is going on in the story by looking at the pictures?"
- The teacher may also choose and prepare "difficult" words from the book ahead of time and put them on a "vocabulary" list for students to learn.
- The teacher then reads the book aloud, stopping at various points to ask questions. These questions are mainly to see if the students are understanding the story, comprehending the plot line, are able to recall incidents from the story, and so on.
- If this is a preprimary class, then the read-aloud is mainly used for teaching phonemic awareness and high frequency words, letter recognition, sentence pattern, and so on.
- Once the book has been read aloud, another book is chosen for a different lesson.

Rarely are children in middle or high school read aloud to and rarely are children's books used abundantly in these age groups. Although the aforementioned outline works well, in order to fully make use of the wealth of multicultural children's literature available to us today, methods that are more interactive and based on reader-response theories may be used for a critical read-aloud format. However, before describing a critical read-aloud format, it is important to describe and explain the reader-response theory on which it is based, in the following paragraphs.

READER RESPONSE

Foremost amongst reader-response theories is Louise Rosenblatt's *transactional theory,* which describes the relationship between a reader and a text. Long before people began thinking about the reader having a stake in the reading process, Rosenblatt formed and described her transactional theory in her work, *Literature as Exploration,* published in 1938, later republished in 1968, 1976, 1983, and most recently in 1995 (Karolides, 2005). Although Rosenblatt does not consider her transactional theory a part of reader-response theories, this work has been the foundation for many other reader-response theories that flourished later in the 20th century (Karolides, 2005). Simply put, Rosenblatt's transactional theory is based on the belief that "meaning is being built up through the back-and-forth relationship between reader and text during a reading event" (Karolides, 2005, p. xix). At a time (1930s) when objective and impersonal approaches to science were the norm, Rosenblatt discovered that her students' readings of literature and their discussions were built on their personal interchanges with the text.

In other words, when people read and responded to texts, they brought in their life experiences, assumptions about the world, and their cultural orientations. This observation was the key factor in forming her transactional theory.

In this theory, Dr. Rosenblatt explains that there are two kinds of transactions that take place when we read a text: *Efferent* and *Aesthetic*. Both of these have to do with the way we read and comprehend the text and "the kind of meaning produced," whatever that text may be (Rosenblatt, 2005, p. xxv). Efferent reading is when we read for informative purposes only, such as instruction labels, directions, "how to" manuals, and so on. In such a reading, the emphasis is on the end result, what we can understand or make meaning of for a particular purpose. We carry forward the meaning we gain from an efferent reading into our actions by following what the text tells us to do, as efferent in Latin means to "carry away" (Rosenblatt, 2005). In such readings, therefore, we do not invest any emotion, personal feelings, or personal preferences; rather, we look for the "actions to perform after the reading ends" (Rosenblatt, 2005, p. xxvi). In other words, an efferent reading happens when we are looking for facts and ideas that we may use for a particular purpose.

Aesthetic reading, however, is diametrically opposite to efferent reading and is highly personal and private. It is a "lived through" experience that happens during the *process* of reading rather than at the end. Aesthetic reading is a transaction between the reader and the text that happens in the duration of the reading and involves "the images, the sensations, the feelings, the changing moods . . . and attitudes surrounding it" (Rosenblatt, 2005, p. xxvi). In such a reading transaction, the end result is a "poem" that is produced between the reader and the text. This "poem" may be interpreted as the "meaning gleaned" or the "experience of" the reader.

Dr. Rosenblatt further puts these two ways of reading on a continuum that she calls the transactional theory, mentioned earlier. In her transactional theory, efferent and aesthetic are on opposite ends of the same pole, which may be drawn as a straight line. All reading may be placed on this line or continuum, and depending on what kind of transaction the reading experience gives us, we can place it on this continuum. For example, we may read the newspaper in the morning to know about what is happening in the world. In the process of reading the newspaper, we unconsciously make selections on what we engage personally with and what we read for information. Perhaps a news item touches us more deeply than another, or perhaps we learn something we had never heard of before from another news item; in other words, we transact differently with different news items, and during our reading, we may move between aesthetic and efferent reading on the same continuum. This transactional theory with its efferent and aesthetic continuum explains what happens in the process of any reading event, especially between the reader and the text.

In terms of teaching reading in the classroom, if the transaction can become one that is closer to an aesthetic reading, children's responses and engagement with the text become more involved, personal, and critical.

READING ALOUD AND TRANSACTIONAL THEORY

In most classroom situations, especially given the push for meeting the standards, time constraints, and accountability, teachers are simply pushed to do efferent transactions rather than strive for an aesthetic transaction. Even 75 years after Dr. Rosenblatt pioneered the transactional theory, many classrooms are still places where students are expected to learn mainly facts and information through reading various texts, rather than become involved in constructing a collaborative curriculum. The traditional read-aloud follows such a curriculum, where students are expected to learn and answer questions about the story or literature selection they read. In fact, Dr. Rosenblatt (2005) herself put it this way:

> The tendency in the teaching of literature has been to turn the student's attention away from the actual experience, and to focus on presenting a "correct," traditional interpretation, and on knowledge about technical devices or biographical or historical background. (p. xxvii)

Similarly, after reading a literature selection, students doing a traditional read-aloud are usually expected to answer specific questions regarding the story's facts rather than reflect on the feelings produced by the story and how those feelings and interpretations affect their attitudes about the story in relation to their worlds. In fact, it may be said that the importance of Rosenblatt's transactional theory lies in its basic principle of reflective practices, that of paying attention to and encouraging students to take deeper and more critical stances in their readings of all school texts and materials.

The Critical Read-Aloud

Based on Dr. Rosenblatt's transactional theory and her philosophy of encouraging students to take more critical stances in their readings of school materials, a "critical read-aloud" may be fashioned using available multicultural children's literature. In a critical read-aloud, books are chosen using the two criteria mentioned in the beginning of this chapter: books with wide audience appeal and possibilities for critical analysis. Further, teachers could also consider the following in choosing books:

- Pick books that connect with the current topic in the classroom and have relevance to the students in the classroom.
- Read the book several times before reading it aloud to the classroom, to
  - Find a specific angle or specific topic that will hook the interest of students in the class. This may be a current event, a fact, a picture, a question, or anything that the students and the teacher could discuss before the read-aloud.

> — Set the book or story in a larger context than just the classroom. As mentioned here, finding an angle to hook students allows students to anticipate what the story is going to be about while also seeing how the story fits with the class curriculum, what they are learning and wondering about, and why it is important to learn about this topic. A simple "I wonder what . . . " sets the context for the read-aloud. This also allows students to participate by doing their own wonderings, a way to meet the requirements of "predicting" without making it mundane.
> — Set the time and pace, and decide where to pause, put emphasis, ask questions, stop for discussion, and so on.
> — Note down major points of the story that can be used for further discussion or for student response activities.

- Decide what responses will be reasonable to ask of students during and after the read-aloud (this depends on age, development level, and ability).
- Strive for responses that help students gain a more aesthetic reading of the book rather than for information or efferent purposes only.
- Prepare open-ended questions that help students to

  — *Connect* with the story (whole story, parts, with a character, etc.)
  — *Discuss* among themselves (whole class or small groups)
  — Understand what they *felt* about the story (Was it sad, happy, etc.) and why
  — *Facilitate intertextual connections* (Do they know of similar stories in their real lives or in what they have read or heard before?)
  — *Develop deeper understandings* of the story (Why do you think an incident happened?)
  — *Provide information* about the author, illustrator, time period, and setting
  — *Critique the story:* Critique does not mean only ripping it apart; it also means getting at critical points in the story that may be difficult to understand. It means helping students understand why something happened the way it did. It means helping students question "either-or" theories or cut-and-dried facts (e.g., Why did the Indians have to sign the treaty and give up their lands? Were all the Indians bad? Were all the settlers bad? What really happened when Columbus "discovered" America?).

As many educators and teachers are aware, open-ended questions are not just questions that don't have a one-word answer or a yes or no answer; rather, they are questions that help students begin thinking about the topic at hand. In terms of doing a critical read-aloud, questioning is an essential process in furthering students' engagement with authentic literature. Although much has been written about questioning and the process and motives of asking questions, it would be useful to go through some techniques of questioning.

QUESTIONING

In a critical approach to learning, students are recognized as contributing members of the curriculum, constructing and shaping it. Empowering students with the ability to construct their curriculum requires that teachers provide the basis for students to build that knowledge through opportunities and "openings" in the curriculum. Questioning is at the core of such a curriculum because through asking productive questions, students are empowered into action. However, asking productive questions is a skill that needs to be constantly honed. Morgan and Saxton (1994) said that "effective teaching depends primarily upon the teacher's skill in being able to ask questions which generate different kinds of learning" (p. 3).

In a traditional read-aloud, the teacher questions students so they can assess if the students are able to comprehend the story. So in a picture walk, students may be asked, "What do you think this book is about?" This activates prior knowledge or tells the teacher how much the students already know about the topic or book. However, rephrasing the same question with a context will help assess various other areas over and above simply activating prior knowledge. For example, say the book being read aloud is *Grandfather's Journey,* by Allen Say, and the teacher asks students, "What do you think this book is about?" Students may answer, "about a grandfather's journey," or something close to that. As can be seen, the question did not invite a longer or more in-depth answer than that. Rather, the teacher might set the context by opening a short discussion on journeys, perhaps asking something like, "Do any of you know anyone who has come from a different country? Have they told you their story?" or "I wonder why people leave their countries to go settle in another country?" After a brief discussion in which students will be able to make various connections to journeys, particularly those of an immigrant, their answer to "What do you think this book is about?" will be more involved. They will now know that this book may be about a grandfather's journey from one country to another. This kind of activation of prior knowledge is more rounded in that it is helping students do multiple learning activities at the same time. The discussion sets the context in helping them do the following:

- *Comprehend* what they are going to read about
- *Anticipate* what may happen in the story, thereby *involving* them
- Make *intertextual* connections with what happens in the story because they have heard others in the class discuss people they knew who may have left their country
- *Synthesize* what is being read to them because they have a context to base it on
- *Analyze* what is happening because the earlier discussion set the foundation for their further understanding of the story

- Be *empowered* as the teacher began a question with, "I wonder . . . " showing them that she may not have all the answers
- *Apply* what they know from the discussion and from the read-aloud to set the stage for further learning and wonderings (Morgan & Saxton, 1994)

As can be seen, it is crucial to word the open-ended question in a way that invites students to participate fully in the read-aloud. A useful strategy in wording the question is to ask oneself the following: "What learning principle do I want my students to gain from their answers to this question?" So for example, when the read-aloud calls for students to be able to "predict," the teacher could ask herself or himself this: "What do I really want them to learn when I ask them to predict?" Does the teacher want to see simply if the students can anticipate or guess? Or is it something deeper? Does the teacher want to know if the students are capable of following visual cues in the story to anticipate what may come next? If this is the case, then rephrasing with a series of questions to lead the students up to the answer may be more useful. So rather than asking, "What do you think will happen next?" one could say the following: "Can you think of another story that was similar to this one? What does this picture tell you? I wonder if we could guess what may happen by looking at the picture." In other words, asking ourselves, "What learning principle do I want my students to gain from their answers to this question?" will help teachers analyze what category or kind of information they are looking for when they phrase a question. That is, what is the function of asking a particular question?

Functions of Questioning

Morgan and Saxton (1994) came up with some very useful categories or kinds of questions. Breaking down questioning techniques by these functions helps us as teachers to understand why we may ask a certain question. In other words, it helps us in the process of understanding what learning principles we want our students to gain by the questions we ask. Making bare these processes and functions clarifies for us teachers the language and procedures to use not only in critical read-alouds but in most lessons that we strive to teach in classrooms. As Morgan and Saxton did such a fantastic job of enumerating and describing this methodology, most of what follows is reproduced and adapted directly from Chapter 5 of *Asking Better Questions* by Morgan and Saxton, originally published in 1994 (a second edition was published in 2006). They classify questions by the function or purpose that they serve when asked. Broadly they classified the following three categories:

- Questions which elicit Information
- Questions which shape Understanding
- Questions which press for Reflection

Rather than classify questions by type, which may limit student participation because the *type* of question may be teacher directed—it may be factual or evaluative—Morgan and Saxton classify questions by what the question is *intended to do*. So they ask, "What do I want this question to *do?*" (1994, p. 41, emphasis in original), which may be a natural shadow to the question that is asked earlier: "What learning principle do I want my students to gain from their answers to this question?"

Elicit Information

Questions that elicit information can further be classified by the function that they serve:

- *Function:* To Establish Rules
  - Rules of behavior (in a classroom, in the playground, during a read-aloud, etc.). For example: "What do we need to remember when we are listening to a story?"
  - Develop discussion skills/take responsibility/give responsibility (to make new rules, to establish parameters, to judge fairness, etc.): For example, "What do we do when we have a problem?"
  - Checking to see if everyone is on the same page/checking for comprehension/checking to see if students are attentive, and so forth. For example: "Did everyone understand what we are going to do now?"

- *Function:* To Establish Procedure
  - Go over procedure, for order, to form groups, to set productive ways for work, and so on. For example: "What do we do first before we go out to play?" "What do we do to form a group?" "How shall we form this group?"
  - Develop organization of time, space, or method of work. For example: "Do we have enough information to come to a conclusion?" "What more do we need to know and how do we go about finding out?"
  - To stimulate research and establish engagement in the material. For example: "Who in real life can give us this information?" "What do we need to know to move on?" "What would happen if . . . ?"

- *Function:* To Establish Control/Group Discipline
  - To help students work independently and efficiently. For example: "How shall we arrange the classroom?" "Who will be responsible for notes?" "Who will keep time?"
  - To unify class to help students feel like a community/togetherness. For example: "Are we all agreed that . . . ?" "Are we ready to move on now?" "Did everyone understand?" "Does anyone have any other questions or comments or anything to add?"

- *Function:* To Focus on Recall of Facts
  — Establish curricular foundation, go over what has been learned, establish facts, and so on. For example: "Could someone summarize the plot?" "Could we recall what happened so far in the story?" "What happened to this person?"

- *Function:* To Supply Information and/or Suggest Implications
  — Prepare students to deal with a possible challenge, pose a possible challenge to help them focus attention or think of implications. For example: "What are we prepared to give up if we choose to do this?" "Did the Indian Tribes in . . . really understand the treaty they were signing?" "What may happen if no one recycles?"

- *Function:* To Reveal Experience
  — To discover what students are bringing into the classroom. For example: "Can you think of a time when you may have been in the same situation?" "Has there been a time when you couldn't/were not allowed to . . . ? What did you experience?"

Shape Understanding

Questions that shape understanding can also be further broken down by the function that they serve.

- *Function:* To Make Connections
  To require students to use what they know and apply it to the material at hand; to bring students today into a relationship with the past and/or future. (Morgan & Saxton, 1994, p. 45)
  — *Personal Connections.* For example: "Has anyone had a similar experience?"
  — *Intertextual Connections.* For example: "How is this similar to something you have heard/read/seen/or been told about?"
  — *Cultural Connections.* For example: "How would it change your lives if . . . ?"

- *Function:* To Reposition (to help students rethink, restate, or reposition a situation so that they are able to understand the depth or concept more accurately). For example: "What does the author really mean when he/she states . . . ?" "Do you really think this person means what is said here?" "What would you do if . . . ?"

- *Function:* To Promote Understanding From Multiple Perspectives (to help students develop their own attitudes, to think through and decode for themselves, to view an area of study from multiple perspectives and under-standings). For example: "Is it okay to want revenge?" "What does war really do?" "Who are the victims of war?" "If it were happening in your own backyard, would you feel differently?" or "Is it possible to live in an area of conflict and belong to no side?" (Morgan & Saxton, 1994, p. 47)

- *Function:* To Enhance Inference and Interpretation, Focus on Underlying Meaning Making (to help students infer from, conclude or deduce, probe for deeper comprehension, especially from written materials that they will use to think). For example: "What is this paragraph really saying?" "What does the statement/situation really tell you about . . . ?" "How will you explain . . . ?" "What is the implication of this on that?"

Press for Reflection

Questions that press for reflection are crucial to a critical literacy curriculum as this is the part where teachers can really lead students into critical thinking. Questions that press for reflection function in the following ways:

- *Function:* To Develop Supposition or Hypothesis (to help students think creatively and laterally rather than literally). For example: "I wonder what would happen if Snow White suddenly discovered that her real mother was the witch and not her stepmother?" or "What would you do if you woke up and found that you had become the opposite gender?" or "What if the homeless person in your neighborhood turns out to be the Nobel prize winner?" These are questions that may throw one off guard, thereby making students think creatively to develop a supposition or a hypothesis.

- *Function:* To Focus on Personal Feelings (Usually questions that press for reflection focus on personal feelings, such as "Which character in . . . was your favorite or did you like this book or story?" may be asked. However, the importance in focusing on personal feelings questions is to give students practice in expressing and sharing these feelings in verbal or written ways.) For example: "Why is it that you sometimes feel homesick even when you are at home?" (Morgan & Saxton, 1994, p. 49). "What is home to you?" or "What might be your concerns . . . ?"

- *Function:* To Develop Critical Assessment/Value Judgments (These questions help to guide students' thinking to examine and recognize their own view-points, biases, feelings, and thinking. The questions are often designed and worded to instigate and stimulate controversy in order to get students think-ing.) For example: "If we woke up one fine day and found that we are no longer a democracy, what would we do?" "Can we justify children working to earn a living?" "Does it really matter if we recycle or not?" "Where would you place value? Or "What would be priority—eradicating hunger in the world or poverty in the United States?"

Morgan and Saxton (1994) also reminded us that these questions and their functions are not hierarchical and do not represent any kind of taxonomy. In other words, during a lesson, a teacher may shift easily between these three categories, using questions from any of the functions, and lead according to the objectives of the lesson: The focus should always be on the needs of the students and "what you want the question *to do*" (p. 51). This classification of questions, according to these two educators, follows the common practice of "low-order" and "high-order" questioning and thinking but by not using those limiting terms, it allows teachers to form their own questions using the functions of questions as a guideline. In other words, we go back to asking ourselves as teachers, "What learning principle do I want my students to gain when I phrase and ask this question?"

Ask the Experts: Authors, Parents, Educators, and Teachers

The usefulness of reading aloud to children at an early age was discovered and formulated mainly by parents, when they saw their children learn how to read and write as a result of being read to, and by teachers, who discovered that students were engaged the most when they were read aloud to in an interesting fashion. In fact, Mem Fox, who is the author of several children's books, began writing and lecturing about the qualities of reading aloud when she saw that her own daughter had gained a grasp of reading because of being read to (Fox, 2001). Similarly, Jim Trelease, considered one of the popular authorities on reading aloud for children, with over a million copies sold of his book, *The Read-Aloud Handbook* (1982, 1985, 1989, 1995, 2001), said that he began reading aloud to his children back in the 1960s when this practice was unheard of: "Each night I read to my daughter and son, unaware of any cognitive or emotional benefits" (Trelease, 2001, p. xv).

Fox, who is also a prolific children's book author, said very similar things in her book on reading aloud, called *Reading Magic: Why Reading Aloud to Our Children Will Change Their Lives Forever* (2001). However, Fox concentrates on an imperative aspect of reading aloud, that of creating an emotional bond with children: "Reading aloud shouldn't be thought of as a grimacing This is Good For Your Child event for mothers and fathers"; rather, she emphasizes that when reading aloud to children, one should concentrate on having a "rollicking good time" so that it becomes "a delicious 'chocolate' kind of experience" (pp. 10–11), reminding us of Rosenblatt's transactional theory, where a "poem" is formed. Further, Fox said,

Engaging in this kind of conspiracy with children is perhaps the greatest benefit of reading aloud to them. As we share the words and pictures, the ideas and viewpoints, the rhythms and rhymes, the pain and comfort, and the hopes and fears and the big issues of life that we encounter together in the pages of a book, we connect through minds and hearts with our children and bond closely in a secret society with the books we have shared. The fire of literacy is created by the emotional sparks between a child, a book, and the person reading. It isn't achieved by the book alone, nor by the child alone, nor by the adult who's reading aloud—it's the relationship winding between all three, bringing them together in easy harmony. (p. 10)

Along with the emotional aspect of reading aloud, Fox cites brain research to support her theory on oral language development. She rightly says that the more we talk with our children about books and with books through reading aloud, the sharper their brains get at helping them figure out language. Through simple logic she says that while programs on television such as *Reading Rainbow* in the United States and *Book Place* in Australia "have great merit because they teach children about stories and how they work . . . it doesn't develop children's ability to speak. . . . Television doesn't talk to children—it talks at them and they can't talk back, and talking back is what learning language is all about" (Fox, 2001, p. 18). In emphasizing the importance of "talking back," Fox touches on the necessity for interaction, the need for contact, and the constant back and forth of enjoying a read-aloud together.

Interaction, as we know, has been at the heart of many tried and trusted learning theories, such as Vygotsky's (1939) "zone of proximal development," the crucial time when a child is on the verge of learning something new but cannot achieve that without interaction with a more knowledgeable peer who is present at the zone of proximal development to push the limits of the zone. In a read-aloud, the more knowledgeable peer reads aloud as the child listens and questions, interacts with gestures, learns new terms for and connects with the reading peer. This interaction in a read-aloud is critical to the learning process.

Amongst the words of wisdom on reading aloud that this prolific children's author gives us are "Mem Fox's Ten Read-Aloud Commandments," which can be accessed at her Web site: http://www.memfox.com/ten-read-aloud-commandments.html (Fox, n.d.). These include some well-known read-aloud necessities such as reading aloud for at least 10 minutes a day every day, as well as some that are refreshing, like "Read aloud with animation . . . don't be dull, flat, or boring. Hang loose and be loud" (Fox, n.d.).

In conclusion, although educators and teachers know the fabulous advantages of reading aloud, often they get caught up in the quagmire of the lesson, checking to see if students understood the plot rather than enjoying the story itself. As Fox (n.d.) said in her commandments, "Never ever *teach* reading or get tense around books";

rather, showing students the fun of reading and how enjoyable it is makes reading something that they would want to do rather than have to do.

Each year, there are countless reports, research articles, books, and chapters that are published by educators that talk about the importance of reading aloud. Many well-known journals publish peer-reviewed articles on children's books, reader responses in the classroom, or simply the innovative ways in which classroom teachers have used reading aloud and what purposes these have served. Although it is not in the scope of this chapter or this book to go into details of these, the bottom line that should be emphasized is that when students are read aloud to, at any age, within any group, they become better readers and writers. When students are read to with the principles of a critical read-aloud in mind, they also become critical learners and questioners.

REFLECTION QUESTIONS FOR THE TEACHER

1. What criteria can I come up with to analyze and choose books that have wide audience appeal and possibilities for critical analysis?

2. Before asking a question, ask yourself this: "What learning principle do I want my students to learn when I ask . . . ?"

3. What do I want this question to do (for me, for the students)?

4. How can I build a context for my read-aloud so that students will be more engaged?

5. What books have possibilities for me to use an animated voice, expression, gestures, and so on?

6. What criteria could I use to find that "special angle" or point of view to hook my students into the reading?

SAMPLE RESPONSE LESSON 3.1
Change Is Not Easy

Primary Grades (Pre-K to K): In the Classroom, by Teachers, Parents, or Tutors

Duration: 1 to 2 Hours

Overview

The teacher picks a book that has wide audience appeal and possibilities for critical analysis, such as *Clara Caterpillar* by Pamela Duncan Edwards, illustrated by Henry Cole. The teacher begins by starting a discussion on change: "Has there been a time when you were told you had to do something but you didn't want to?" For this age group, the teacher may need to give a few examples for students to understand. After a brief discussion, the teacher begins the read-aloud by saying, "Well today we are going to read a book about Clara, who also didn't like change."

The teacher will read aloud and stop at two points in the story to help students understand Clara's reluctance to change. The teacher then shows a prewritten letter from Clara's mother, which asks for their help in getting Clara out (example shown later in this lesson).

Students discuss and brainstorm what should be done to help Clara get over this change. Students may be put into small groups to make drawings and crafts for helping Clara. After the discussion, the teacher continues the read-aloud to finish the story. The teacher helps students make connections to other books on caterpillars, like Eric Carle's *The Very Hungry Caterpillar.*

Materials

Large, prepared letter, addressed to students; *Clara Caterpillar* book; markers; scissors; paper; glue; and other craft materials as needed

Key Vocabulary and Terms

Courageous, Contented, Curious (and many other C words), Caterpillar, Chrysalis, etc.

Anticipatory Set

1. *Focus:* Students learn to solve a problem that they can relate to: "change." Students learn to work together in a group to brainstorm and solve a problem.

2. *Objective:* By the end of the lesson, students learn to creatively address a situation and find ways to help Clara accept change from an egg to a caterpillar and to go inside the chrysalis to become a butterfly. They also learn the life cycle of a butterfly.

3. *Transfer:* As students brainstorm about how to help Clara change smoothly, they may begin to understand that change and transitions are necessary for them to grow, just as for Clara.

Instructions

1. The teacher gathers students around or at a designated read-aloud spot and begins a discussion on change. The teacher may give an example from her own life when change was good for her but she was reluctant. The teacher asks for input from students about similar stories in their lives.

2. The teacher begins the read-aloud and stops at the point where the other caterpillars are trying to get Clara out of her egg. She stops after Clara says, "But I'm comfortable in here" (p. 4). The teacher then stops and asks students, "What should we do? Clara

(Continued)

(Continued)

doesn't want to come out!" The teacher has a short discussion and continues reading aloud until she comes to the page that says, "Then one day Cornelius called, 'Clara come and make your chrysalis'" (p. 11). The teacher stops again and asks students the following: "Do you think Clara is going to make her chrysalis? She loves being a caterpillar; hmmm, I don't know...." The idea here is to get students excited and anticipate what will happen next.

3. The teacher then shows the big prewritten letter and says, "You know, I received this letter from Clara's mother. Let's see what it says." The letter, written on big chart paper so that all children can view it, may say something like this:

Dear Class _____

My name is Mrs. Cabbage and I am Clara's mother. I have a problem and I hope you can all help me! You see, Clara, my daughter, won't go into her chrysalis because she loves being a caterpillar. And if she doesn't go into her chrysalis, she won't grow up to be a beautiful butterfly. Please help! I heard you all are experts on butterflies and know all about them.

I hope you will help me.

Sincerely,
Mrs. Cabbage

4. The teacher then asks students, "Do you think we can help Mrs. Cabbage?" The teacher brainstorms with the whole group and then divides it into smaller groups so that students can work on their ideas. The teachers allows time for students to complete their arts and crafts.

Independent Practice

Students showcase their group work and the class may work on a butterfly project. Students may read other books on butterflies and connect to this one.

Closure

Students enact being inside a chrysalis. They may use expressions from the book such as, "I'm crushed, I'm creased, I'm crumpled," and so forth (see pp. 15–16 in the read-aloud book). The idea is to be silly and have fun.

Example of Response to Lesson 3.1

Butterfly Project Created by a Preschool Class (ages 3–5): One 4-year-old student suggested that they make a "rainbow" chrysalis so that Clara finds it more interesting to go and explore inside. The rest of the class decided this was a good idea and made it a class project by making a huge rainbow chrysalis. They used butcher paper, which they painted with rainbow colors as a class, and then the teacher helped them glue it up to look like a chrysalis. This was hung in the middle of the class for all to see. Throughout the week, students pretended to talk with Clara (who had apparently gone into the chrysalis) to encourage her and ask her how she was doing and when she planned to come out as a butterfly.

SAMPLE RESPONSE LESSON 3.2
Negotiating a Deal

Elementary Grades: (1st to 5th): In the Classroom, by Teachers, Parents, or Tutors

Duration: 1 to 2 Hours

Overview

The teacher begins with a discussion to set the context for the read-aloud by asking a series of well-chosen questions around negotiating a deal. The teacher may want to connect this with a real-life or current issue, such as a union negotiating a deal (e.g., teachers' union, grocery store workers' union, Writers Guild of America negotiating a deal with big studios, Screen Actors Guild, etc.). Students may be familiar with these as they see these things on television or hear about them in the news. The teacher begins to read aloud a popular picture book like, *Click, Clack, Moo: Cows That Type,* by Doreen Cronin. The teacher reads with great animation until the end.

Students are asked to recall a time in their lives when they had to negotiate a deal. This may be inconsequential like, "Eat your vegetables and you get ice cream for dessert," or it may be much more important. Students are given scenarios where they would want to negotiate a deal with the classroom, with the school, or with their teacher. The students are asked to create points to discuss in small groups that they could then use to persuade the deal to go through.

Materials

Large butcher paper, markers, read-aloud book (*Click, Clack, Moo: Cows That Type,* by Doreen Cronin)

Key Vocabulary and Terms

Typewriter, Ultimatum, Strike, Neutral Party, Deal, Negotiation

(Continued)

(Continued)

Anticipatory Set

1. *Focus:* The students learn that we use negotiation techniques every day in our lives for inconsequential as well as consequential things. Students learn to become persuasive writers and thinkers, especially in terms of what is fair and unfair. Students learn to view things from various perspectives and think from the framework of lawyers who may negotiate on a daily basis.

2. *Objective:* By the end of the lesson, students know all the processes that go into negotiating a deal. They learn about labor unions and how and why labor unions work within a democracy.

3. *Transfer:* By the end of the lesson, students are shown the connections between this funny story and real-life issues, such as Cesar Chavez's struggle to negotiate a fair deal for farmworkers through their union and other such real-life examples. Students also make connections to political negotiations and issues that are current in today's world.

Instructions

1. The teacher begins with setting the context for the read-aloud by asking students if they have ever heard of people in a labor union or if they have ever heard of negotiating a deal, and so forth. The teacher gives some information and examples from real life that are current.

2. The teacher reads aloud *Click, Clack, Moo: Cows That Type,* by Doreen Cronin.

3. The teacher asks selected open-ended questions to lead the students to make connections between the story and real life. The teacher also provides other books to help students make intertextual connections. The teacher may use a books such as *Harvesting Hope: The Story of Cesar Chavez,* by Kathleen Krull.

4. The teacher provides students with preset scenarios that would be relevant to them and that they could then negotiate with the class, the school, or with the principal. This could be class-lead by asking the students the following: "If there was something you wish you could have in school, what would it be?" "In small groups, how could you begin to negotiate for this?"

Modifications: Middle and Secondary Grades

The lesson would be very similar except the read-aloud used could be books such as *Animal Farm,* by George Orwell, or *Kids at Work,* by Lewis Hine, or other nonfiction works that discuss labor unions.

SELECTED ANNOTATED BIBLIOGRAPHY

Brown, A. (1998). *Voices in the park*. New York: DK Children's Books.

Although this is a simple tale of a mother who takes her son and dog to the park, the illustrations are so layered and full of possibilities for critique, analysis, and meaning-making, that it is actually a very complex book. Children of all ages and even adults will find interesting and stimulating images on each page. Recommended age 0 and up.

Duncan, A. F. (2005). *Honey baby sugar child*. New York: Simon & Schuster Children's Publishing.

With beautiful colors and realistic action pictures, this book shows a mother and her baby playing throughout the day. The words depict the African American language as the mother says, "I wanna kiss ya, squeeze ya till the sugar's gone. . . . Child I wanna eat you up." Recommended age 0 and up.

Fleischman, P. (1997). *Seedfolks*. New York: HarperTeen Books.

This vignette-style short novel tells the story of a community that is brought together by the beauty of a garden. The garden is started by one girl who plants some seeds in a plot of land that is until then used as a landfill. Latino(a), Korean, Haitian, young, old, and sick all come together and gain something out of this garden. Each vignette is told from the point of view of a new character as we are introduced to everyone who lives in the apartment next to the plot. Recommended age 9 years and up.

Lionni, L. (1973). *Swimmy*. New York: Knopf Children's Paperbacks.

Swimmy is a small black fish who leads a carefree life in the deep ocean with his friends until the tuna fish starts eating them when they go out to play. Swimmy teaches his friends to swim in formation so that the tuna fish think they are one big fish. It teaches a lesson on camouflage. Recommended age 0 and up.

Lionni, L. (1995). *Little Blue and Little Yellow*. New York: HarperCollins.

Little Blue and Little Yellow are friends and like to follow each other around. One day they lose each other and when they find each other again they hug so much that they turn green. This is a sweet tale of friendship that also shows primary colors and changes when colors mix. Recommended age 0 and up.

Levine, E. (2007). *Henry's freedom box*. New York: Scholastic Inc.

This story is based on a true story first retold in an 1872 publication about the Underground Railroad. Excellently illustrated by Kadir Nelson, the book shows the beauty, dignity, and integrity of the Black people: "Do you see those leaves blowing in the wind? They are torn from the trees like slave children are torn from their families," says Henry's mother in the story. In it, Henry, a slave, hides himself in a box and mails himself to freedom. Recommended age 4 years and up.

Mora, P. (1994). *Agua, agua, agua.* Tucson, AZ: Good Year Books.

This is a popular fable about a raven who is thirsty but cannot reach the water it seeks. Told in simple language yet vibrant colors, this makes a great read-aloud for a beginning Spanish reader. Recommended age 0 and up.

Mora, P. (1996). *Confetti poems for children.* New York: Lee & Low Books.

This book contains short narrative poems; some are bilingual, using both Spanish and English words, showing various scenarios in the Southwestern way of life. Vibrant illustrations by Enrique Sanchez make this a wonderful read-aloud book for an early childhood audience. Recommended age 0 and up.

Taylor, M. D. (1998). *The friendship.* New York: Puffin Books.

This is one of the tales told through the eyes of the Logan children. Set in 1930s Mississippi, it reflects the racism and struggles of the African American community. In this story, Tom Bee and Wallace are friends but Tom Bee is African American and Wallace is White. The Logan children witness the betrayal of this friendship as Wallace shoots Tom Bee. Recommended age 8 years and up.

Taylor, M. D. (2003). *Song of the trees.* New York: Puffin Books.

This is another tale of the Logan family, this time told through the voice of Casey as she witnesses racism against her family that owns some land. There are suspenseful moments as Casey happens to hear a plot to illegally cut down trees on her land. Recommended age 8 years and up.

REFERENCES

Fox, M. (2001). *Reading magic: Why reading aloud to our children will change their lives forever.* San Diego, CA: Harcourt.

Fox, M. (n.d.). *Mem Fox's ten read aloud commandments.* Retrieved October 20, 2009, from http://www.memfox.com/ten-read-aloud-commandments.html

Karolides, N. (2005). Theory and practice: An interview with Louise M. Rosenblatt. In L. Rosenblatt (Ed.), *Making meaning with texts: Selected essays* (pp. xv–xxxiv). Portsmouth, NH: Heinemann.

Kiefer, B. (2010). *Charlotte Huck's children's literature* (10th ed.). New York: McGraw-Hill.

Morgan, N., & Saxton, J. (1994). *Asking better questions: Models, techniques and classroom activities for engaging students in learning.* Markham, Canada: Pembroke.

National Endowment for the Arts. (2004, June). *Reading at risk: A survey of literary reading in America* (Research Division Report No. 46). Washington, DC: Author.

Rosenblatt, L. M. (2005). *Making meaning with texts: Selected essays.* Portsmouth, NH: Heinemann.

Trelease, J. (2001). *The read-aloud handbook* (5th ed.). New York: Penguin Books.

Vygotsky, L. (1939). Thought and speech. *Psychiatry, 2,* 29–57.

Part II

Exploring Issues in Multicultural Children's Literature

Chapter 4

Responding to Censorship, Book Banning, and Controversies

As long as the written word has survived, there has been some sort of censorship, more often than not for political, religious, or sexual content. Historically, censorship goes back to ancient times and has been tied to notions of protecting the society from immorality. People have been burned at the stake, jailed, tortured, and banished from their lands for their different views by those who think of themselves as protectors, those acting on behalf of the larger good of the society. From Socrates to Salman Rushdie, censorship and book banning is nothing new to the human race. In the field of children's literature, book banning and censorship have been even more rampant, with almost everyone who has a child or is in any way connected with the care of a child taking the responsibility of shaping what the child views. What then is censorship? What is book banning? Who are the censors and what does censorship really do? How does one react to censorship and what steps could be taken? What are the views of authors, publishers, parents, and teachers in terms of censorship? These are some of the questions that are discussed in this chapter.

Although censorship, book banning, and controversies may not seem like topics for a book that focuses on multicultural children's literature, it is an important topic to include in such a text, as many trade books that have been censored are usually books that talk about the experiences of people who may have been marginalized, underrepresented, or otherwise ignored. As one will see in the course of this chapter, often the authors whose books have been banned or censored are those who portray a different world, alternate lifestyles, unique viewpoints, or topics that we would not be aware of, if not for these books. In keeping with the central theme of approaching multicultural children's literature through a critical issues approach, this chapter is an inherent part.

What Is Censorship?

A useful definition of censorship in relation to children's literature comes from the American Library Association (ALA):

> Censorship is the suppression of ideas and information that certain persons—individuals, groups, or government officials—find objectionable or dangerous. It is no more complicated than someone saying, "Don't let anyone read this book, or buy that magazine, or view that film, because I object to it!" (ALA, n.d., "Intellectual Freedom and Censorship Q&A")

Further, the ALA explained how censorship happens, especially in relation to children and materials such as books, videos, and films for children:

> Censorship occurs when expressive materials, like books, magazines, films and videos, or works of art, are removed or kept from public access. Individuals and pressure groups identify materials to which they object. Sometimes they succeed in pressuring schools not to use them, libraries not to shelve them, book and video stores not to carry them, publishers not to publish them, or art galleries not to display them. Censorship also occurs when materials are restricted to particular audiences, based on their age or other characteristics. (ALA, n.d., "Intellectual Freedom and Censorship Q&A")

In terms of literature in general, broadly censorship is "suppression of information" (*Academic American Encyclopedia*, n.d.) or the "restriction of expression" (Riley, 1998), including, but not limited to, freedom of speech. The *Academic American Encyclopedia* describes censorship as follows:

> Suppression of information, ideas, or artistic expression by anyone, whether government officials, church authorities, private pressure groups, or speakers, writers, and artists themselves. It may take place at any point in time, whether before an utterance occurs, prior to its widespread circulation, or by punishment of communicators after dissemination of their messages, so as to deter others from like expression.

This definition explains the kinds of censorship that there may be, broadly: political, social, sexual, and religious. Thus, in ancient times, Socrates was given the death penalty in Athenian society for airing his political views, despite the fact that this society was known for its intellectual freedom. Thus, the Catholic Church censored Galileo, the great scientist, for saying that the earth moves around the sun. In recent times, political leader and winner of the Nobel Peace Prize, Aung San Suu Kyi, has been house arrested for the past 6 straight years and censored so that her democratic views do not affect the people of Myanmar. Bangladeshi author Taslima Nasreen has been banished from her country and even personally attacked, and author Salman Rushdie had a *fatwa* or death warrant placed on him, for the controversial books that they have written, which have been banned in many countries with a large Muslim population. Children's books, such as the following, have also been banned, challenged, or censored by various groups: *And Tango Makes Three* (2005), about two male penguins who adopt another penguin in the New York Zoo for its social inappropriateness; *Forever* (1975/2007), about teenage love for its sexual content; *Are You There God? It's Me, Margaret* (1970/1986), about menstruation and body changes, for obscene language and antireligious concerns; *Daddy's Roommate* (1990), and *Heather Has Two Mommies* (1990/2000), about homosexual families, for social inappropriateness.

In fact, as we become globally smaller in terms of information dissemination, censorship takes on new meanings in regard to the World Wide Web. With the multitude of information available at our fingertips in less than a nanosecond, it becomes an even more complicated arena. The power of the Internet to disseminate information is so feared that "the Internet was banned in some countries, such as Saudi Arabia and owning a modem became a capital offense in others, such as Burma (Myanmar)" (Simmons & Dresang, 2001, p. 10).

As the various aforementioned definitions state, censorship goes across all media: books, newspapers, television, movies, Internet, and so on. As the field is too vast, this chapter is limited to discussing only the censorship of children's and young adult books.

Book Banning, Book Challenge, and Censorship

Although censorship overarches book banning and book challenges, it is useful to make a distinction between the two in order to clarify the various terms that are used in this chapter. While censorship includes all forms of suppression of information, whether in the form of speech, video, actions, and so on, as explained by the previous definitions, book banning specifically takes place when the book that is being objected to is removed and not made available for reading as a result of the objections raised against the book. A book challenge is when a person objects to a book and then the person takes action to try to remove the book, resulting in a debate about the issue, whether or not the book is successfully removed. The ALA defines a book challenge as "a formal, written complaint, filed with a library or school requesting that materials be removed because of content or appropriateness"

(ALA, n.d., "Terms & Definitions"). Therefore, the "attempt to remove or restrict materials" is termed a challenge, whereas the actual removal of the material is termed a ban (ALA, n.d., "About Banned & Challenged Books"). Both of these terms are forms of censorship. As mentioned previously, this chapter concentrates on books that pertain to children and young adults and both the terms *challenging* and *banning* are used, where appropriate. Further, the term banning may also be used interchangeably with the term *censoring*.

INTELLECTUAL FREEDOM AND THE FIRST AMENDMENT

The First Amendment of the Bill of Rights of the U.S. Constitution states:

> Congress shall make no law respecting an establishment of religion, or prohibiting the free exercise thereof; or abridging the freedom of speech, or of the press; or the right of the people peaceably to assemble, and to petition the government for a redress of grievances. (Cornell University Law School, n.d.)

In other words, in the United States, everyone has the right to practice the religion of their choice and the right to free speech and free press without interference from the government or any other body or institution. Wachsberger (2006) said that the First Amendment is "America's greatest gift to civilization" and has inspired countless people all over the world to fight against censorship (p. vii). Closely related to the First Amendment is the concept of *intellectual freedom,* defined by the ALA as follows:

> Intellectual freedom is the right of every individual to both seek and receive information from all points of view without restriction. It provides for free access to all expressions of ideas through which any and all sides of a question, cause or movement may be explored. Intellectual freedom encompasses the freedom to hold, receive and disseminate ideas. (ALA, n.d., "Intellectual Freedom and Censorship Q&A")

These two statements could be construed as essentials of any democratic system, thereby clarifying that any sort of censorship may be deemed illegal. However, the censors are also protected under these laws and therefore have the right to express their opinions and take action, which may or may not lead to litigation.

In terms of children's literature, there are issues of intellectual freedom and First Amendment rights that come into play when confronted by censorship. For example, when a librarian or a teacher selects only certain kinds of books to avoid controversy in the classroom or among parents, are they "selecting" or are they "censoring"? McClure (1995) went to the heart of all censorship when she rightly identified the motivation as not so much protection, but perception: "Censorship is not a problem of good versus evil but 'your' perception of good versus 'my' perception of good" (p. 4). And this seems to be the issue in most book challenges and censoring activities. It is not so much that someone has an opinion about a certain book but that the person wants to suppress the information for everyone else. It becomes a First Amendment issue when others are not given a choice to make up their own minds. It becomes an issue of intellectual freedom when one person's objection to certain topics results in the removal of materials thereby forcing others access only to those materials that are not banned.

Ultimately, censorship maybe interpreted as a form of power wielded by one group over the other, whatever the goal or motivation is and however serious or mild the censoring may be. Therefore, when a parent objects to a certain book being read to her child and takes action by demanding its removal for everyone in the class, she is wielding her power to censor. When dictators or leaders suppress information for a nation or for a society, they are wielding their power to censor. Of course, there are various justifications for censorship depending on the case and situation; some types of censorship appear more justified than others, like if parents choose for their child. However, the point here is that it is still censorship, whether the restriction affects one individual or a nation, as it takes away the basic right to choose from the individual or the society or the nation.

Types of Censorship

Simmons and Dresang (2001) further classified censorship issues not only by the most common reasons for censoring but also in the ways that censorship manifests itself. They said that censorship may fall into the following categories: classic or traditional, proactive, abridgement or adaptation, student journalism, student creative writing, and self-censorship.

Classic or traditional censorship occurs when a teacher assigns a text to students to read and a parent or caregiver objects to it with or without reading it and with or without discussing it. The parent or caregiver immediately demands that the book or text be removed from the school, class, or reading list. The ensuing action could be between the parent and school officials or parents and district, and it may turn into a litigation. Some examples are books such as the *Harry Potter* series, about a young orphan turned wizard, by J. K. Rowling, banned or challenged due to religious beliefs; and the *Alice* series, about a teenage girl, Alice McKinley, and her trials and tribulations of growing up without a mother, by Phyllis Reynolds Naylor, both of which have been challenged and recommended for removal by PABBIS (Parents Against Bad Books In Schools) for explicit and inappropriate language.

Proactive censorship is when the censors remove material even before it is published. Objections are raised at the publishing phase, calling for certain materials to be suppressed before they even reach the public through textbook and publishing houses. Some broad examples of censorship in historical texts include ignoring actual events involving Native American incidents, the Japanese internment, African American contributions, de-emphasizing evolution as a study topic in certain science texts, and so on (Simmons & Dresang, 2001).

Abridgement and adaptation are censoring from the author's side or from the publisher's side through obvious omission. The difference between proactive censorship and abridgement or adaptation is that the latter maybe done after the original work is published. For example, *Heather Has Two Mommies* (1990/2000) is a story about a lesbian couple who have a daughter named Heather. In the original version, it is explained to Heather that she was conceived by artificial insemination. However, in subsequent versions of this book, the part about artificial insemination has not only been removed, but the story has also been changed into merely a feel-good story of family diversity. Lesléa Newman, the author, mentions in the afterword that she wrote this book initially for a friend's daughter, as there were no children's books that reflected her world, that of having two mothers.

The next two types of censorship, student journalism and student creative writing, are explained by Simmons and Dresang (2001) as the other side of censorship, that is, "the limits placed on students' written expression" (p. 34) by censors. This kind of censorship "reflects a certain irony in U.S. schooling: From their earliest years as public school students, young people are taught about freedom of expression in general and the significance of a free press in particular" (Simmons & Dresang, 2001, p. 34). Some examples that Simmons and Dresang (2001) give of topics censored for student journalism and creative writing are attitudes toward HIV/AIDS and a 1968 piece by a young, Black Vietnam war returnee on his experiences (see pp. 34–35). SLATE newsletter (Supporting Learning and Teaching of English), a subcommittee of the National Council of Teachers of English (NCTE), mentions cases such as the Hazelwood School District, where students sued their principal for suppressing articles written by them in the school newspaper on teenage pregnancy and divorce affects on children (McNabb, 1994).

Self-censorship is the practice of suppressing information or materials by the author or maker of that material in deference to the current authority. For example, media specialists such as Amanpour and McArthur say that news agencies practiced self-censorship in regard to the Iraq war in deference to the Bush administration, as reported in *USA TODAY,* a popular newspaper (Johnson, 2003). Simmons and Dresang (2001) said that often self-censorship is practiced by school authorities, administrators, faculty, and staff.

WHY ARE BOOKS CENSORED?

While there are many meanings attached to the word censorship, and many avenues by which it may be implemented, the reasons for censorship are almost always the same: protecting oneself or society from apparent ill effects. Over the centuries, the four most common reasons for banning or censoring books have been on political, social, religious, or sexual grounds, when we take all literature into consideration (Karolides, Bald, & Sova, 1999).

The Office of Intellectual Freedom (OIF), a subgroup of the American Library Association (ALA), identified further reasons that pertain to children's literature, which may be clubbed under the aforementioned four broad reasons: anti-ethnic, insensitivity, racism, sexism, homosexuality, nudity, antifamily, offensive language, drugs, the occult or satanism, inaccurate, graphic violence, and so on (ALA, n.d., "Challenges by Initiator, Institution, Type, and Year"). According to the OIF, only about 20% to 25% of challenges are actually reported. Although the four broad categories are not at the top of the list for children's literature, it is useful to discuss these, as many of the books banned or censored in these categories are often on middle and high school reading lists.

Literature Suppressed on Political Grounds

Karolides et al. (1999) explained that books suppressed on political grounds are the result of actions by a government to block "its citizens from receiving information, ideas and opinions that it perceives to be critical, embarrassing or threatening" (p. 1). For example, John Steinbeck's *Grapes of Wrath* (1939) has been censored and banned at various points since its publication and has been on the list of the 25 most censored books until as recently as the year 2000. *Grapes of Wrath* is the story of the Joad family, set during the Great Depression, whose members have lost all their land in the Oklahoma dust bowl and they begin traveling westward to California. The book takes us through their arduous journey, and once in California, they face even more hardships and discrimination trying to find work in the farmlands. This book has been censored for its political commentary through the family's story, for its language set in the local dialect, for its reality in showing the abject poverty and hopelessness of the many people who were lured westward (Karolides et al., 1999). Another book that has been censored at various points on political grounds is *Animal Farm* (1945/1996) by George Orwell, about a group of animals whose rebellion results in the pigs taking over the running of a farm. The famous phrase, "All animals are equal but some animals are more equal than others," comes from this book. Both of these books have also appeared on the *100 Most Frequently*

Challenged Books of 1990–2000, published by the ALA (see http://www
.ala.org/ala/issuesadvocacy/banned/frequentlychallenged/challengedbydecade/
1990_2000.cfm).

Although data from the OIF show that between the years 2000 and 2005 there
were only 144 instances in which books were censored for their political viewpoints,
as opposed to 728 instances of censorsing due to offensive language, politics do crop
up in children's books, and these are objected to strongly by parents. As the OIF
reports, for every challenge that is reported, four or five go unnoticed. For example,
many online reviewers have strongly objected to Doreen Cronin's popular book,
Click, Clack, Moo: Cows That Type (2001), about a farmer whose cows demand
electric blankets because the barn is cold. When the farmer refuses, they get together
with the hens to strike. Words such as "strike," "ultimatum," "neutral," and so on,
suggest the union trouble that Farmer Brown has. Online reviewers have said that
they object to the union propaganda, the political organization of the book, whereas
many teachers see it as a hilarious avenue to discuss current politics with their
students, and some media specialists commend the book for its political views
("Audio File," 2000).

Literature Suppressed on Social Grounds

This reason is one of the broadest in terms of what books it includes. In short, literature suppressed on social grounds includes anything that is against the social sen-
sibility of a society and is "socially motivated censorship" (Sova, 1998, p. 334). So
topics such as offensive language, racism, drugs, violence, and so on, would fall
under this category. Karolides et al. (1999) also included sexual orientation and differences because of class in this category. They specified that authors and their
works have been included in this category if these did not "conform to the social
expectations of their censors, or because they contain socially unacceptable ideas or
speech" (p. 334). For example, *The Adventures of Huckleberry Finn* (1884), by
Mark Twain, has been censored several times since its original publication in 1884,
beginning in 1885 when the Concord Public Library (Massachusetts) banned the
book for offensive language and obscenity. Since then it has remained on the list of
the top 10 most frequently banned books, as late as even 2007, although it was off
the list in 2006 (Doyle, 2007).

To Kill a Mockingbird (1960), by Harper Lee, was her only book, and it won a
Pulitzer Prize in 1961, a year after it was published. This is a story told through the
eyes of 8-year-old Scout Finch and what happens in the sleepy, fictional town of
Maycomb, Alabama, over 3 years, when her father, Atticus Finch, takes on the case
of a Black man, Tom Robinson, accused of raping a White woman. Set in the 1930s,

this book touches on issues of race, class, prejudice, and justice. In those 3 years, Scout grows from a small gullible girl into a "young lady," along with her brother Jem and cousin Dill. Censored frequently since 1977, the book has remained on the ALA's *100 Most Frequently Challenged Books of 1990–2000* for offensive language and racism. Other books that have been banned at various times on social grounds include the following: *Anne Frank: The Diary of a Young Girl* (1947), by Anne Frank, a compilation of the journals and diary left behind by a 15-year-old Jewish girl in hiding from the Nazis during World War II, which was censored for sensuality and topics such as menstruation. Some passages were also abridged and adapted or changed so that they do not hurt the sensibilities of German readers (Karolides et al., 1999, p. 340). *The Canterbury Tales* (1400), by Geoffrey Chaucer, a collection of short stories written in verse, was banned and censored for "risqué language and sexual innuendo" (Karolides et al., 1999, p. 359). *The Catcher in the Rye* (1951), by J. D. Salinger, was censored for obscene language.

A recent case of banning on social grounds was the Newbery Medal winner of 2007: *The Higher Power of Lucky* (2006), by Susan Patron, because of the word "scrotum" on the first page, describing a dog's scrotum (Bosman, 2007). Dav Pilkey's series about a silly hero called "Captain Underpants," created by two bored, elementary school children, has caused controversy since the first book in the series came out in 1995. Based on his own childhood experiences, Pilkey's *Captain Underpants* series, with books such as *The Adventures of Captain Underpants* (1997), *Captain Underpants and the Attack of the Talking Toilets, Captain Underpants and the Perilous Plot of Professor Poopypants*, to name just a few, have all been banned by various school administrators, parents, and staff for insensitivity, antifamily content, disobeying authority, and encouraging unsuitable behavior. For example, it was banned in 2001 by Naugatuck, Connecticut, school officials for causing unruly behavior, and it has been on the list of the top 10 most frequently challenged books, as reported by the ALA ("Banned Book Week," 2006).

Other books that fit this category include *Mommy Laid an Egg*, by Babbette Cole, a hilarious picture book showing stick figures of how a baby is conceived, censored for age-inappropriateness; *Where the Wild Things Are*, by Maurice Sendak, a picture book about young Max who goes on an imaginary "wild rumpus," for being psychologically harmful to children; and *Scary Stories*, by Alwin Schwartz, for graphic violence.

Literature Suppressed on Religious Grounds

Amongst books that have been censored or banned on religious grounds come the Bible and the Qur'an, two of the ancient treatises of two major religions of the world. Although censorship in religious circles can be traced back to ancient times, when opposing views led to the suppression of different interpretations of the same text, more recently these interpretations have extended to fundamentalist orders such as the death warrant on Salman Rushdie for his book, *The Satanic Verses*, by the religious leader Ayatollah Khomeini. Karolides et al. (1999) contended that after the invention of the printing press in 1450, which led to "unauthorized Bible translations," giving rise to further disagreements in terms of interpretation, the church "expanded its censorial functions" (p. 169). They also referred to an "Index of Forbidden Books" that endured four centuries of existence before it was abolished completely by the Vatican in 1966. They called this "the most successful censorial device of modern times" (p. 170).

What is surprising in terms of literature suppressed on religious grounds is that this reason seems to be the only one that disregards the First Amendment rights of individuals. Karolides et al. (1999) stated the following:

> Though the First Amendment prevents government authorities from practicing religious censorship in the United States, individuals and organized religious fundamentalist groups have successfully pressed to remove books viewed as Anti-Christian from public and school libraries and curricula. . . . Their targets have included textbooks that teach evolution without presenting the alternative theory of "creationism," books said to promote the religion of "secular humanism" and, in a growing trend, material with references to Eastern religions, "New Age" thought, witchcraft or the occult. (p. 170)

Hence the *Harry Potter* series, by J. K. Rowling, has been on the list of the 10 most frequently challenged books published by the ALA since the very first book came out in 1998. The stories in the series revolve around an orphan named Harry Potter who discovers, when he turns 11, that his parents were wizards. He goes to Hogwarts School of Witchcraft and Wizardry, and he makes two very close friends, Ron and Hermione, with whom he fights the dark Lord Voldemort. While the series is credited with making the most reluctant readers read, it has also provided ample fuel for censors. A few instances of challenges regarding the Harry Potter series include: parents in Gwinnett County, Georgia, who objected to these books, saying that they encourage the Wicca religion, witchcraft, and the occult. This contention was ruled baseless by the Georgia Board of Education in 2006 (Doyle, 2007). In San Gabriel, California, several books in the Harry Potter series were removed and banned by the Wilsona School District on recommendation by the parent-teacher committee (Doyle, 2007).

Literature Suppressed on Sexual Grounds

Over the years, the reasons for suppressing books on sexual grounds have changed, as people's ideas of what constitutes erotic or pornographic material, especially in books, have also changed. As Sova (2006) mentioned, sometimes books that were banned became required reading in college classrooms and young adult classes within a span of a few years. Unlike the aforementioned three broad reasons, books suppressed on sexual grounds are elusive in what is included. Books that may have at one point been considered pornographic may now be considered classically erotic, and as Sova pointed out, it is sometimes difficult to distinguish between the cheap mass-produced works and those termed classically erotic. Further, it has been very hard to correctly define what is obscene and what constitutes obscenity (Riley, 1998; Sova, 2006). Although the First Amendment protects free speech, obscenity does not come under it (Riley, 1998). Rather, several laws have come and gone to protect society at large against obscenity, showing the difficulty in pinning down a definition of what constitutes obscenity. Riley (1998) mentioned the Obscene Publications Law of 1865, the first law passed in the United States, later replaced by the Federal Anti-Pornography Act of 1873, also known as the Comstock Act, both of which applied to the U.S. Postal Service and were revoked in 1915. Other legal activity led to the Federal Communications Commission Regulations on Indecency and Censorship and the Communications Decency Act, both of which censored telephone and media (Riley, 1998, pp. 40–44).

Although these laws are extremely important in terms of protecting children against child pornography and sexual violence, the difficulty has always been the vagueness with which obscenity is defined, especially in legal terms. Therefore, many state and local statutes have been put in place regarding what constitutes obscenity and what is objectionable (Riley, 1998). Often, what is sex education to one community may be considered obscene by another society, or what is experienced by certain members of society may be censored because to it is too risqué to publish. For example, Maya Angelou's autobiographical tale, *I Know Why the Caged Bird Sings* (1969), has been listed repeatedly on the ALA's list of the 10 most frequently challenged books, making it to the list even in 2007 for obscenity, sexual explicitness, and violence. In it, Angelou describes the tumultuous life she led between the ages of 3 to 16, the racism and violence she faced when she was sent to live with her grandmother in Stamps, Arkansas, how she was raped by her mother's boyfriend when she was 8, and her struggles with her sexuality, leading to her becoming pregnant at 16. Although this book has been challenged frequently, it is also an award-winning book and is recommended reading for young adults because it is autobiographical and historical. Similarly, *Always Running: La Vida Loca:*

Gang Days in L.A. (1993), by Luis Rodriguez, is based on his life, written as a memoir about his childhood and teenage years, on how he struggled to stay in school living in one of the poorest sections of Los Angeles, Watts, where "life was crazy" for him and his siblings. The book depicts many real instances filled with violence, drugs, sex, racism, and death, as children, as young as 11, who sometimes feel that these are the only groups they can belong to, are initiated violently into gangs. Written in explicit and powerful language, *Always Running* is shocking and saddening, painting a vivid picture of gang life. In the prologue, Rodriguez dedicates his book to his son Ramiro, whom he realized may also be swept into the gang culture. *Always Running* has been on the ALA's list of the 100 most frequently challenged books since it first came out in 1993.

Many works of fiction have also been identified as banned or challenged for being sexually explicit and obscene, such as the *Alice* series, by Phyllis Reynolds Naylor. This young adult series of 16 books tops the list of books to be challenged or banned by the PABBIS association. Published between 1985 and 2005, this series centers around the character of Alice McKinley, who loses her mother at age 4. Growing up without a mother figure in her life, Alice goes through what every adolescent girl may go through in terms of boys, menstruation, buying a bra, body image, and so on. Although they have frequently been on the ALA's list of most challenged books, not all the books in the series have been banned; however, many school boards and libraries have decided to remove the entire series from their reading lists (Sova, 2006).

Other books that have been banned include the following: Judy Blume's *Are You There God? It's Me, Margaret* and *Forever,* for obscenity and strong sexual content; and Toni Morrison's *The Bluest Eye* (1970/2000), for "graphic sexual description" and "vulgar," "obscene" language (Sova, 2006, p. 27). *The Bluest Eye* is the sad story of Pecola, a young African American girl living in the 1940s who, because of circumstances, is convinced that having blue eyes is more beautiful. She is raped twice by her father, becomes pregnant, and is driven to madness when a priest who wants to rid himself of a dog takes advantage of her need and tells her to look for a sign to gain blue eyes when she unwittingly feeds the dog poison. *The Bluest Eye* is also on the ALA's 2008 list of most frequently challenged books, having been challenged in a Michigan school district (Doyle, 2008). Khaled Hosseini's *Kite Runner* (2003) has also been challenged in Morganton, North Carolina, for depicting a sodomy rape (Doyle, 2008). *Kite Runner* is Hosseini's debut novel of two friends, Amir and Hassan, spanning a time from the end of the monarchy in Afghanistan until the Taliban's rule. A complicated cultural tale of a boy's coming of age and two friends' loyalty to each other divided by classism, where one escapes to the United States while the other dies in Kabul trying to save their home, *Kite Runner* is perhaps the only Afghani novel written in English by an insider of the culture and has been on the New York Times bestseller list since its publication.

Literature Suppressed on Other Grounds

The OIF, a branch of the ALA, publishes essential materials and data on censorship each year. In its database, compiled by year, are the various reasons for literature to be suppressed. The database is geared mainly toward children's literature, including young adult literature from high school readings lists. The OIF gathers information on challenges, book banning, and other forms of censorship, which is published yearly in a newsletter called the *Newsletter on Intellectual Freedom.* As mentioned previously, the reasons mentioned by the OIF are more detailed than the four broad reasons that are given earlier. It is interesting to note that "sexually explicit" and "offensive language" score the highest in terms of number of challenges or bans in every year from 1990 to 2005. There were 1,607 challenges or bans that cited sexually explicit as a reason between the years 1990 and 2000 and 1,427 that cited offensive language. Between 2000 and 2005, there were 811 challenges that cited offensive language and 714 that cited sexually explicit as the reason. Following close behind are "unsuitable to age-group" at 1,256 and "occult/satanism" at 842 from 1990 to 2000 and "unsuitable to age-group" at 504 from 2000 to 2005. "Violence" scored relatively low between 1990 and 2000 at only 737, whereas it was much higher from 2000 to 2005 at 405 (ALA, n.d., "Challenges by Initiator, Institution, Type, and Year").

WHAT DOES CENSORSHIP REALLY DO?

Norma Mazer, the prolific young adult novelist, relates a story about a *Chicago Sun-Times* columnist who wrote a book that was on the New York Times best-seller list and received information that his book was being challenged by a parent due to the word "hell." Mazer said that the columnist's response was to "call the family and promise them his support in their attempts to have his book banned" (Mazer, 1993, p. 23), because he felt that there was no greater opportunity than this to create interest in the book and sell a lot of copies. In fact, Mazer went on to explain, that he also wrote to the family about his next book and requested that "if there was anything at all they could do about getting that one banned too, he'd really appreciate it" (Mazer, 1993, p. 23). The irony that Ms. Mazer is pointing to here is that children's books that are banned or challenged usually create so much attention and curiosity that often it ensures that more children want to read the book. In fact, librarians often report that they get more requests for books that are on restricted, challenged, or banned lists than for books that can be checked out easily. Censorship hence does not meet its goal effectively (McClure, 1995).

However, the flip side of censorship and the more serious side is that restricting access to materials results in much more than merely causing the materials to become more popular. If stories are not told, then how can we learn from the experiences of others? For example, *Always Running* and *I Know Why the Caged Bird Sings* are both autobiographical, albeit portraying some extremely disturbing images of childhood. Further, one of the purposes of writing them may have been to portray these authentic stories as cautionary tales or evidence of some of the evils of our society so that children who may be in similar situations may find resonance with these stories and solutions if possible. Judy Blume, children's author, and one of the most censored authors of our time, got to the heart of the matter when she said, "It's not just the books under fire now that worry me. It is the books that will never be written. The books that will never be read. And all due to the fear of censorship. As always, young readers will be the real losers" (Blume, n.d.). As British author Nicky Singer (2006) said, "The least our children deserve, is a context for the events they witness around them. . . . The usefulness of fiction in this process is that it can offer a 'safe space' for that discussion. Terrible events can be realistic but not real" (p. 310).

Perhaps books are the "safe space" that can be controlled amidst the vast majority of media images; then again, perhaps schools are one of the few final frontiers that parents feel they can control for their children through censorship.

What Do Authors, Publishers, Teachers, and Parents Say About Censorship?

Generally speaking, after the 1940s, when laws such as the Obscene Publications Law and The Comstock Act were imposed, many authors and editors were themselves the censors, afraid that their works might not be published and that these works would not sell (Karolides, Buress, & Kean, 1993; West, 1988). There was also another kind of censorship that editors and publishers practiced during the later part of the 19th century and the earlier part of the 20th century. This had to do with the race and gender of the author. Often, authors with names that might identify them as belonging to certain races or cultural groups were forced to change their names to appear more White. Women authors were forced to change their names so that they might appear male or gender neutral, which happens to this day. For example, K. A. Applegate, J. K. Rowling, Enid Blyton, and George Eliot are all women authors.

According to many educators, children's book censorship, as we know it today, became more rampant after the mid-1970s (Karolides et al., 1993; Warchsberger, 2006; West, 1988). Some of the most censored and prolific contemporary children's authors began their careers in the 1960s and 1970s, such as Maurice Sendak, Judy

Blume, Katherine Paterson, Robert Cormier, Roald Dahl, Rudolfo Anaya, Shel Silverstein, and Norma Klein, to name just a few. Of these, Judy Blume and Maurice Sendak top the list in terms of the number of times they have been censored for their various books. So what do these authors have to say about censorship? What are their opinions, and what is their side of the story in terms of the books they choose to write?

"Censorship grows out of fear" rather than a motivation to protect children, according to Blume (n.d.). As described earlier by many others, censorship is a form of power that is held by someone over others, and Blume feels that in order for censors to feel in control of their children's lives, censorship is usually "disguised as moral outrage." In a revealing interview with Mark West (1988), Blume said that she did not start off writing about controversial topics; rather, she wrote about what she thought young children and teenagers should be able to discuss responsibly— sexuality (*Forever*), puberty (*Are You There God? It's Me, Margaret*), bullying (*Blubber*), masturbation (*Deenie*)—which then became some of her most controversial and frequently challenged books.

Author Nicky Singer (2006) voiced similar opinions when she said that books should be avenues that children and young adults have to openly discuss topics that they see often on television and in other media. For example, she began to write about diverse sensitive topics such as suicide bombers (*Innocent's Story*) and hazing or initiation experiences (*Feather Boy*) by gang members and came under fire by publishers themselves. She cautioned that censorship causes a silence and silence in turn causes a false legitimacy to the situation. Speaking about her book, *Innocent's Story,* and the difficult process of proactive censorship that she faced from American publishers who had great reservations to her story, she said, "If we say nothing about the bombs to our young people it gives terror a kind of legitimacy, makes it ordinary, not something worthy enough to be remarked upon" (p. 310).

Maurice Sendak, controversial picture book author of such well-loved classics as *Where the Wild Things Are* and *In the Night Kitchen,* feels that censorship is a form of promoting silence and ignorance that is unfounded. He feels that when children are already very aware of certain topics like their own body parts, why ignore that awareness and create shame? *In the Night Kitchen* is a picture book of a small boy's dream of being baked into a cake, and it shows the child completely naked tumbling through the air. Censored for showing the genitals of a boy, Sendak called it "ridiculous." "They (censors) seem to think that children are in complete ignorance of their genitals and they (censors) dislike my book because it threatens this ignorance," as quoted in an interview with West (1988, p. 88). In other words, Sendak feels that censoring what is real is ignoring what is realistic in life.

Katherine Paterson, realistic fiction author, goes to yet another aspect of censorship and says that stories are meant to be open-ended and told in such a way so that the readers can find themselves somewhere in the story. When censored, the invitation to be part of the story and identify and empathize with it is lost. Paterson (in an interview with Chattaway, 2007) said that "books give us emotional practice" to go through realistic experiences like death and learn how we may react to it, as in her book, *Bridge to Terabithia* (1977). *Bridge to Terabithia* is not just about death; rather, it is about the friendship of a boy and girl who make up an imaginary land called Terabithia, where the girl dies one day alone, leaving the boy to grieve. Paterson's other highly censored book, *Great Gilly Hopkins,* about 9-year-old Gilly Hopkins, who is a reluctant and sassy foster girl and her current family that consists of an older woman and a 5-year-old boy, has been highly censored for racial slurs and bad language. Paterson said that in order to make the book realistic, she had to give Gilly real words that portrayed her (character's) real interactions with the world (McClure, 1995).

Many publishers, while they by and large support these authors, say that it is their duty to look for words and passages that may be considered potentially controversial. For example, Phyllis Fogelman, longtime editor of Dial Books for Young Readers, said that her strategy is to be aware of what might cause controversy and help the author identify whether the language and actions of the character are seminal to the story or if they are peripheral. For example, if the character uses the word "damn" only once, is it really characteristic of the character? Ultimately, she feels that editors and publishers are only guides and that the work belongs to the author (West, 1988).

Other publishers see censorship, especially in the world of children's books, as the "kiss of death" (West, 1988, p. 119), because the actual buying of books is not by children, but by adult librarians, school officials, and other public servants, who do not generally want to invite controversy. Therefore, it seems that publishers of children's books are more aware of and against censorship in general. Publisher Steven Roxburgh, of Farrar, Strauss & Giroux, warned that censorship, especially in children's books, is very concerning as it subconsciously affects the decisions of publishers, editors, authors, and illustrators. Roxburgh's argument goes back to Blume's refrain that censors are driven by fear: "The fear of controversy makes people involved in producing children's books more and more conservative" (West, 1988, p. 122).

PABBIS, an organization formed by parents called Parents Against Bad Books In Schools, believes that parents of school children have the right to exercise their First Amendment rights in relation to their children. In other words, PABBIS feels that parents who uphold their rights to defend their values and beliefs in accordance with the First Amendment are not practicing censorship. On the PABBIS Web site is an extensive list of books that have been challenged or banned. Also listed are phrases, sentences, and passages pulled from each of these books to illustrate this point. The main topics objected to by PABBIS are sexuality, religion, and violence. PABBIS sees its work as selection rather than censorship and offers a disclaimer that these are only suggested lists and passages that may be objectionable and that parents need to make their own decisions for their children (see http://www.pabbis.org). This is a very useful

Web site, especially for teachers, as some of the posts are very well-informed. It would be beneficial for teachers to consult such Web sites to make sure that they reorganize their lessons to address the concerns that parents might have.

Looked at in any way, censorship does cause controversy, especially when it is related to choices for minors. More than others, parents, caregivers, and teachers do have the responsibility to create an educational environment that encourages critical awareness, as Naidoo (1995), censored author of *Journey to Jo'Burg,* emphasized. McClure (1995) also cautioned that "there is a fine line between protection and control, however; protection without love and through fear can lead to over-control and the stifling of a developing mind" (p. 25). She supports the opinions of authors and publishers cited here in that it is better to have open discussions about controversial issues rather than "deny their existence" (p. 25).

Useful Resources

Organizations

Censorship in children's literature is all the more controversial and duplicitous, as parents do have the right to decide what is best for their children, and teachers do have the responsibility to create critical awareness in an educational environment. Organizations such as the National Council of Teachers of English (NCTE) and ALA have therefore created some very useful resources for parents, educators, and the community regarding censorship that address issues in such a way as to keep the best interests of children at the forefront. Some of these resources are given here:

1. *American Civil Liberties Union* (ACLU) is a nonprofit organization that was founded to protect the individual rights of people including free speech, right to religion, equal protection under the law, right to a fair trial, and so on (see http://www.aclu.org).

2. *National Coalition Against Censorship* (NCAC) is an alliance that includes about 50 "literary, artistic, religious, educational, professional, labor, and civil liberties," nonprofit groups that are "united by a conviction that freedom of thought, inquiry, and expression must be defended" (see http://www.ncac.org). These work together to educate its members and "the public at large about the dangers of censorship and how to oppose them." Particularly after the September 11th, 2001, attacks, the NCAC has provided important resources and education against censorship cases, especially those that arise based on fear.

3. *Citizens Internet Empowerment Coalition* (CIEC) is an organization that was founded solely to stop government censorship of the Internet. The

Communications Decency Act, a law that censored Internet activity, was found to be unconstitutional in 1997, and the CIEC was founded to uphold that decision. It provides important resources and educational tools to fight against censorship on the Internet and also provides resources for parents to educate themselves about protecting their children (see http://www.ciec.org; see also http://www.getnetwise.org, an online resource guide for kids' safety, protection, privacy, etc.).

Formats and Guides

The NCTE provides five helpful resources about censorship (see http://www .ncte.org/action/anti-censorship): These are mentioned briefly in the following points:

- *Students' Right to Read:* This models procedures and rules backed by law for teachers to respond to challenges. It provides such useful information as "Citizens' Request for Reconsideration of a Work"—a format for gathering information about a challenge, Procedures for Book Selection, Community's Responsibility, Legal Action, Defending the Book, and much more.
- *Guidelines for Selection of Materials in English Language Arts Program:* Prepared by the joint subcommittee, Support for the Learning and Teaching of English (SLATE), and the Standing Committee Against Censorship, these thorough guidelines define what is considered instructional materials, the importance of those materials, and the criteria to select instructional materials in connection with educational objectives and relevance to students' needs. Further, they outline the procedures for the selection of instructional materials, including responsibility, cultural relevance, and so on.
- *Rationales for Teaching Challenged Books:* This section includes specific criteria and rationales available in a two-CD set, with over 300 rationales developed in association with the International Reading Association (IRA), and an instructional sheet on what to include in a rationale, with two samples to teach *Bridge to Terabithia* and *The Color Purple* and a rationale to the Teach Challenged Books index.
- *Guidelines for Dealing With Censorship of Nonprint and Multimedia Materials:* This is one of the few resources for practices and principles regarding nonprint materials, including those related to media literacy, the Internet, motion pictures, and so forth.
- *Defining and Defending Instructional Methods:* This is a detailed guide to defining instructional materials such as written expressions, oral expressions,

reading, response to literature, nonprint materials, and so on. It is an extremely valuable resource for teachers.

The OIF of the ALA also has forms for Reporting a Challenge, Dealing With Challenges, and other useful forms and resources. The following is a brief list of points adapted from the OIF to cope with challenges:

1. *Communicate effectively,* be open, and listen more than talking; avoid giving personal opinions. Explain in simple language (without jargon) that the library or school or class has certain policies that will be made public.

2. *Distribute facts* about the book in an easy to read format in bullet points and simple, to the point language.

3. *Distribute the school's or library's policy* in writing. You may include the Library Bill of Rights terminology given on the ALA Web site, including First Amendment Rights (see http://www.ala.org/ala/aboutala/offices/oif/ statementspols/statementsif/librarybillrights.cfm).

4. *Explain the rationale* for including instructional materials. The library, school, or class should have a policy for what counts as instructional materials; show how this book fits that rationale.

5. *Prepare a clear explanation* of the procedures to follow for registering a complaint. Ask for a written complaint, give a precise procedure of when a reply can be expected, and perhaps have a committee review the complaint and provide a written response.

REFLECTION QUESTIONS FOR THE TEACHER

Encountering censorship in the classroom is always a challenging situation, especially for teachers who may feel that it is up to parents to introduce certain issues, and for those who are concerned about their job security. Here are some questions to ask yourself before you read a controversial book or make choices for your class's reading list:

1. What issues does this book bring up in my classroom, given the population of students in this class?

2. What steps can I take to educate myself about a certain topic or banned book or censored book so that I may give my students the most comprehensive information?

3. Where do I stand, personally, in regard to a particular controversial or censored issue?

4. What am I willing to do to defend a certain topic or controversial book? How far am I willing to go? What will this "cost" me?

5. What support does my school, district, community, or the law give me to defend myself and support my case?

6. What is my responsibility as a teacher in terms of critical literacy to my students, to make them more aware of issues and controversy?

Teachers can also adapt the following worksheet for a defense against a possible challenge. Adapted from various sources such as SLATE, NCTE, and ALA, this form has been rewritten to include what may be important to say. Teachers may adapt this form to suit their purposes.

TEACHER'S RATIONALE

School: Curriculum plan for:

Title of book:

Grade or course:

Summary of book:

Educational significance of book:

Purpose and method of using book:

Objectives of lesson(s) that this book will meet:

Why is this book especially appropriate for this unit or course?

Potential problems that may arise in relation to the book:

Teacher's plans to address potential problems:

Curriculum plans to address potential problems:

Alternate books:

Check all that apply:

Required _____ Recommended _____ For Whole Class _____ For Special Group _____ For Individual _____ For Class Reading List _____ To Be Included in Class Library _____ Other _____

This book is part of a permanent class collection _____. This book is part of the school library _____.

WEB SITES OF ORGANIZATIONS

American Civil Liberties Union: http://www.aclu.org
American Library Association: http://www.ala.org
Citizens Internet Empowerment Coalition: http://www.ciec.org
National Coalition Against Censorship: http://www.ncac.org
National Council of Teachers of English: http://www.ncte.org
Parents Against Bad Books In Schools: http://www.pabbis.org
Educational information for parents on Internet protection: http://www.getnetwise.org

---

SAMPLE RESPONSE LESSON 4.1

Censorship

Primary Grades: In the Classroom, by Parents, Tutors, and Librarians

Duration: 1 Day or 1 Week

Overview

The teacher will read aloud a short picture book or chapter book that is already popular with students, such as the *Captain Underpants* series, by Dav Pilkey (for Grades 2–4) or the *Goosebumps* series, by R. L. Stine (for Grades 4–6). The teacher will collect articles and opinions from the World Wide Web on censorship activity that has been initiated for these books. After the read-aloud, the teacher can conduct a discussion on various issues around censorship, such as the following: What is censorship? What is choice in reading? What is free speech? The teacher may also want to give information on First Amendment rights.

Materials

Captain Underpants series, by Dav Pilkey; poster board, paper, markers, journals

Key Vocabulary

Censorship, Free Choice, First Amendment

Anticipatory Set

1. *Focus:* Students will have the opportunity to discuss what their opinions are in terms of censorship: Should they be allowed to read certain materials and why? Students will have an opportunity to discuss with the teacher in a safe environment the opinions of the

(Continued)

(Continued)

censors and voice their opinions of whether they agree with critics and what the consequences may be.

2. *Objective:* By the end of the lesson, students will have a clear idea of the First Amendment, especially regarding free speech rights. Students will have the opportunity to discuss and voice their opinions on the pros and cons of being exposed to materials that some adults think they should not be reading.

3. *Transfer:* These conversations will help students voice their doubts, opinions, and feelings in a safe space under the guidance of a teacher who will facilitate these discussions. These will give them the opportunity to gain valuable persuasive techniques that they may use in the future.

Instructions

1. After the read-aloud, bring in popular media reports of the censorship activity around these books. Talk to students about what it means to censor. Cite censorship activities not only in terms of books and reading children's literature but also in terms of government, lifestyle, current issues, and so forth, so that students may see the relationship between what they are learning and what is happening in real life.

2. Direct the lesson through a series of critical questions such as: "What topics are you not allowed to view, talk about, read about, and so on?" "Why do you think your parents or teachers may not want you to read or talk about these topics?" "What do you think would happen if everyone was always given their free choice?" "Would some people's choices harm other people?" Conduct a discussion so that students see the pros and cons of censorship and that as young children, they also have a certain degree of choice. As they discuss these issues, the teacher can write notes on a poster board so that students may refer to the points later.

Independent and Group Practice

Later the students can break into small groups or pairs and read popular fiction that may have been censored at some point, such as *Where the Wild Things Are* or *In the Night Kitchen*, by Maurice Sendak; or *Halloween ABC*, by Eve Merriam, illustrated by Lane Smith, and prepare a "defense" or persuasive speech against censoring this book.

Closure

Students share their persuasive speeches. Teachers can give more information about censorship, especially about Banned Books Week, which is always celebrated the last week of September.

Extension

Have the school librarian or principal talk to the class about the school's policies on censorship and selection. Talk to parents about selection.

SELECTED ANNOTATED BIBLIOGRAPHY

Angelou, M. (2009). *I know why the caged bird sings.* New York: Ballantine. (Original work published 1969)

In this autobiographical tale, poet laureate Maya Angelou talks about her painful childhood filled with abuse, an unwanted pregnancy, and tragedy. Recommended age 12 years and up.

Blume, J. (1986). *Are you there God? It's me, Margaret.* New York: Yearling Books. (Original work published 1970)

Margaret, a young preteen, wonders when she is going to fill out her training bra. This is a wonderful book about puberty and the anxiety that young girls face during that time. Recommended age 8 years and up.

Blume, J. (2007). *Forever.* New York: Simon Pulse. (Original work published 1975)

Katherine and Michael, two high school teenagers, fall in love and discover their sexuality and passion for each other. Recommended age 12 years and up.

Cole, B. (1996). *Mommy laid an egg.* San Francisco: Chronicle Books.

In this comical tale of where babies come from, a set of parents decide to tell their young children all about the birds and the bees, but they give them all the wrong information. The two children then proceed to give the parents the right information, complete with stick figure drawings. Recommended age 3 years and up.

Cronin, D. (2001). *Click, clack, moo: Cows that type.* New York: Scholastic.

When the cows discover the old typewriter, they begin communicating with Farmer Brown, demanding electric blankets. This is the hilarious tale of the farm animals that stage a strike when the farmer refuses to give in to their demands. Big words such as neutral party, deal, and ultimatum make this a wonderful learning experience. Recommended age 4 years and up.

Hosseini, K. (2003). *Kite runner.* New York: Riverhead Books.

Kite Runner is Hosseini's debut novel of two friends, Amir and Hassan, spanning a time from the end of the monarchy in Afghanistan until the Taliban's rule. A complicated cultural tale of a boy's coming of age and two friends' loyalty to each other divided by classism, where one escapes to the United States while the other dies in Kabul trying to save their home, *Kite Runner* is perhaps the only Afghani novel written in English by an insider of the culture and has been on the New York Times bestseller list since its publication. Recommended age 14 years and up.

Lee, H. (1960). *To kill a mockingbird.* New York: Harper Perennial.

This is the story of 8-year-old Scout and her brother Jem, who live in the small town of Maycomb, Alabama, in the 1930s. Scout's father, Atticus Finch, defends Tom Robinson, a Black man accused of raping a White girl. Issues of racism, justice, color, class, and growing up enmesh in this Pulitzer Prize winning novel. Recommended age 12 years and up.

Morrison, T. (1970). *The bluest eye.* New York: Vintage.

This is the sad story of Pecola, a young African American girl living in the 1940s who, because of circumstances, is convinced that having blue eyes is more beautiful. She is raped twice by her father, becomes pregnant, and is driven to madness when a priest who wants to rid himself of a dog takes advantage of her need and tells her to look for a sign to gain blue eyes when she unwittingly feeds the dog poison. Recommended age 12 years and up.

Naidoo, B. (1988). *Journey to Jo'Berg.* New York: HarperCollins.

This is the story of a sister and brother who travel to Johannesburg in apartheid-ridden South Africa. Naidoo writes this story when she acknowledges the sheltered existence she leads as an upper class person in South Africa. Recommended age 9 years and up.

Naylor, P. R. (various years). *Alice series.* Atheneum Books.

The *Alice* series, which began many years ago, is about an everyday girl going through life as a junior in school. The series originally had books that dealt with such things as Alice's first dates in junior high and high school. Recently, the author has also added "prequels" that show Alice in her growing years, beginning in primary and elementary school. There are more than 16 books in this popular series. Recommended age 9 years and up.

Neuman, L. (1990). *Heather has two mommies.* Los Angeles: Alyson.

This is the tale of Heather, who has two mommies and does everything with them. Recommended age 3 years and up.

Orwell, G. (1945). *Animal farm.* New York: Penguin Books.

This is the allegorical story of the farm where the animals stage a coup and oust their human master. Although they run successfully for a while, the pigs become self-proclaimed leaders who are no better than the human masters they ousted. A story of communism, this is an interesting and engaging read of leadership gone wrong. Recommended age 13 years and up.

Parnell, P., & Richardson, J. (2005). *And Tango makes three.* New York: Simon & Schuster Children's Publishing.

This is the charming true story of two male penguins in the Central Park Zoo in New York City, who "adopt" an egg (with the help of a zookeeper) and care for it until it hatches. This "different" penguin family can still be seen in the zoo today. Recommended age 0 and up.

Patron, S. (2007). *The higher power of Lucky.* New York: Atheneum.

In this Newbery Award winning book, 10-year-old Lucky grows up in a very small town in California. Having lost her mother suddenly, she is always prepared for the unexpected and is a high energy, always questioning young girl. Recommended age 9 years and up.

Rodriguez, L. (1993). *Always running: La vida loca: Gang days in L.A.* New York: Touchstone.

In this autobiographical tale, Rodriguez recounts real events from his childhood growing up in Watts, a south Los Angeles community filled with drugs, gangs, and violence. Recommended age 13 years and up.

Rowling, J. K. (2007). *Harry Potter box set* (books 1–7). New York: Arthur A. Levine Books.

This seven-part series follows Harry Potter and his friends Ron and Hermione through their growing years from 11 to 17. The first book begins with Harry discovering that he is a wizard and not a poor orphan who has been left to his cruel aunt and uncle. The rest of the books follow him as he fights evil and triumphs. Recommended age 8 years and up.

Singer, N. (2007). *Innocent's story.* New York: Holiday House.

Originally published in the United Kingdom, this story is the chilling tale of a young girl who dies in the subway bombing in England and as a ghost lodges herself in the brain of a suicide bomber. The book brings up issues of religion, faith, understanding, and what is right. Recommended age 13 years and up.

Steinbeck, J. (2002). *Grapes of wrath.* New York: Penguin Books. (Original work published 1939)

This is the story of the Joad family's journey west to become migrant farmworkers. Set in the Depression Era of the 1930s, it was controversial even when it was published, as it brings up questions of justice, government, capitalism, power, and so forth. Although required reading in many high schools, it still remains very controversial. It has been republished many times. Recommended age 15 years and up.

Willhoite, M. (1990). *Daddy's roommate.* Los Angeles: Alyson.

Mommy and Daddy get a divorce and Daddy lives with his roommate Frank. This is a very simplistic tale of two gay men who have custody of their son. What the book lacks in its illustration in terms of sophistication, it makes up for in its simple message that "being gay is just another form of love." Recommended age 3 years and up.

REFERENCES

Academic American Encyclopedia. (n.d.). *Definitions of censorship.* Retrieved October 21, 2009, from http://www.thefileroom.org/documents/Definitions.html

American Library Association. (n.d.) *About banned & challenged books.* Retrieved December 7, 2007, from http://www.ala.org/ala/issuesadvocacy/banned/aboutbanned books/index.cfm

American Library Association. (n.d.). *Challenges by initiator, institution, type, and year.* *Retrieved* December 7, 2007, from http://staging.ala.org/ala/aboutala/offices/oif/banned booksweek/bbwlinks/challengesinitiator.cfm

American Library Association. (n.d.) *Intellectual freedom Q & A.* Retrieved December 7, 2009, from http://www.ala.org/Template.cfm?Section=basics&Template=/ContentManagement/ ContentDisplay.cfm&ContentID=60610

American Library Association. (n.d.). *100 most frequently banned books.* Retrieved December 7, 2009, from http://www.ala.org/ala/issuesadvocacy/banned/frequently challenged/challengedbydecade/1990_2000.cfm

Audio file of interview about *Click, Clack, Moo* by Doreen Cronin. (2000). Retrieved July 15, 2008, from http://www.npr.org/templates/story/story.php?storyId=1069209

Banned book week: *Captain Underpants* controversy. (2006). Retrieved July 14, 2008, from http://www.marshall.edu/library/bannedbooks/books/captainunderpants.asp

Blume, J. (n.d.). *Judy Blume talks about censorship.* Retrieved October 22, 2009, from http://www.judyblume.com/censorship.php

Bosman, J. (2007, February 18). With one word, children's book sets off uproar. *New York Times.* Retrieved October 22, 2009, from http://www.nytimes.com/2007/02/18/books/18newb.html

Chattaway, P. (2007). *An "unsafe" bridge.* Retrieved October 22, 2009, from http:// www.christianitytoday.com/ct/movies/interviews/2007/katherinepaterson.html

Cornell University Law School. (n.d) *First Amendment of the Bill of Rights of the U.S. Constitution.* Retrieved July 4, 2008, from http://www.law.cornell.edu/constitution/ constitution.billofrights.html

Doyle, R. P. (2007). *Books challenged or banned in 2006–2007.* Retrieved December 7, 2009, from http://www.ila.og/pdf/2007banned.pdf

Doyle, R. P. (2008). *Books challenged or banned in 2007–2008.* Retrieved December 7, 2009, from http://www.ila.og/pdf/2008banned.pdf

Johnson, P. (2003, September 14). Amanpour: CNN practiced self-censorship. *USA Today.* Retrieved December 7, 2009, from http://www.usatoday.com/life/columnist/mediamix/ 2003-09-14-media-mix_x.htm

Karolides, N. J., Bald, M., & Sova, D. (1999). *100 banned books: Censorship histories of world literature.* New York: Checkmark Books.

Karolides, N. J., Buress, L., & Kean, J. M. (Eds.). (1993). *Censored books: Critical viewpoints.* Lanham, MD: Scarecrow Press.

Mazer, N. F. (1993). Not laughable, but lethal. In N. J. Karolides, L. Burress, & J. M. Kean (Eds.), *Censored books: Critical viewpoints* (pp. 19–24). Lanham, MD: Scarecrow Press.

McClure, A. (1995). Censorship of children's books. In S. Lehr (Ed.), *Battling dragons: Issues and controversy in children's literature* (pp. 3–30). Portsmouth, NH: Heinemann

McNabb, S. (1994). Censoring student newspapers hurts education. In J. E. Brown (Ed.), *SLATE on intellectual freedom* (pp. 31–32). Urbana, IL: National Council of Teachers of English.

Naidoo, B. (1995). Undesirable publication: A journey to Jo'Burg. In S. Lehr (Ed.), *Battling dragons: Issues and controversy in children's literature* (pp. 31–38). Portsmouth, NH: Heinemann.

Paterson, K. (2007). *Bridge to Terabithia* (1977). New York: Crowell.

Riley, G. B. (1998). *Censorship*. New York: Facts on File.

Simmons, J. S., & Dresang, E. T. (2001). *School censorship in the 21st century: A guide for teachers and school library media specialists*. Newark, DE: International Reading Association.

Singer, N. (2006). Tale of an innocent. *Children's Literature in Education, 37*, 305–312.

Sova, D. B. (1998). *Literature suppressed on sexual grounds*. New York: Facts on File.

Sova, D. B. (2006). *Literature suppressed on sexual grounds* (Rev ed.). New York: Facts on File.

Wachsberger, K. (2006). Preface. In D. B. Sova, *Literature suppressed on sexual grounds*. New York: Facts on File.

West, M. I. (1988). *Trust your children: Voices against censorship children's literature*. New York: Neal Schuman.

Chapter 5

Gender, Sexuality, and Equity

Kimberly Persiani-Becker

> *What is read to children not only leaves an impression behind but also influences the values, and shapes the dreams, of children. It can provide negative images and stereotypes and cut off hopes and limit aspirations. It can erode self-respect through overt and covert racism or sexism. It can also help young people get beyond family troubles, neighborhood violence, stereotyping and prejudice.*
>
> —Kohl (1995, p. 61)

Anyone having taught kindergarten through fifth-grade classes for any number of years may have heard such comments such as "Girls don't play _____" and "Boys don't like that/do that. . . ." In other words, as teachers we constantly overhear stereotypes of what gender should look like, behave like, or be like on a daily basis in schools. For those of us who believe in equity, whether it be in education, sports activities, occupations, and so forth, and for those of us who would like to consistently emphasize to students the importance of equality for boys and girls and men and women, it can be disheartening to listen to one's own students express such remarks. As the quote by Kohl demonstrates, multicultural books that depict boys and girls in various roles and capacities can be excellent starting points in engaging students in dialogue about gender issues. This chapter explores issues of gender, especially related to the inequities in children's trade books that have had very few good role models for girls and that sometimes still perpetuate gender stereotypes.

Closely related to the issues of gender and perceptions of what each gender is capable of or allowed in society is the issue of sexuality and how this plays out in society. Given the recent political controversy around gay marriage and individual rights, books that show different lifestyles are also included in this chapter as a part of multicultural children's books that are inclusive. An analysis of gender issues as portrayed in children's books is explored, along with a discussion of popular stories such as folktales and fairy tales and gender inrequity in these.

GENDER ROLES PORTRAYED IN CHILDREN'S LITERATURE

Many studies have lamented the gender inequity in children's books citing more male protagonists than females (Ernst, 1995; Singh, 1998; Temple, Martinez, & Yokota, 2006). Although there has been a concerted effort by children's authors and educators to bridge this gap in the last decades, especially in contemporary realistic fiction and specific historical fiction (see, e.g., such books as the *Dear America* series and the *Dear Diary* series), there are still fewer books that have girls as the main character than books that have boys as protagonists. Studies have also speculated and reported on the effects of this gender inequity, specifically on adolescent girls, which result in a flawed self-image, lack of motivation or drive, and gender stereotyping (Fox, 1993; Pipher, 1994; Temple et al., 2006). The changes in perceptions and understanding of gender roles seem to happen around the preadolescent and adolescent ages when children are going through many developmental transformations. As Tomlinson and Lynch-Brown (2002) said, "The stereotyping of females in traditional roles is a debilitating message to convey to today's girls" (p. 15).

However, children begin to form their ideas of gender well before preadolescence, in their early formative years. At this age, children are considering their "gender schema, that is, an organized pattern of behavior which they use to sort information about the world with regard to gender" (Trepanier-Street & Romatowski, 1999, p. 155). They are beginning to understand what it means to be male or female as they view how society classifies people and the roles they play by gender. They are developing attitudes toward the appropriateness of toys, activities, and occupational roles based on gender.

A quick look at children's books in any collection shows the gender roles portrayed in the average children's books as reiterating many of the stereotypes of society. Men fix things; women are caretakers or homemakers; boys don't cry and need to be tough, whereas girls need boys to rescue them. Many children's books continue to depict women in gender specific roles such as housewives, but not as much as in the more traditional literature, which often portrays helpless, vulnerable female characters waiting for strong, capable men to rescue them, especially in the ever popular fairy tales like *Snow White* and *Cinderella*. At the same time, these stories also stereotype men as perpetually strong, capable, and competent. This is alarming, especially given the fact that most **traditional tales** are usually read to children at an early stage in their

old + outdated concepts

lives as the first stories they hear. Further, these traditional tales are also perpetuated by glossed-over movies for young audiences such as those by Disney. Gender stereotypes are more apparent in these stories than many others. Although it can be argued that Disney could hardly be considered quality children's literature, for the average person, Disney versions of traditional tales are most common and most widely read because of their popularity and mass appeal. While many current titles are changing these stereotypes, it is still true that most of the children's trade books published today still have boys as their protagonists, doing all the exciting things. This is alarming, because when attitudes toward gender are slanted due to inaccurate representations of society, it is possible that the potential and motivation of individuals can be stifled (Trepanier-Street & Romatowski, 1999).

[handwritten marginal note: Michael Jordan vs. Mia Hamm commercial 1997]

CHILDREN'S READING PREFERENCES

"What kinds of books are our children reading? What images are we offering boys and girls in the literature they read?" (Ernst, 1995, p. 66). As recently as 20 or 30 years ago, girls were stereotyped as working in the kitchen, whereas boys were riding bikes. The images often showed boys in more positive images than those of girls. Boys were generally shown as independent, active, problem solvers, and in charge of situations, whereas girls were often portrayed as dependent, passive, problem causers, and as followers.

Gilbert (1989) stated that when much of the past literature was written, gender bias was not a consideration. In fact, if children were introduced to such literature, it's possible they might believe the following: (a) men fix things, (b) animals are male or neuter, (c) women rarely have jobs, (d) fathers make decisions, (e) women serve food but don't eat food, and (f) girls have dolls.

However, there is hope; in a recent survey of girls' reading preferences, Gopalakrishnan and Ulanoff (2005) found that in spite of the imbalance in children's trade books with regard to gender, girls preferred reading about strong and independent women characters who were resilient, resourceful, and clever, such as Hermione in the *Harry Potter* series, Violet from the *Lemony Snicket* series, and many characters from *Shojo Manga* or Japanese girl comics. As a result, many recent authors are recognizing the need for gender equity and much of the current literature for young people includes more relevant issues. We are beginning to see girls in more active roles, such as in *Amazing Grace*, by Mary Hoffman; *Under the Quilt of Night*, by Deborah Hopkinson; *A Chair for My Mother*, by Vera Williams; and *America Is Her Name*, by Luis Rodriguez. America is a strong Latina girl who is a wonderful poet and an independent, well-mannered young lady who overcomes many family struggles with grace and dignity. She is a lovely model for young girls and teens to look up to.

In addition to active female characters, boys are being viewed as friendlier toward girls than in the past, with stories such as in *Angel Child, Dragon Child,* by Michelle Surat, and "Gloria Who Might Be My Best Friend," from *Stories Julian Tells,* by Ann Cameron, where the main male characters in these two stories each befriend a girl and enjoy sharing in her activities.

GENDER EQUITY AND FINDING A BALANCE

With children's literature being such a powerful tool in today's classrooms, libraries, and homes, how gender is portrayed in children's books can contribute to the image children develop of their own role and that of their gender in society. What they read about and see in illustrations has a strong impact on their own identity if they are not exposed to varying portrayals. Gender bias is often embedded in the content, language, and illustrations of a large number of books. This bias may be viewed as how gender is represented by the main characters in children's books. "A book reflecting gender equity shows equal opportunities for both genders in the workplace and depicts multiple and diverse personal roles for individuals of both genders" (Temple, Martinez, Yokota, & Naylor, 2002, p. 111). As teachers, becoming aware of this in society is important, as gender stereotypic thinking may limit children's choices, interests, and abilities. Reading books that do not stereotype roles and occupations by gender might encourage children to think critically about gender roles. Children's "gender schemas" could then shift to incorporate several possible occupations and roles for men and women in society (Trepanier-Street & Romatowski, 1999). It's also important that children have the chance to compare contemporary gender portrayals with the more traditional portrayals as a way to compare the two and provide more options in the way of careers, adventures, friendships, home lives, and so on, that are made available to them.

As we know, early on, children begin receiving messages about their place in society. What do the messages found in books say about their role in society today? There are several stories that include nonstereotyped gender roles and are equitable in nature. *William's Doll,* by Charlotte Zolotow, portrays a young boy who wants his dad to buy him a doll. His father wants to buy him "boy toys" and his brother refers to William as a sissy. When the grandmother buys William a doll, the family realizes it really is no big deal if boys play with "girl toys." *Toby's Doll's House,* by Ragnhild Scamell, and *Swish!* by Bill Martin, also portray characters in various roles other than those previously seen as boy roles or girl roles. In *Toby's Doll's House,* Toby wants a dollhouse for his birthday, but the family takes that to mean what he really wants is a fort. This causes him to take the situation into his own hands and he builds his own dollhouse. In *Swish!* two girls' teams compete against one another in an intense and close final championship game with a "no-holds-barred" attitude. Both of these books tweak gender stereotypes and are a bit edgy considering the mainstream of books out there today. On the other hand, a past favorite like *Pippi Longstocking*, by Astrid Lindgren, is still popular today. However, with stories such as this one, it can cause a problem when books try too hard, meaning when stories depict the opposites of the stereotyped gender roles in hard-to-believe ways or are edifying in presentation. A more reasonable title might be that of *The Butterfly*, by Patricia Pollaco, which is a story about two girls who become friends, face prejudice, and find their own strength, as one of the girls is being hidden from the Nazis in the other's basement.

Realistic fiction like *The Butterfly* is something female readers can relate to directly as they struggle to move through difficult situations while leaning on their girlfriends for support in facing their fears head-on. Such picture books are quite powerful. In addition, for upper elementary (Grades 5 and 6) through middle school (Grades 7–9), teachers who want to expose their students to strong female characters coming to terms with their identity and overcoming familial obstacles will find *Becoming Naomi Leon* and *Esperanza Rising*, by Pam Muñoz Ryan, perfect choices. For high school–age students, rich multicultural novels like *Snowflower and the Secret Fan*, by Susan Lee, and *A Thousand Splendid Suns*, by Kaleil Hosseini, are exceptional portrayals of young women finding themselves, even though their circumstances are often tragic, and of the boys and young men in their lives who model gentlemanly behavior for the women, who have seen evil in their gender counterparts.

SOME CONSIDERATIONS AND RECOMMENDATIONS

It's most important to create a library collection that balances both males and females in a variety of roles; however, there is still an ongoing trend in children's literature that highlights active male protagonists, making this difficult at times. While newer books are beginning to address this imbalance, the bulk of books available to children in libraries and classrooms reflect decades of accumulated literature, including the more traditional type, which tends to stereotype gender roles. In contemporary literature, women are presented in many different career positions, including but not limited to caretaker. They are also portrayed as smart, independent, self-assured individuals. When men and boys are not stereotyped, they are portrayed as sensitive people with varying emotions. Both men and women should be portrayed positively in a variety of careers, with a variety of emotions, and as self-confident, independent beings. In turn, children will be exposed to boys and girls, men and women with whom they wish to identify. Just making sure to have female and male gender tags in titles of books does not mean that the books are about characters of that gender or that the portrayal is positive. "How many books with male characters could we substitute with a female and in how many books with female characters could we substitute a male? This would be an intriguing critical response to a book in which to engage our students in order to examine gender balance" (Ernst, 1995, p. 74). Teachers might decide to try this out using a handful of titles from their own classroom library and have the students do the analysis in small groups. This will not only help the teacher choose appropriate titles, but it will certainly get the students to begin thinking consciously about the books they are currently reading and choosing and those they plan to choose in the future.

A balance of male and female characters is necessary in meeting the needs and interests of children of both sexes and helps these members "understand more fully the perspectives, problems, and feelings of members of the opposite sex" (Tomlinson & Lynch-Brown, 2002, p. 34). Classrooms, homes, and libraries need collections to include a wide range of topics with a combination of male and female characters portraying a variety of occupations, sports achievements, emotions, family dynamics, and the like. Having such titles available to children helps them see alternative gender behaviors as opposed to their traditional book counterparts. Because "books serve as a touchstone to which children compare their realities and from which they form their sense of the world" (Mitchell, 2003, p. 172), it is important to remember that when adults choose books for children, they also need to discuss these books with them, and they need to be aware that children see books as reflecting how the world really is and should be.

A way to find balance when pulling together a collection of books for children and young adults is to consider female characters who are strong and independent but still sweet and kind, as well as male characters who are sensitive and compassionate yet capable and intelligent. Here are some guidelines: (1) Analyze gender assumptions in the text, (2) raise questions about the portrayal of the male and female characters, and (3) reverse the genders of the main characters to decide if the switch can work and keep the storyline intact (Rudman, 1995). Using these few guidelines can serve as a beginning for developing a balance of male and female characters portrayed positively in books.

CHILDREN'S BOOKS AND SEXUALITY

More than other types of books, picture books provide visual aids as role models for children. Of course, having stories available that depict boys and girls in a variety of ways will help in providing positive models to emulate, especially since gender stereotypes and sexism act as limits to children's potential growth and development (Narahara, 1998). With this in mind, it is a great responsibility to choose books for children in which they can see themselves as strong, hardworking, and successful individuals. The development of the self-concept and identification is when an individual accepts the characteristics and beliefs of another as his or her own. A boy may begin to talk like his father or a girl may begin to walk like her mother. This early identification with the parent of the same sex leads to sex typing, the adoption of the sex roles considered acceptable in a particular culture (Brewer, 1997). As sex roles become far less restricted, children should be provided with ways of identifying their own sexuality while remaining free from stereotypes (Glazer & Giorgis, 2005).

Books present models for sex role identification. If children are only exposed to books with female characters as passive and male characters as active, they are learning what kind of behavior is expected of them. Fortunately, many books have been moving away from sex role stereotyping. One can now see female characters as career minded and successful in the working world. Males are now showing tenderness and sensitivity in children's books. No longer are we seeing women working only in the home wearing aprons and raising the children, while men go off to the office wearing suits or working at physical-labor jobs. However, to choose only books that show women working at exciting and interesting careers is "creating an imbalance as much as it is to present only books that show women functioning as mothers or homemakers" (Glazer & Giorgis, 2005, p. 211).

With this in mind, it is important to provide a variety of characters that are not stereotyped. If children are acting or perpetuating stereotypes, one may want to introduce evidence that conflicts with their current beliefs. The teacher who presents *Sleeping Beauty,* about a young woman who waits to be kissed by her brave prince, may also want to present *Jo Jo's Flying Sidekick,* by Brian Pinkney, which presents a young girl taking on her personal demons and challenges by conquering her fears through karate, as a way to show the difference between the behaviors of girls in children's literature. According to Glazer and Giorgis (2005), "Literature allows you to provide a great variety of possible behaviors to broaden children's conceptions of possibilities for themselves" (p. 212). It is then the responsibility of those making literature accessible to children to see to it that an assortment of story lines is available where boys and girls, men and women, are represented in a variety of capacities.

SEXUALITY PORTRAYED IN CHILDREN'S BOOKS

Anyone who has worked with or spent time with children in sixth, seventh, and eighth grade, when youngsters struggle with "raging hormones" and "feelings of inadequacy" while developing physically and experiencing potentially intimate feelings for their peers, knows that it can be one of the most confusing periods in an adolescent's life. Often, preteens and teens find themselves alone, vulnerable, and fearful of confiding in family or friends about such emotions, because going through this time period can be a very lonely experience as children begin to identify with peers of the same sex and opposite sex. Having characters in books whom readers can associate with closely offers boys and girls other people, places, and events familiar to them so this loneliness is not as blatant. It's quite calming to find a relevant story to escape into when the real world is confusing and overwhelming for boys and girls going through such a difficult stage, especially when a topic like intimate relationships is on the table.

Because of this, secondary teachers might want to examine their school curriculum and consider incorporating literature that includes the concept of healthy relationships, be they heterosexual or homosexual. Teachers might also want to explore the history and role models in said relationships, just as has been done with relevant literature about diverse cultures, women, and people with disabilities. The dilemma over whether books with sexual themes and characters should be used in middle and high school is one that will continue to be debated for years to come, but choosing appropriate stories that reflect the youngsters being taught can provide models for our youth. And although American schools have actively and appropriately addressed cultural issues related to ethnic and gender discrimination, one can expect these same schools to face the dilemma associated with close relationships and the possibility of discrimination based on sexual orientation (Whittingham & Rickman, 2007). Meeting youngster's questions head-on, through appropriate literature and in a safe environment for discussion, will likely be more productive in the long run.

Seeing as romance stories are popular with preteens and teens, especially girls, who find themselves becoming more aware of their growing sexuality, it is important, once again, to maintain a balance of books addressing identity issues. Some stories for preteens show attraction between members of the opposite sex as well as members of the same sex. More often than in the past, there are more stories available that portray the struggle of young people coming to terms with a homosexual or lesbian sexual orientation, whereas other stories show the cruelty toward young homosexuals or lesbians (Tomlinson & Lynch-Brown, 2002). The book *Annie on My Mind,* by Nancy Garden, is the perfect example of relevant literature for young people who have the need to identify with characters they are reading about in stories. Although *Annie on My Mind* is one of the censored books during the 1990–1999 decade, according to the American Library Association, it is still one that addresses a key issue about sexual identity. Coming to terms with falling in love is difficult enough, but when it's with someone of the same sex, it is even more confusing. *Annie on My Mind* is a wonderfully engaging book for anyone who has dealt with the oppressive and ignorant nature of those who would otherwise wish to ignore the issue of sexual identity. It addresses the topic without hitting the reader over the head in an obvious way or crude manner.

[handwritten margin note: Seems very judgmental for those with strong Christian values]

Although it is important to maintain the more subtle approach, books such as *Kissing Kate*, by L. Myracle, and *Keeping You Secret*, by J. Peters, raise important points about the ramifications of coming out and the concept of homophobia and how teens today have the pressures of such issues to contend with. In *Keeping You Secret*, a young lady, Holland, begins an intense relationship with CeCe, a girl who identifies as a lesbian. Holland experiences serious consequences attached with being a lesbian, but ultimately she is proud to have taken the risks. In *Kissing Kate*, 16-year-old Lissa's relationship with her best friend of 4 years changes after they kiss at a party. Kate had leaned in to kiss Lissa, and Lissa kissed her back. Then, Kate pretends Lissa doesn't exist. Confused and alone, Lissa is left questioning everything she thought she knew about herself. Luckily, with the help of a new friend, Lissa begins to find the strength to realize that sometimes falling in love with the wrong person is the only way to grow in this regard. In both books, the story line is less subtle than in the previously mentioned books, but they are just as important all the same. Our youth today often feel alone and isolated. Without books such as these, that feeling of loneliness only can be intensified. When young people know they are not alone during highly stressful situations, they are more likely to talk to others in their same situation or seek help for questions they have. They only want to be accepted, and having like-minded people to share with is the first step in moving forward.

That being said, teens who identify as heterosexual and are also coming to terms with their sexuality and feelings of attraction at this stage in their lives go through just as many changes and have just as many concerns in regard to falling in love, having their heart broken, questioning their own sexual behavior and choices, questioning their masculinity and femininity, wondering if they are pretty enough or handsome enough, and wondering whether anyone will ever love them.

A coming of age story that was popular in the late 1960s but still holds true today and is still read by teens all over the world is *The Outsiders*, by S. E. Hinton. Realities that perplex today's youth are no different than 40 years ago and can be found in this story. Such concerns include dating and love, masculinity, life and death, and many other issues our youth deal with today. It's a story that most likely will never go out of style and is continuously reprinted. While this book has a stronger, masculine quality to it, it is read by both girls and boys and carries with it strong and meaningful discussions for both genders.

Two other titles that concern themselves with heterosexual identity and experimentation with love in the teen years are *Someone Like You*, by Sarah Dessen, and *Too Soon for Jeff*, by Marilyn Reynolds. In *Someone Like You*, Halley and Scarlett, girls who have been friends for a long time, deal with the struggles of friendship once Scarlett finds out she is pregnant with her boyfriend's baby after he is killed in a motorcycle accident. This story is one young women will read and feel less alone, whether the reader is pregnant, in a new relationship and considering sex, trying to be a good friend, or simply worrying about such issues. In *Too Soon for Jeff*, aspects of the teen pregnancy problem stem from the young man's point of view. In this story, Jeff, just 17 years old, has decided that he must be honest with his girl-friend Christy and tell her that he no longer wants to have a relationship with her. Then he is shocked to find out that she is pregnant. This really throws off his plans of college and freedom. However, by the end, both Jeff and Christy have matured enough to be parents to their baby son. Both of these books are strong choices available for teens in the midst of going through such experiences.

More current young adult novels do tend to deal directly with issues of sexuality. These issues often surround coping with sexual behavior and its consequences, including the identity of sexual orientation as well as physical growth changes (Temple et al., 2002). A book that deals with these types of issues includes the often censored and challenged book, *Are You There God, It's Me, Margaret?* by Judy Blume, which addresses female menstruation to the dislike and discomfort of many in terms of the appropriateness in consideration for young girls. Other titles, such as *Caddie Woodlawn,* by Carol Brink, and *The Sisterhood of the Traveling Pants,* by Ann Brashares, also address such concerns related to identity.

In *Caddie Woodlawn,* an 11-year-old tomboy would much rather run around the woods playing with her brothers and being adventurous than become a "lady." It's one of the stories that supports girls coming to terms with their identity as equals to boys, while still maintaining their feminine traits. In *The Sisterhood of the Traveling Pants,* four female best friends each assume their individual identities over their summer vacation as they all spend it apart from one another. Each finds that she is unique, strong, capable, sexy, and smart. These two books couldn't be more different, but they are both effective in introducing young girls to several different individuals, all who are self-identifying their sexuality and their place in the world.

With regard to sexism in literature, its subtleness can be dangerous if not approached and delivered carefully. It can subtly condition boys and girls to accept the way they see and read the world, which might reinforce gender images (Fox, 1993). This reinforcement influences children to not question existing social relationships, thus accepting what they are presented. At the same time, books containing images and story lines that conflict with gender stereotypes provide children the opportunity to reconsider their gender beliefs and assumptions. "Texts can provide children with alternative role models and inspire them to adopt more egalitarian gender attitudes" (Singh, 1998, p. 3) as they begin to form their identities.

Gay and Lesbian Families Addressed in Children's Books

Those who have taught for several years and have worked with a variety of non-traditional families may find it difficult to find appropriate curriculum to address the needs of children stemming from same-sex parent homes. In the last decade or so, children's literature always seemed to be a place one could turn to in order to make the learning environment more inclusive and relevant for the children who identify with said families, be it as the child of the same-sex parents, a friend, cousin, and so on. Through the years, more and more book choices depicting families with parents who are gay or lesbian have become more readily available and accessible as well as necessary, especially as we see the need increasing in the future.

Things have changed in the more current literature available to children and young adults today that lends itself to addressing such issues. These issues include divorce, stepparents, stepsiblings, and the like, but it's only part of the real-life circumstances children of same-sex parents might have to face. Thirty or so years ago, the feelings of loneliness, guilt, shame, and fear were rarely depicted in the story lines children were privy to through the curriculum at that time. Having characters to relate with who shared similar circumstances would have made all the difference between keeping attentive at school, because students might no longer feel alone or lose focus while worrying more about their home lives. Luckily, children's literature portraying idyllic family structures of the past have slowly given way to more realistic depictions of families of divorce, blended families, foster children, adoptive children, and single parenthood. For the most part, these books have been viewed as enriching the literature selection possibilities and are a welcome reflection of the various family structures and issues that exist in today's society (Mitchell, 2003). However, a family structure that continues to be excluded is one in which there are same-sex parents. Because there are children who live with two moms or two dads, it's important that they are mirrored in book selections and collections.

Over the decades, schools have become populated with children whose home life does not fit the nuclear family model. Unfortunately, books such as *Heather Has Two Mommies,* by Leslèa Newman, and *Daddy's Roommate,* by Michael Willhoite, have hardly been embraced by schools, libraries, and parents. In fact, both books are on the ALA's list of 100 most challenged books during the 1990–1999 decade for various reasons, and they continue to make that list today. However, there are children who desperately need to be able to see themselves reflected in what is being read to them or what is accessible for their own reading. These two titles are only a couple that are appropriate for opening discussions with children who can relate to the story line in one way or another.

There are several books available that depict such families, and with more and more publishers making note of this literature, there will continue to be more books written and published. Unfortunately, fear of censorship as well as the displeasure of teachers, librarians, and parents about the topics, are likely to keep them out of the hands of young people. There are many children living in loving families with gay or lesbian parents, siblings, or other family members, but they are often excluded when it comes to being reflected in the stories they read at school, the library, and at home.

Books validate for children that their lives are normal and that they are part of the culture. If they are exposed only to books with two-parent families, they might question whether something is wrong with their single-parent family. If they see only a mom and a dad as parents, children might question what is wrong with their two-mommy or two-daddy family; just as if they see only families that are happy all the time, children might wonder what is wrong with their family because their parents argue, as do their siblings. Succinctly stated by Diana Mitchell (2003), "Children expect the world as they know it to be represented in some of the books they read. If they see no reflections of themselves or the world they live in, they begin to wonder about themselves" (p. 172).

Many characters in picture books and novels for children face moments of crisis, situations of difficulty, or circumstances in which life-changing decisions must be made. The situations often reflect what children will face in their own lives (Tomlinson & Lynch-Brown, 2002). Nontraditional family dynamics including children with lesbian or gay parents face said crisis. Through stories, children can understand more fully these difficult life-changing issues that the characters face and can then dialogue about the consequences and outcomes that may result from the circumstances or the character's choices. For teachers, parents, and librarians, these kinds of books will open the door to rich discussions that may otherwise have been avoided. Such books are also vehicles with which to solicit discussion should topics of concern be at the forefront of children's lives.

In *Oliver Button Is a Sissy,* by Tomie dePaola, children are introduced to Oliver, who is portrayed as a sissy because he takes dance lessons instead of playing ball or the like. This is often the case when young children veer from the stereotypical norm of what boys usually play and what girls usually play. This book invites children to meet Oliver and celebrate his talent with him rather than ridiculing him for doing what the girls like to do. Although *Oliver Button Is a Sissy* is not specifically designated for discussing homosexuality, it does imply that if boys and girls veer away from their stereotypical activities, their peers may label them gay or lesbian. This is one of those books that would encourage dialogue should a situation of sorts be occurring with one's children.

Additionally, same-sex parents have had few resources to turn to in the way of children's literature in order to meet the needs of their children. This, too, is changing over time with publishers like Two Lives, which was launched by Bobbie Combs, a former buyer for Koen Kids, and Sally Lindsay, the vice president of merchandising and marketing at Koen. The publishing company focuses primarily on children's books with gay, lesbian, bisexual, and transgender themes. Their target audience is children in gay and lesbian families. With publishers such as Two Lives, gay and lesbian families will have access to more relevant and more appealing literature for their children. Bobbie and Sally saw a "real need for this kind of publishing as more and more gay, lesbian, bisexual, and transgender people are starting families, and they want to provide a continuous output of books for them" (Britton, 2001, p. 19). One title that serves children trying to grapple with the fact that they have same-sex parents is *Zack's Story,* by Keith Greenberg. This is one of those stories that comes directly from an 11-year-old's perspective as he describes what his life is like having two moms. Books like these that are more realistic in nature make the text more relevant and accessible to the reader. On the other hand, fairy tales that depict a prince and a princess getting together to live happily ever after do not support those coming from families where the prince and prince or the princess and princess live happily ever after. *King & King,* by Linda deHaan and Sern Nijland, is a suitable example to use for those whose families veer from the traditional fairy tale. In addition, *King & King & Family* carries on the story to include an adopted child from another country, making it an even more reflective choice for children with same-sex parents. However, the illustrations and text might confuse a younger crowd (0–8 years old), but older children (9–14 years old) and young adults might enjoy the creative pictures, quick pace of the story line, and nonsubtle point. Finally, this story's appeal lies in its fairy tale narrative, making it possible for those who live a life outside of the tidy prince and princess package like that of Cinderella or even Shrek, to identify with. At least with Shrek, the characters aren't perfect in the way of looks and make the best of a situation. That's exactly what *King & King* opens the door for, a different story line with varying possibilities.

USING CHILDREN'S BOOKS TO PROMOTE EQUITY AND UNDERSTANDING

Because children are in the process of developing their identities, it seems that children's thinking is open to environmental influences. It is vital, then, that teachers, parents, librarians, and the like acquire children's literature that will encourage a more equitable and reflective view of the world. If we want children to view a variety of occupations, activities, identities, family structures, and their roles in society, roles not limited because of stereotypic views, it is important that in the early years they be exposed to nonstereotypic models. A valuable resource for exposing children to such nonstereotypic models is high quality children's books. The use of children's literature is a powerful medium for influencing their attitudes.

Oftentimes, new teachers, especially, inherit classroom libraries that are older and disjointed. Parents aren't always certain which books are appropriate or interesting for their children. Unfortunately, libraries don't always have the available funds to increase their collections year to year. Ideally, all children's literature should include well-rounded male and female characters. Although that is not always the case, it is possible to take active steps to ensure the use of books that promote gender equity among the sexes, address sexual identity, and include nontraditional families such as gay and lesbian households.

*Oxford Academic Journal article states that studies showing that women are biologically predisposed to being more nurturing, recognizing visual + auditory cues

When selecting books, one might want to consider the following:

- Individuals are portrayed with distinctive personalities irrespective of their gender.
- Achievements are not evaluated on the basis of gender.
- Occupations are represented as gender-free.
- Clothing is described in functional rather than gender-based terms.
- Females and males participate equally in physical activities.
- Individuals are logical or emotional depending on the situation.
- Families are not solely distinguished as two-parent or male and female couples.
- Characters are encouraged to self-identify.
- Both female and male characters are shown as having a wide range of sensibilities, feelings, and responses.
- Traits such as strength, compassion, initiative, and courage are treated as human rather than gender-specific (Narahara, 1998; Rudman, 1995).

disagree ←

Books can also be selected that have countersex attitudes embedded in them that can help children recognize stereotypical messages. Also, one might choose to combine traditional and contemporary books to elicit discussion of how genders and family dynamics are portrayed in different books. Also, the message of respect for both genders and various lifestyles should be subtly contained in the texts. It is important to avoid books that have preachy messages on gender equity, as readers tend to reject books that "hit the reader over the head" with the point of the story line.

When discussing books with children, it is important to validate both feminine and masculine voices and to listen to opposing opinions. Some children already embody attitudes that are stereotyped toward certain issues. They need to be encouraged to make choices that are consistent with their own personalities and that are self-empowering. It is also important to keep in mind that rethinking stereotypes, be it toward gender roles, sexual identity, or the like, is an ongoing process, one that can continue only if presented with material to keep the discussion and reflection going. Rich, meaningful, and appropriate children's literature is such a tool to keep this happening and children engaged.

Reflection Questions for the Teacher

1. What is the ratio of girl protagonists to boy protagonists in the books that I have in my classroom?

2. In the illustrations and in the content of these books, what gender stereotypes are propagated?

3. What criteria can I set and look for in a book with gender equity?

4. Using many of the points given in this chapter, how can I portray a balanced view of gender roles through children's books in my classroom?

5. What are my views and limitations on using books with gay and lesbian families in my classroom? How can I implement an equitable approach given this view?

6. What are my biases and limitations in terms of addressing any questions that may arise in my classroom due to my having books that show every type of family?

not in today's world

SAMPLE RESPONSE LESSON 5.1

Gender Roles

Primary Grades: In the Classroom, by Parents, Tutors, and Librarians

Duration: 1 Day

Overview

On a two-column chart paper divided into "boy roles" and "girl roles," the students will break down stereotypical and traditional gender roles before the read-aloud of *Oliver Button Is a Sissy*, by Tomie dePaola. After, students will use the revisited gender role chart to illustrate and label the interchanging activities for boys and girls. Having an immediate awareness about how and what one's children perceive to be male and female roles helps create a rich dialogue about the appropriateness of such roles. Other titles can be used for this same activity, or in addition to it, such as *William's Doll*, by Zolotow; *Jo Jo's Flying Sidekick*, by Pinkney; or *Toby's Doll's House*, by Scamell.

Materials

Two pieces of blank chart paper, markers, blank white paper folded in two (vertically), a copy of *Oliver Button Is a Sissy*, by Tomie dePaola (preferably in big book format)

Key Vocabulary

Sissy

(Continued)

(Continued)

Anticipatory Set

1. *Focus:* Students will identify stereotypical and nonstereotypical gender roles.

2. *Objective:* By the end of the lesson, students will illustrate and label an activity for a boy and for a girl that is typically reserved for the opposing gender.

3. *Transfer:* Students will use this information as a foundation for discussion as more books are read aloud to them about nonstereotypical gender roles.

Instruction

1. Prior to a read-aloud of *Oliver Button Is a Sissy,* by Tomie dePaolo, the teacher will lead children through an activity of breaking down typical gender roles. On chart paper segregated into two columns labeled "boy roles" and "girl roles," have students share out and categorize typical male and female roles. Start by asking children who they perceive certain roles to belong to, such as being a teacher, a doctor, a mechanic, a professor, a dancer, an artist, a basketball player, and so forth. Place these titles in the column the children express.

2. Give a very brief explanation about what this story is about, then read aloud *Oliver Button Is a Sissy,* by Tomie dePaolo. Read the story from cover to cover and avoid stopping to review, predict, summarize, or clarify. Just read the story without interruptions because the children have already begun the lesson by building schema about what the point of the story will be.

3. Following the read-aloud, dialogue with children about whether they can swap the gender titles on the chart paper and then assign and the roles in each column to the new gender. Reflect on the story to make the connection for the children by referencing the many "boy activities" that Oliver did not relate to but the "girl activities" that he demonstrated extraordinarily.

Guided Practice

1. Fold a piece of blank chart paper in two (vertically), then tape it to the board. Label the sides "Boy" and "Girl."

2. On the first side, "Boy," have the students choose a nonstereotypical activity for a boy (e.g., ballet dancer or caregiver). The teacher will then illustrate and label the activity.

3. On the second side, "Girl," have the students choose a nonstereotypical activity for a girl (e.g., firefighter or race car driver). The teacher will then illustrate and label the activity.

4. Review the updated gender chart one more time and ask the students if there are any more nontraditional activities that can be assigned to each side of the gender role chart. Add these activities.

Independent Practice

Have students refer to the updated gender role chart. Hand out blank white paper and have the children fold it in half vertically and label the sides "Boy" and "Girl." Have the children replicate the activity modeled by the teacher using the gender role chart as a reference.

Closure

Having children discuss the misconceptions about male and female roles in society brings the issue to life and makes concrete meaning of this topic to them. Children's literature such as this story is the perfect vehicle with which to extract discussion. Although it is important to dialogue about equitability among the genders, it is also important to do the following:

1. Refrain from saying that "boys can do anything girls can do" and vice versa. In many regards, not all girls will be strong enough to be football players or fire fighters, and not all boys will be flexible and graceful enough to be ballet dancers.

2. Explain that heredity and genetics play a key factor in what we physically and intellectually can and cannot accomplish as easily as others. This is neutral in terms of gender, because clearly there are male dancers and nurses as well as successful female basketball players and scientists.

3. Finish by reviewing with the children that (a) *Oliver Button Is a Sissy* allows for a boy to be successful in a role typically reserved for girls. His achievement, as celebrated by his family and peers, demonstrates and celebrates nontraditional gender roles, and (b) it is just as acceptable to embrace the more traditional gender roles as portrayed in many of the books available to them, although in the United States today, boys and girls, men and women have more choices than once offered.

Evaluation

Using a 4-point rubric, teachers will review student's illustrations and labels, looking for their understanding of nontraditional gender roles.

Modifications: English Language Learners

English language learners (ELLs) will be paired with peers of higher English language development (ELD) levels for translation to support student understanding and practice. In addition, if possible, use *Oliver Button Is a Sissy* in "big book" format to ensure that all students can see the pictures, because the illustrations strongly depict the text.

Sample Response Lesson 5.2
Gender and Coming of Age

Secondary Grades

Duration: 1 Day to Open and Several Days to Read and Act Out the Play

Note to the teacher: As important as it is to distinguish gender equity in children's literature, it is also essential that children have "coming of age" books available to them, which depict their realities as they struggle to come to terms with their sexuality and sexual identity. Gary Soto's *Novio Boy* does just that. Not only is it a book about young men and young women engaging in the dance of first dates and unfamiliar emotions, it does so in play format. This book offers a lovely story portraying the real experiences of boys and girls coming to an age when they find themselves interested in one another but awkwardly so.

Overview

Novio Boy can be broken down into characters and performed as a play. Group work and summaries for each section of the play will be included for comprehension, prediction, and critical thinking purposes and will be assessed accordingly. Students will rewrite, in play format, the outcome of the story.

Materials

Class set of *Novio Boy*, by Gary Soto, and reflection journals for each student

Key Vocabulary

Novio

Anticipatory Set

1. *Focus:* Students will identify a variety of perceptions both boys and girls have about dating through the characters' actions in the play.

2. *Objective:* By the end of the book, students will have summarized scenes and predicted actions in upcoming scenes from daily readings. Mixed or gender groups will work together to rewrite, in play format, the outcome of the story.

3. *Transfer:* Students will use this information as a foundation for discussion as the class reads more books about relationships and considers how it relates to their own lives as they consider the dating scene.

Instruction

1. In small groups, have the students focus their dialogue on the rituals of dating and the perceptions boys have about girls and vice versa. Set some boundaries for discussion (i.e., be polite, respectful, realistic, etc.).This can be accomplished as either a mixed or a gender group. Oftentimes, having the genders separated helps to elicit more honest discussions without the fear of backlash from the opposite gender group. However, mixing the groups opens the door for the other to hear directly about misconceptions and understandings of one another.

2. Have students come together as a whole group and share ideas that were formulated in small groups. Chart responses on a graphic organizer such as a Venn diagram or a Double Bubble Thinking Map from each of the mixed or gender groups as a way to make their thoughts concrete and organized. The teacher should add any ideas that the students may have left out.

3. Over the next several days, students will use the text to act out the play. The teacher will assign character roles each day so that all students get a turn to perform.

4. At the end of each day, have students get into their mixed or gender groups and reflect on that day's reading. After 5 to 10 minutes, give students time to summarize that day's reading in their reflection journal and predict what they think will happen in tomorrow's scene.

Guided Practice

1. Using the graphic organizer with students' ideas, the teacher will model how to use their comments to either confirm what is happening in the scenes or refute the realism of the scenes. This will model how to write an appropriate summary and prediction. The first one will be done together so the students get a clear idea about what the teacher expects. After the first day, students will do this on their own following their discussion groups for that day's reading.

2. Have two or three volunteers share their summary and prediction each day as examples for those who are struggling.

3. After the sharing of information, ask the students if they would like to add to the Venn diagram about how boys and girls perceive dating rituals or what they expect from one another given what they have read in the story so far.

Independent Practice

At the end of the book, students will use their summaries as reference tools to rewrite, in play format, the outcome of the story. They will develop a new ending scene with their mixed or

(Continued)

(Continued)

gender group to be acted out in front of the class. The students in the audience will be part of the evaluation process.

Closure

After performing the plays, have students revisit the charted responses on the graphic organizer one last time. If the gender groups were separated, bring them together. Using the book as a reference point, the participants can decide if their perceptions of one another have changed or been confirmed. Keeping the dialogue going as a mixed group, chart the changes or new thoughts the students have about the opposite gender in regard to coming of age, dating, emotions, and the way in which they might want to be considered by one another in the future. *Novio Boy* brings to life characters and scenes with which many students can relate immediately and specifically. This book may be a catalyst for change in their lives when it comes to considering how they want to be treated and how they want to treat others when it comes to dating and relationships.

Evaluation

As students perform their rewritten scenes, the students in the audience will write a reflection on the realism of the changes, the level of interest using a 1–4 star scale, and ways they could have improved the scene. This can be done on a half sheet of paper prepared in advance by the teacher. These will be turned in to the teacher to be used for evaluation of those who performed and also by those who critiqued. In addition, on completion of the book, every student will write a book report (format to be decided on by the teacher) to be turned in a week later as a formal evaluation.

Modifications

English Language Learners

ELLs will be paired with peers of higher ELD levels for translation to support student understanding and practice.

Parents, Tutors, and Librarians

A scaled-down version of this lesson can be implemented in your practice at home or at school. If you are working with one student or a small group, continue with the discussions (though they may be one sided if there are only two of you and of the same gender), use of the graphic organizer (again, could be one-sided), summaries, predictions, scene rewrites, and book report.

SELECTED ANNOTATED BIBLIOGRAPHY

Brashares, A. (2003). *Sisterhood of the traveling pants*. New York: Delacorte Books for Young Readers.

A strong friendship lies at the heart of this coming-of-age novel, in which a pair of jeans has some kind of magical quality and can fit each of four girls, all of varying shapes and body types. During the first summer the four girlfriends are separated from each other, they share a pair of second-hand jeans. They experience happiness, heartbreak, and all the complications of growing up apart from one another.

Brink, C. (1997). *Caddie Woodlawn*. New York: Simon & Schuster.

Eleven-year-old Caddie grows up with her six brothers and sisters on the Wisconsin frontier in the mid-19th century. She infuses herself into a variety of activities that aren't thought of as being "ladylike." She would much rather run through the woods with her brothers, cross a lake on a raft, visit an Indian camp, or listen to the stories of the circuit rider. Caddie's wonderful adventures provide an exciting picture of life on the Wisconsin frontier in the 1860s. Caddie learns what growing up truly means, that it is not so very different today.

Cameron, A. (1981). *Stories Julian tells*. New York: Random House.

This book relates episodes in 7-year-old Julian's life, which include getting into trouble with his younger brother, Huey, planting a garden, trying to grow taller, losing a tooth, and most importantly, finding a new friend, Gloria, a girl, in "Gloria Who Might Be My Best Friend."

deHaan, L., & Nijland, S. (2002). *King & king*. Berkeley, CA: Ten Speed Press.

When the queen insists that the prince get married and take over as king, the search for a suitable mate does not turn out as expected. The prince is introduced to several suitable women but only has eyes for the brother of one of the ladies he encounters. It does turn out to be "Happily Ever After," but not as originally planned by the queen.

deHaan, L., & Nijland, S. (2004). *King & king & family*. Berkeley, CA: Ten Speed Press.

Newlyweds King Lee and King Bertie travel on their journey into the noisy jungle. The kings are greeted by wild animal families, but the royal couple comes upon something more significant in the trees. King and King soon discover that there's no adventure more wonderful than starting a family of their own and when they return to the castle, they introduce the new addition to their family.

dePaola, T. (1979). *Oliver Button is a sissy*. Orlando, FL: Harcourt Brace.

A little boy must come to terms with being teased and ostracized when his brother, father, and classmates expect him to be more like a "boy" and play sports or more "boy" types of games rather than read books, paint pictures, and tap dance. He shows his family and peers that he can be just as successful at the activities he enjoys most.

Dessen, S. (2004). *Someone like you.* New York: Penguin Group.

Halley and Scarlett have been friends for a long time. Scarlett is known to be popular and outgoing whereas Halley's the quieter soul and happy that way. In the beginning of their junior year, Scarlett's boyfriend is killed in a motorcycle accident and she soon finds out that she is pregnant with his child. For the first time, Scarlett really needs Halley and although this is a difficult time of adjustment, they remain friends.

Garden, N. (1992). *Annie on my mind.* New York: Farrar, Straus & Giroux.

Two teenage girls, Liza and Annie, fall in love with each other, and even after a disaster at school, they allow love to triumph over the ignorance of people.

Greenberg, K. (1996). *Zack's story.* Minneapolis, MN: Lerner.

Zack is 11 years old. He lives in New Jersey with his mom and Margie. Margie is his second mother. His mom and Margie identify as lesbians. They love each other and have a relationship together. Sometimes kids say mean things about gay people, and some kids think that having lesbian mothers is different and even weird. But Zack thinks they live the way every family does. They do the same things most families do when they spend time together.

Hinton, S. E. (2006). *The outsiders.* New York: Penguin Young Readers Group.

In this book first published by Viking in 1967, three brothers struggle to stay together after their parents' death, as they search for an identity among the conflicting values of their adolescent society in which they find themselves "outsiders." This coming-of-age story includes issues related to dating and love, masculinity, life and death, and many other issues our youth deal with even today.

Hoffman, M. (1991). *Amazing Grace.* New York: Dial.

Grace loves to act out stories. One day, her teacher asks who would like to play the lead in the play *Peter Pan.* Grace raises her hand, but Raj tells her she isn't a boy, and Natalie tells her she can't because she is Black. Her grandmother sets her straight: She can do anything she sets her mind to. With this thinking, Grace tries out for the play and wins the part.

Hopkinson, D. (2001). *Under the quilt of night.* New York: Atheneum.

A young slave girl leads her loved ones away from the slave master who worked them hard. We read about how part of her family is about to be sold off so they must escape right away. Readers are also exposed to the good, kind people along the Underground Railroad who help the runaways find safety in Canada.

Hosseini, K. (2007). *A thousand splendid suns.* New York: Penguin Group.

This is a story set against the volatile events of Afghanistan's last 30 years—from the Soviet invasion to the reign of the Taliban to post-Taliban rebuilding—that puts the violence, fear, hope, and faith of this country in intimate, human terms. The depiction of Mariam and Laila's plight is a sadly accurate version of what many Afghan women have experienced.

The romantic twists and fairy-tale turns make it fiction, but they are precisely what make the novel such a compelling read. Childhood promises are sacred; true love never dies; justice will be done; sisterhood is powerful.

Lee, S. (2006). *Snowflower and the secret fan.* New York: Random House.

In 19th-century China, in a remote Hunan county, a 7-year-old girl named Lily is paired with a *laotong* ("old same") in an emotional match that lasts a lifetime. The laotong, Snow Flower, introduces herself by sending Lily a silk fan on which she's painted a poem in *nu shu*, a unique language that Chinese women created in order to communicate in secret, away from the influence of men. Over the years, the girls send messages on fans and compose stories on handkerchiefs, reaching out of isolation to share their hopes, dreams, and accomplishments. Together, they endure the agony of foot-binding and reflect on their arranged marriages, loneliness, and motherhood. The two characters in this story find solace, developing a bond that keeps their spirits alive. But when a misunderstanding arises, their deep friendship is suddenly threatened.

Lindgren, A. (1976). *Pippi Longstocking.* New York: Penguin Putnam for Young Readers.

At the edge of a Swedish village, Tommy and his sister, Annika, have a new neighbor, Pippi Longstocking. She has crazy red pigtails, no parents to tell her what to do, a monkey for a friend, a horse that lives on her porch, and a way of getting into one adventure after another.

Martin, B. (1997). *Swish!* New York: Henry Holt.

Two girls' basketball teams, the Cardinals and the Blue Jays, play a close and intense game as they fight for the championship.

Muñoz Ryan, P. (2002). *Esperanza rising.* New York: Scholastic.

Esperanza and her mother are forced to leave their life of wealth and privilege in Mexico to go work in the labor camps of Southern California, where they must adapt to the harsh circumstances facing Mexican farmworkers on the eve of the Great Depression.

Muñoz Ryan, P. (2005). *Becoming Naomi Leon.* New York: Scholastic.

Naomi Soledad Leon Outlaw has been through a lot in her young life. Besides her clothes, sewn in polyester by Gram, her difficulty speaking up, and being "nobody special" at school, her Gram says most problems can be overcome with positive thinking. And with Gram and her little brother, Owen, life at Avocado Acres Trailer Rancho in California is happy, until their mother reappears after 7 years to claim her. Naomi runs away to Mexico with her great-grandmother and younger brother in search of her father.

Myracle, L. (2004). *Kissing Kate.* New York: Penguin Young Readers Group.

Sixteen-year-old Lissa's relationship with her best friend changes after they kiss at a party. Kate was Lissa's best friend for 4 years. Then one night at a drunken party, Kate leans in to kiss Lissa, and Lissa kisses her back. Then, Kate pretends Lissa doesn't exist. Confused and alone, Lissa is left questioning everything she thought she knew about herself. With the help of a new friend, Lissa begins to find the strength to realize that sometimes falling in love with the wrong person is the only way to grow.

Newman, L. (2000). *Heather has two mommies*. Los Angeles: Alyson Wonderland.

After visiting her playgroup, Heather feels bad because she has two mothers and no father. She eventually learns that there are lots of different kinds of families and the most important thing is that all the people love each other.

Peters, J. (2005). *Keeping you a secret*. New York: Megan Tingley Books.

This book raises important points about the ramifications of "coming out." The main character, Holland, is experiencing a tough school schedule, responsibilities as student council president, college applications, a serious boyfriend, and a meddling mom when open lesbian, CeCe, transfers to her school. Their immediate connection begins as flirtation and then moves to an intense relationship. Holland is thankful she "risked change," despite the serious consequences.

Pinkney, B. (1995). *JoJo's flying sidekick*. New York: Aladdin.

A young girl takes on her personal demons and challenges by conquering her fears through karate. She is strong physically and mentally, just like the boys in her karate class and at home.

Polacco, P. (2000). *The butterfly*. New York: Philomel Books.

Monique and Sevrine, a young Jewish girl hiding from the Nazis in Monique's basement in her French village, become secret friends, whispering and giggling late at night after their families have gone to bed. Eventually, Monique's mother finds out about Sevrine and her family hiding during the Nazi occupation. The emphasis is on friendship and heroism and is relatable to any reader, as two friends experience prejudice and learn of their own strength.

Reynolds, M. (1994). *Too soon for Jeff*. Buena Park, CA: Morning Glory Press.

Aspects of the teen pregnancy problem stem from the young man's point of view. In this story, 17-year-old Jeff has decided that he must be honest with his girlfriend, Christy, and tell her that he no longer wants to have a relationship with her. Then he is shocked to find out that she is pregnant. This really throws off his plans of college and freedom. However, by the end, both Jeff and Christy have matured enough to be parents to their baby son.

Rodriguez, L. (1998). *America is her name*. Willimantic, CT: Curbstone Press.

Set in the Pilsen barrio of Chicago, a Mixteca Indian from Oaxaca, Amâerica Soliz, survives the poverty and hopelessness of her circumstances and surroundings, made more endurable by her desire and determination to be a poet. This book gives a heartwarming message of hope. Amâerica is a student who is unhappy in school until a poet visits the class and inspires the students to express themselves creatively, in Spanish or English. This story deals realistically with the problems in urban neighborhoods and has an upbeat theme: You can succeed in spite of the odds against you.

Scamell, R. (1998). *Toby's doll's house*. London: Levinson Books.

What is wrong with wanting a big doll's house for your birthday? Well, in Toby's house, nobody's listening. His dad, auntie, and grandpa think he would like things such as a toy fort, a barnyard filled with animals, and a multistory parking lot. But that's not what Toby wants.

Soto, G. (1997). *Novio boy*. Orlando, FL: Harcourt Brace.

Rudy anxiously prepares for and then goes out on a first date with an attractive, older girl, Patricia. He can't believe she even agreed to go out with him. Rudy has to come up with the money, the self-confidence, and the right conversation to go through with it. This one-act play is heartwarming and heart-wrenching, as it follows Rudy from his search for guidance from family and friends, through the date itself, to its successful conclusion.

Surat, M. (1990). *Angel child, dragon child*. New York: Scholastic.

Ut, a Vietnamese girl attending school in the United States, is lonely for her mother left behind in Vietnam, but she makes a new friend, a boy named Raymond, who presents her with a wonderful gift.

Willhoite, M. (1991). *Daddy's roommate*. Los Angeles: Alyson Wonderland.

This straightforward story of a young boy discusses his divorced father's new living situation, in which the father and his gay roommate share regular everyday events like eating, shaving, sleeping, arguing, doing chores, playing, loving, and living. This new concept is explained to the child as "just one more kind of love."

Williams, V. (1982). *A chair for my mother*. New York: William Murrow.

A child, her mother, and her grandmother save coins to buy a comfortable armchair after all their furniture is lost in a fire.

Zolotow, C. (1985). *William's doll*. New York: HarperCollins.

William is a happy little boy who wants only one thing: a doll. His brother thinks he's a sissy, and his father buys him "boy" toys like a basketball and a train, but these do not make him want a doll less. Then, when William's grandmother learns what William wants, she takes him to the store and chooses a doll for him. She knows that William needs the doll to cuddle and love and to help him become a caring father one day.

REFERENCES

Brewer, J. (1997). *Introduction to early childhood education: Preschool through primary grades* (3rd ed.). Boston: Allyn & Bacon.

Britton, J. (2001). New publisher to focus on gay families. *Publishers Weekly, 248,* 19.

Ernst, S. B. (1995). Gender issues in books for children and young adults. In S. Lehr (Ed.), *Battling dragons: Issues and controversy in children's literature* (pp. 66–78). Portsmouth, NH: Heinemann.

Fox, M. (1993). Men who weep, boys who dance: The gender agenda between the lines in children's literature. *Language Arts, 70,* 84–88.

Gilbert, P. (1989). *Gender, literacy and the classroom.* Melbourne, Australia: Australian Reading Association.

Glazer, J., & Giorgis, C. (2005). *Literature for young children.* Columbus, OH: Pearson.

Gopalakrishnan, A., & Ulanoff, S. (2005). Resilient divas and incredible escapades: What a pilot survey of adolescent girls' reading preferences revealed. *SIGNAL Journal, 28*(1), 20–25.

Kohl, H. (1995). *Should we burn Babar? Essays on children's literature and the power of stories.* New York: New Press.

Mitchell, D. (2003). *Children's literature: An invitation to the world.* Boston: Allyn & Bacon.

Narahara, M. (1998). *Gender bias in children's picture books: A look at teachers' choice in literature.* East Lansing, MI: National Center for Research on Teacher Learning. (ERIC Document Reproduction Service No. ED 419247)

Pipher, M. (1994). *Reviving Ophelia: Saving the selves of adolescent girls.* New York: Putnam.

Rudman, M. (1995). *Children's literature: An issue approach.* New York: Longman.

Singh, M. (1998). *Gender issues in children's literature.* Bloomington, IN: Office of Educational Research and Improvement. (ERIC Document Reproduction Service No. ED 424591)

Temple, C., Martinez, M., & Yokota, J. (2006). *Children's books in children's hands: An introduction to their literature* (3rd ed.). Boston: Allyn & Bacon.

Temple, C., Martinez, M., Yokota, J., & Naylor, A. (2002). *Children's books in children's hands: An introduction to their literature* (2nd ed.). Boston: Allyn & Bacon.

Tomlinson, C., & Lynch-Brown, C. (2002). *Essentials of children's literature.* Boston: Allyn & Bacon.

Trepanier-Street, M., & Romatowski, J. (1999). The influence of children's literature on gender role perceptions: A reexamination. *Early Childhood Education Journal, 26,* 155–159.

Whittingham, J., & Rickman, W. (2007). Controversial books in the middle school: Can they make a difference? *Middle School Journal, 38,* 41–45.

Chapter 6 Understanding or Justifying Violence

Kimberly Persiani-Becker

Violence, it seems, is an inherent part of our lives. History is peppered with violent acts in every step of humankinds' evolution, whether they were fights for freedom or justice, personal fights, genocides, or natural disasters. What is worrisome in recent times, however, is the permeation of violence into every walk of life: on TV, in the media, in games, and so on. What are the consequences of this? Given the amount of violence in and around children's lives, should we really be worried about the violent images children read about in books? Don't they see worse in movies, on TV, or in video games depicting graphic violence? Or is this just the status quo for children in the 21st century, which we ought not be concerned with? Are children more desensitized to violence these days? It is important to bear in mind when and why violence is appropriate in children's and young adult literature and if there is any justification to violence in their stories and what warrants it. Even many of the traditional "classics" contain images and story lines of violence. It follows that

> violence cannot be avoided in literature, even literature for children [and young adults], for literature serves to explain the human condition. . . . The issue is not whether violence has a place in children's literature, because history has shown it has, but whether violence in children's books can be justified. (Tomlinson, 1995, p. 40)

In this chapter, many of these issues are discussed in terms of understanding violence or justifying violence, if at all possible. Further, this chapter also explores how violence can be mediated in children's books and if this is justifiable. We begin with trying to define violence.

DEFINING VIOLENCE

Violence can be defined in a multitude of ways. When we think of violence, immediate images fill our heads. Right away, some might think of gang violence, including physical beatings, gun and knife use, and territorial fighting. Others may consider the gore, blood, and guts portrayed on TV, the movies, and in videos games. Many find violence in books, newspapers, and magazines. Some may associate violent images and events with war and history, as well as with natural disasters.

In fact, it can be surprisingly difficult to define violence: Is it only physical or does it include verbal and psychological aspects? Although physical violence is very visual, the other two types of violence are more subtle, yet they may lead to more danger. In other words, what counts as violent abuse? There could be dangerous consequences to physical abuse, such as bullying or hazing. Subtler yet just as dangerous is psychological abuse, such as brainwashing, that may lead children to become suicide bombers; or verbal abuse, such as libel and defamation; or even emotional abuse that forces people to do things they don't normally want to do. In other words, defining what violence is and does becomes important, because sometimes violence and its consequences may not be obvious, visual, or perceptible, but they do affect each and every one of us.

Some may think of violence and believe it could never happen to them. This may be due to how they view their socioeconomic status (SES), their neighborhood, city, state, or the country they live in, their religious affiliation, their race culture, their gender, their sexual orientation, and other sociocultural aspects. But violence does not always discriminate, and none of us are exceptions. Violence caused by fire, floods, and other natural disasters don't see race, SES, gender, and so on. Violent accidents and death are not isolating of culture either. Violence can be perpetuated because of religion, race, sexual orientation, and other reasons, so none of us are immune.

JUSTIFYING VIOLENCE IN CHILDREN'S BOOKS

No matter how one defines violence, children and young adults are exposed as much as, and sometimes more than, adults. Being able to discuss what they see and hear in this regard is a step closer in helping them make sense of it all by being more critical about it as a way to distinguish between entertainment, history, and real-life current events, as well as why and how to avoid violence toward or against oneself. Picture and chapter books are a means for introducing and digesting these situations and also working toward resolutions. The challenge is getting readers to pick up such rich pieces of literature, especially in a quick-paced, media-related time.

It seems likely that violence in children's books is something that won't go away anytime soon, but in choosing quality books for the classroom that will connect with the children who are used to such images, be it through picture books, video games, TV, movies, and the like, one can be cognizant of the appropriateness of the illustrations in matching the text or topic, without scaring the reader or introducing inappropriate images to the learner. Picture books such as *It Doesn't Have to Be This Way,* by Luis Rodriguez, or *Cool Calvin's No Bandanas for Me: Staying Gang Free,* by Ralph Burgess, are two examples of stories about gang violence and why children should avoid such activity. Each book portrays two different race cultures, both of which are dealing with the same question of whether to join a gang. Potential violence in these groups and situations is not unique to any one culture. While both stories are compelling, culturally relevant, and written for two different age groups, they may not be appropriate for all learners. Real-life circumstances of one's students plays a huge role in choosing appropriate curriculum and stories, and having books like these available is critical in getting youngsters to identify with characters, even though violence is included. With many of our youngsters residing in urban areas where violence might be prevalent, such stories draw readers in, as they can relate in some respect.

Because of this, when choosing titles that support curriculum, especially when it has to do with teaching history or introducing the concept of cultures, similarities and differences, families, children, young adults around the world, and more, violent images and story lines might be necessary to make the point. In *The Culture of Violence and Picture Books,* Vandergrift (2008) stated the following:

> The children of the world today live in a culture of violence. Some of them actually dodge rocks and bullets in war-torn regions of the world; others are barricaded in comfortable homes where they bombard themselves with the sounds and images of guns, war, and violence on TV and in the games they play. In recent years there have also been an increasing number of picture books that deal with violent subject matter as a means to cry out, either directly or indirectly, for a more caring, nonviolent world. These picture books make powerful statements, but they also raise important questions to consider when choosing books:
> - What messages do young people actually take from these books?
> - Does the impact of the truly aesthetically powerful composition imprint the violence on young minds rather than the message of peace?
> - Do children reading these books need the assistance of an adult intermediary to understand and make sense of them? (p. 1)

These critical questions might be used as one decides which books to assign for student reading, reading aloud, sharing of illustrations, adding to the classroom or school library, or making books available for children and young adults to read on their own. One must also consider whether the violence depicted in the book chosen for the classroom, home, or library "can be justified in terms of the deeper understanding it provides of past events and present conditions" (Tomlinson, 1995, p. 40). Knowing that youngsters are becoming more and more desensitized to violent images because there is so much stimuli available through a variety of mediums, some might choose to go in the other direction when choosing books for the classroom and libraries, although it is also important to consider whether this might be a detriment to their learning of real situations and events.

Popular Images in Media

Should children be exposed to any violence in the various mediums available to them? Is it realistic to believe that any and all violence is inappropriate for children to experience in books, on TV, in video games, movies, music videos, the Internet, and so on? Is it fair to assume that graphic and unnecessary violence is unacceptable at any age, when classic tales have always contained violent elements, which lend context to stories? Think about the bad guys, the villains, and the witches. Do they need slaying? Even in the classic fairy tales like *Cinderella* and *The Three Little Pigs,* evil stepmothers and big bad wolves are taken out, often through violent means.

According to the Web site created by Pasadena Child Care Provider (2008), tales that contain this element of good triumphing over evil is a lesson for children. These stories basically say that you can fight evil and win. But knowing when the violence supports the story and when it is over the top, which is often aggrandized in pop videos, video games, and the Internet, can be confusing to children listening to these stories. In life it is unfortunately not always so easy to know the evil or how to subdue it. When it is popularized in other mediums, it is difficult for children to recognize it in literature pieces, especially when it's subtle. This desensitization is scary. When the wolf in *Little Red Riding Hood* or *The Three Little Pigs* is seen as a caricature to young children, when it used to be seen as a violent creature, we have to ask ourselves how much violence in children's literature has any effect at all. However, because life is filled with good and bad, it is unrealistic to shield children from stories where good triumphs over evil, which they probably have figured out by the age of 4 anyway. That being said, which medium has the right to foster violence in its story lines? If we want children and young adults to continue to pick up books, how are books to compete with the kinds of images they see today in all forms? How have these other mediums affected our youngsters when it comes to choosing a good book? If there isn't enough violence and intrigue, will they continue to pick up books?

I don't think it's necessarily what children see, but more w/ how they are taught to behave ... polite, respectful, compliant ... violence is taboo + therefore more interesting

Movies and Television

So, how violent are movies and TV? If children and young adults are drawn to the quick and visual violence, should books get more and more blatant about said images? Who would have guessed that book authors would have to consider that their medium competition would include top grossing films that are full of blood, gore, and violence in a way that makes children and young adults see books as "boring"? No wonder it's so difficult to get youngsters to pick up books on their own these days unless they are clearly marketed to entice them with mysticism and aggressive violence.

Although violence has always been in films, really violent movies were seen only by a certain audience, and usually it was more of an adult audience. Families now go together to movie theaters showing R-rated slasher films. And the rest of the audiences watch these same movies when they reach DVD or digital TV. Many of the movies seen at home wouldn't have been shown in theaters 10 to 20 years ago (Anderson, 2002).

Movie violence these days is louder, bloodier, and more anatomically precise than ever before. There was a time in films when a character was shot or stabbed, and we only saw the body falling. Now with slow motion, pyrotechnics, and a penchant for leaving nothing to the imagination, all conspire to make movies and TV shows more gruesome than ever (Anderson, 2002). Although these images and story lines aren't ideal, they do create a situation where some books are less terrifying than they once were. Book series like *Scary Stories,* by Barry Moser, and *Goosebumps,* by R. L. Stine, have been challenged for years, but they are popular with children and young adults. They aren't exactly deep, rich, multicultural stories that readers can relate to, but they are fun and even silly and can hardly be shelved before they're checked out again at school libraries. Even though these are the kinds of books that adults sometimes find violent, children find them enjoyable and intriguing. Is it because of their experiences with violent movies and TV that they are more interested in the scarier, bloodier, gorier story lines? Perhaps, but what adults may want to consider is that their children are reading books with plots, clear beginnings, middles, and endings, as well as imagery and quick-witted characters to analyze.

Children and young adults meet an increasingly violent world with few limits. Children's greatest exposure to violence does not come from books but from movies, TV, and video games. These all expose young children and young adults to a level of violence that would never have occurred to many of us only a decade or two ago. At a very young age, children are seeing a level of violence and mayhem that in the past may have been witnessed only by law enforcement and military personnel. Movies, TV, and video games bring hitting, kicking, stabbings, car chases, shootings, and dismemberment right into homes on a daily basis. With this kind of outright violence being a part of these young people's lives so early on, reading about the effects of war, gang activity, hurricane damage, and classic tales of the past where wolves are seen as scary characters should hardly be a concern in regard to children's books and young adult literature. The question still remains, however: Should authors catch up with the rest of the mediums available to their readers today, if they want children to pick up books on their own? With movies, TV, and video games telling stories as well, but in more violent ways, does that mean all forms of media need to be as obvious in their delivery of a story? Should authors escalate the level of violence and aggressiveness in children's literature in order to compete with the likes of the video game *Grand Theft Auto,* which has seen at least four versions at this point?

Video Games

Choudhury (2003) said the following:

> Violence has always been a part of children's literature. It provides a safe buffer zone where children can clarify their stance on moral issues by exploring alternatives and exercise their responses to the terrible and be prepared for it in real life. (p. 1)

Considering that children today are growing up in a world where information is constantly available to them and they are no longer as sheltered from the anger, frustrations, and violent images of the past, including such tales and images in picture books and chapter books is less concerning than it once was. But of course, choosing quality literature that tells a rich tale and does not scare the reader is a good idea. Bright, vibrant, and quick-paced storylines, such as *Chato's Kitchen,* by Gary Soto, is the perfect example of good literature that captures children's attention and makes a topic such as living in an inner city and being perceived as a gang member seem not as serious due to the obvious stereotyping and witty discourse.

But how do publishers compete with the video game industry, TV, and movies, where violence is considered cool? Should books become more overtly violent in order to get children and young adults to pick them up?

> For now, [Thomas] is content with the fact that, in the next three hours, he'll commit 147 felonies including aggravated assault, murder, attempted murder, robbery, arson, burglary, conspiracy, assault with a deadly weapon, drug trafficking, and auto theft while violating just about every section of the RICO Act, the nation's anti-organized crime law. He'll even be so brazen as to gun down bystanders and police officers and will personally beat someone to death with a golf club. All without ever leaving his room. (Boehm, 2006, p. 12)

In these kinds of games, the player is role-playing a character, similar to how a reader takes on the thoughts, feelings, and persona of characters found in books. However, while many consider these games highly entertaining, we need to be aware that games are becoming more and more violent in their content. How often do adults question books for being so aggressively violent? That isn't to say that some titles aren't being censored and challenged for their violent content, but is it to the same extent as what kids are exposed to in the gaming industry? Not exactly.

This may have more to do with the fact that unlike reading a book or watching a movie or TV show, a child is actively making choices and weighing options when playing video games. He or she is rewarded for certain behaviors, which, depending on the game, may range from solving a puzzle to opening fire on a group of bystanders. How can this be said of books? These games are violent, and although there is violence depicted in books, wouldn't parents rather have their child read a book, where the violence is placed in a learning context, than see apparent violence, which becomes a rewarding experience when one takes out more people who get in their way?

"Video games today are vast and dazzling environments that seek to create an 'immersive experience' for the player," said Boehm (2006, p. 12). Isn't that how most authors, publishers, storytellers, readers, librarians, and others who have a love for books consider the reading experience? And shouldn't we attempt to get children and young adults to embrace this quote for books rather than video games and the like? Even the more traditional tales of long past have enough grit and intrigue to keep the imaginative child busy. Although even those tales have their share of violence, it is nothing compared to what kids see in video games.

STEPS TO COUNTER VIOLENCE IN THE MEDIA

No matter how parents, teachers, administrators, and the like feel about allowing young people access to violence through a variety of media, including books, there are some simple ways to find out how much violence is projected in certain films, TV shows, music, and so on, by tapping into available online resources. For those making decisions for children and young adults in terms of how much violence they ought to be exposed to, there are some useful Web sites that offer reviews or ratings about such content in various forms of media. With the use of industry ratings serving as a good tool and general guide, the sites listed here offer more detailed descriptions of content that can help in the selection process:

- *Center for Media Literacy:* http://www.medialit.org/focus/par_home.html
- *Common Sense Media:* http://www.commonsensemedia.org

- *Kids in Mind:* http://www.kids-in-mind.com
- *Media and Children—Taming Television:* http://www.parenting247.org/article .cfm?ContentID=83&AgeGroup=4
- *Media Awareness Network*: http://www.media-awareness.ca/english/index.cfm
- *PBS Parents guide to children and media:* http://www.pbs.org/parents/issues advice/childrenandmedia/index.html
- *Screen It! Entertainment Reviews:* http://www.screenit.com

The same kind of meaningful information is just a click away in regard to books. It's quite easy to Google a book title to find reviews from those who have read the books in order to carefully choose for classroom read-alouds, suggestions to students, school libraries, and the like. With that said, answering the question about whether authors ought to enhance their stories with more overtly violent story lines in order to get children and young adults to pick up those books is still one that teachers, administrators, librarians, and parents might have an opinion about. For those of us who seek and choose rich literature that we hope interests children and young adults, the answer is no. There is already enough tragedy and aggressiveness found in some of the earliest of books and even more so in the recent published titles. There is nothing wrong with leaving the reader to imagine the potential violence of characters who are considering joining a gang, or past battles stemming from a war, or the death and destruction of September 11th, 2001. If children and young adults become desensitized to violence in movies, TV, and video games, perhaps we need to avoid letting it filter into good books. Leaving a bit to the imagination is most likely more than enough for young and creative minds to grasp and imagine. With the increase of detailed images accessible to young people today, a little sheltering might be just the thing they need, especially given the life experiences they are witness to on a daily basis.

GANG VIOLENCE

STATS (2022)

Children in poverty....
- In US (15.8%)
- In GA (17.2%)
- In Cobb (8%)

When children and young adults are more and more privy to extreme and immediate violence in their own neighborhoods, having an outlet to discuss and consider alternatives for themselves can be a saving grace for many. Gang violence, especially in urban environments, where many of our students come from, is more prevalent than ever before. Books referring to such topics establish an outlet for readers to relate to characters who look like them and go through many of the same situations but also offer advice and alternative ways of approaching and avoiding gang activity.

As mentioned earlier in the chapter, *It Doesn't Have to Be This Way*, by Luis Rodriguez, is a picture book that creates the perfect story line for discussion about joining a gang and the ramifications associated with doing so. Like this title, *America Is Her Name,* by the same author, is another story that includes gang violence but not so overtly as the previous one. In this story, the main character is negotiating her way through school and living in an urban setting where guns are seen and used, her father drinks excessively, and she doesn't see how an education will benefit a girl. There are several multicultural aspects taking place in this story, all of which are situations relevant to many young people. The potential for discussions about risks and consequences and resolutions is obvious through the use of these read-alouds. They also offer a chance for some readers to relate directly to the issue at hand while introducing the concept to those who can't directly relate but could use the opportunity to understand more clearly how their peers in other areas live each day.

Although some of these stories are not appropriate for certain children and young adults, be it due to age or relevance, there are several who will benefit greatly from knowing they are not alone and from seeing themselves in these stories. One title that any young adult could benefit from reading as a means of seeing success stories of those struggling through challenging and violent lives is *The Freedom Writers Diary,* by Erin Gruwell. In this book, readers witness Erin Gruwell's journey as a teacher at a high school rampant with hostility and racial intolerance. For many of the students she works with, substance abuse, gang activity, homelessness, and physical and sexual abuse are all very real day-to-day experiences. Erin Gruwell was the first person to treat these students with dignity, to believe in their potential and help them see it themselves. Soon, their loyalty toward her and enthusiasm to help end violence and intolerance became a force of its own. Unfortunately, many of our teens in schools today can relate to these circumstances. But this book, full of 150 student voices, offers a place for said readers to connect with someone like them.

For more detailed and realistic gang violence experiences, where those who have been involved in gangs then come out the other side, *Always Running: La Vida Loca: Gang Days in L.A.,* by Luis Rodriguez, and *My Bloody Life: The Making of a Latin King,* by Reymundo Sanchez, are stories that give hope to those either considering or already involved in gangs. These are the kinds of books, although violent, that offer readers prime examples of success stories. While educators might not be comfortable assigning these books as units to be used in the classroom, they may be more open to assigning them for book reports or holiday or summer reading. Again, some settings are less appropriate than others to include such titles into the regular lesson planning but one might consider making them available for independent choice.

Whether the children and young adults we work with are immediately involved in gangs or know much about what it means to be in a gang, most youngsters at least know about this concept and the violence associated with it. Including picture and chapter books that relate to this kind of potential violence creates a space for discussion and consideration about what decisions one might make if ever presented with this topic, be it directly or indirectly, especially when TV, video games, and movies tend to glamorize gang affiliation. This works against us and combats what teachers and parents are trying to do in the classroom: offering students an education as an alternative for their future. With such a serious issue, it's also important to remember to counteract this topic with more subtle stories to keep readers from focusing on only serious or scary tales.

TRADITIONAL TALES AND VIOLENCE

As we know already, violence is hardly a new phenomenon in literature for children and young adults. Although more recent titles relating to violence are on the rise, there are still many traditional stories that are overrun with violent acts and "often with a cruelty and brutality that horrifies the adult perspective" (Choudhury, 2003, p. 1) that can be just as obvious, yet maybe less serious. The favorite Grimms' fairy tales are the perfect example of violent stories, and they are also included in classroom scripted language arts programs today.

With Harry Potter at the forefront of book sales and movie watching, one might ask how a "near iconic boy wizard who grapples with the dark forces, sorcery, witchcraft and black magic, defying death and destruction" (Choudhury, 2003, p. 1) can be so loved by children, young adults, and adults alike. Other popular series of books, like that of *Lemony Snicket* and R. L. Stine's *Goosebumps,* offer gruesome experiences that children love.

In addition, such tales as *Little Red Riding Hood* have endured controversy for many years. In different versions, illustrations and story lines change. Some are more subtle, whereas others are more aggressive and show a violence unlike that of the popular movie *Hoodwinked,* a cute tale of Little Red and her cohorts as they try to find the bakery bandit, a small furry bunny who turns out to be the aggressive one, while the wolf is a hero. With that said, in Kiefer's (1995) article, one is reminded of Sarah Moon's version of *Little Red Riding Hood,* where the very scary wolf is shown to be about to eat Little Red Riding Hood. Children might even have nightmares after such a tale if read before bedtime. Then, of course, there is Montresor's version, where Little Red Riding Hood is stuffed into the wolf's mouth. Again, this would scare many children. So the question goes: Should this version be presented to children?

What about the stepmother who wants to kill Snow White or the stepmother and wicked stepsisters who are mean to Cinderella? Should they be eliminated for fear that this will influence the relationships between stepparents and their stepchildren? Choudhury (2003) answered these questions:

For generations children [have been] entertained with traditional often-violent fairy tales, at home, at school, and often at bedtime reading, and these

[handwritten margin note: this assumes that by removing this content, children will somehow be saved from what is a part of human nature]

stories continue to enthrall. Set in old world kingdoms, forests and fiefdoms, and peopled with evil giants, cruel stepmothers, wicked wolves and of course little children, the violence in the fairy tale, besides adding to the story value and creating a dramatic impact, is today even seen as beneficial for the child. Some argue that exposure to evil characters in fairy tales as well as to their violence and cruelty is actually therapeutic, with good clearly winning over evil in all the stories [such as] the wolf who eats Red Riding Hood. What's also important is that you see the little people win over the bad people by using their wits and with a little judicious help from the good forces in the world, like Jack, Hansel, Gretel, the little pig, or Snow White, being good examples. (p. 1)

In essence, the images of Little Red Riding Hood being stuffed into the wolf's mouth and the stepmother who is violent in *Snow White* and *Cinderella* are showing readers that good triumphs over evil, which we don't always get to see in other forms of media (Choudhury, 2003).

[handwritten margin note: violence serves a purpose — careful with more current events, history is told through perspective which allows the reader to really connect]

REAL LIFE, HISTORY, AND VIOLENCE

With real tragedies like that of the Oklahoma City bombing on April 19, 1995, there were no obvious book titles about circumstances such as this at the time to use as a jumping off point for dialogue. Students had questions, and many educators and parents were struggling for an explanation. Circumstances such as this often create space for books to be written about this kind of violence, but usually after the fact. Sadly, but fortunately, more and more titles are available due to tragedies having occurred in the last couple of decades.

One April Morning: Children Remember the Oklahoma City Bombing is one that would have helped, but of course it didn't exist for those grappling with how to address the students' questions and assumptions. This book speaks to children who watched or heard about the Oklahoma City disaster and others who suffered trauma of their own. In this book, we are introduced to 50 Oklahoma City children, ranging in age from 3 to 14, as they share their memories of and feelings about the bombing of the Federal Building on that day. Though this came out well after the tragedy, and it is highly useful in addressing such situations, the publishing world could be more proactive so that children don't see these horrific events on TV and then have no outlet for discussion. Such events become history and much of what children and young adults learn through picture and chapter books is just that. Being sure to have current and realistic books portraying the true stories as they unfolded in real life is important in ensuring that readers get the facts.

One can hardly pick up a book about a period in history without being exposed to violent events. Children learn history very early on in school, at about the fourth grade. They are quite savvy and they want the truth about the past. This is what educators want to teach so that the same violent episodes can be prevented in the future, but it can be challenging for them if they have no more experience, especially with historical fiction and nonfiction, than what textbooks or mandated curriculum provides. Textbooks are not enough to teach these concepts, and they can be selective to the point of vague and even skewed information, whereas children's and young adult literature is an appropriate and interesting vehicle for filling in the gaps.

Eve Bunting wrote about one Black boy and one White boy as they explore the fields near the construction site of their new homes in *The Blue and the Gray*. The story juxtaposes the Civil War battlefield of 1862 with the same space that will now serve as their new backyards. This story brings the past and the future together to tell a real tale in which violence must be addressed to make sense of the implications of that land. When history can be represented in one's own life, it makes more meaning. In teaching the Civil War, picture books like this can get readers more interested in the facts of such an event so the information in their textbooks is more approachable and comprehensible and sometimes even more appealing.

In particular, authors like Bunting write picture books that lend themselves to a children's audience as well as to one of young adults. Although some of her titles are more severe than others in terms of story line and historical fiction, one that is more suitable and less graphic is *The Wall*, which is about a boy and his father who come from far away to visit the Vietnam War Memorial in Washington, D.C., and find the name of the boy's grandfather, who was killed in the conflict. This is the perfect example of a book to use in teaching about the Vietnam War without having to go into more violent story lines. And although older students may at first balk at the use of a picture book, they quickly forget this as the story unfolds and the illustrations offer context for the words.

Books like these, as well as others, such as *Pink and Say,* by Patricia Polacco, which is about a young man named Say Curtis, a White soldier, and his relationship to Pinkus Aylee, a Black soldier, during the Civil War, show the results of things like uprooted and ruined lives of those who have endured war, along with the suffering and sadness and wasted lives. It is these kinds of stories that create images for readers that may convince them to find peaceful ways to settle their differences, which in turn justifies said violence in the literature (Kiefer, 1995). War is only one part of the violence seen in literature, but there are many other periods of history that need to be told so that children and young adults can make conscious decisions about their own future as they relate it to violent solutions.

In *Smoky Night*, Eve Bunting tells us of a boy and his mother having to learn to get along with people who are different from them when they are forced to leave their apartment for the safety of a shelter at the onset of the Los Angeles riots.

Bunting addresses urban violence in this thought-provoking book inspired by the Los Angeles riots. Teaching children about this event to get them to think consciously about the potential of such an experience in their own neighborhoods may be a bit dramatic, but again, this is the kind of story that relates to children, as many of them may live in precarious situations similar to that in the story. Good literature has this power to encourage children to be a part of the bigger picture and contend that this will never happen again.

UNDERSTANDING VIOLENCE

When is violence justified in books? Are the illustrations separate from the story line or must they go hand in hand? How can one discuss the realities of the civil rights movement without showing the disturbance caused by so much hate and anger toward people of color, through illustrations? Violent passages in literature for children and young adults are more specifically related to historical fiction and nonfiction. These stories are told to provide a deeper, clearer understanding of the events of the past and how those events have affected the present. Because of this, the violence in such books is justified.

On the other hand, "Violence used for its shock value as a device for entertainment is difficult to justify, particularly if this excess serves to blunt young reader's sensitivity to violence in all its forms" (Kiefer, 1995, p. 49). If this is the case, what do we do about the children who would rather spend hours upon hours playing violent video games? "Rather than trying to protect children against any book that contains violence, adults would be better advised to seek out and read those that are worthy of children's attention and then offer these titles to children as alternatives" (Kiefer, 1995, p. 49).

A book to do just that might be *I Never Knew Your Name,* by Garland (1994). In this story, we hear of a lone teen as reflected on by a young boy. After reading about a variety of very telling instances in this teen's life, the story ends with him committing suicide. The young boy then recalls the teen being left out on the basketball court, feeding a stray dog before it was hauled off to the pound, and being spurned by a girl that he had a crush on. The narrator's own lost opportunity to reach out provides a regretful contrast echoed in others' reactions to the death. Although this story is sad and ends in suicide, it is the kind of violence teens can relate to. Having an adult share this book with them and follow with discussion is ideal.

Why are books with violent images and story lines so popular? Is it simply the excitement of the unknown found in these books? Or is it the clearer picture of an event in history as it really happened? What is the effect such violence could have on the reader? Librarians, teachers, parents, children, and others might agree that violence in literature doesn't have to be bad. In fact, it doesn't even have to pertain to purposeful violence. There are all kinds of violence children experience and view. Much of this can stem from automobile accidents or natural disasters.

The 2004 Asian tsunami was caused by an earthquake deep in the Indian Ocean that occurred on December 26, 2004, with an epicenter off the west coast of Sumatra, Indonesia. The earthquake triggered a series of devastating tsunamis along the coasts of most land masses bordering the Indian Ocean, killing more than 225,000 people in 11 countries and inundating coastal communities with waves up to 100 feet. It was one of the deadliest natural disasters in history. This was not purposeful violence, but these images were spread across various media outlets and publications for several weeks and months.

And none of us will forget similar images seen in the same medium after Hurricane Katrina. The storm surge caused severe damage along the Gulf Coast, devastating several Mississippi cities. Nearly every levee in metropolitan New Orleans breached as Hurricane Katrina passed east of the city, flooding most of the city and many neighboring areas for weeks. Almost 2,000 people lost their lives during the hurricane and in the subsequent floods, making it one of the deadliest U.S. hurricanes ever.

For those of us who had no words to describe these kinds of devastation, how were we to talk about this violent and sad tragedy? For many of us who use books to dialogue with our students about such things, there were few nonfiction titles available that included real stories and even less historical fiction available to show people experiencing something similar. Fortunately and unfortunately, since the time of Hurricane Katrina, several books have been published about hurricanes. However, most of them are nonfiction experiences, such as Dudley's *Hurricane Katrina* for secondary students, which includes discussions of the government's preparedness and response and whether New Orleans should be rebuilt, various stories stemming from news reporting, as well as discussions of racism and global warming as factors in the disaster.

For younger children, *When the Hurricane Blew* is a book written by fourth graders who have personally experienced two major hurricanes as well as the resulting devastation to their Gulf Breeze, Florida, community. They know what it's like to be a kid, watch a hurricane approach, and then experience the aftereffects it can cause. This would have been a great choice following Hurricane Katrina and will no doubt serve those children who consistently endure the fear of this kind of natural disaster, given their place of residence.

The best teaching for children is to help them think for themselves. We give them tools so they can think about things and then make conscious decisions after analyzing critical issues. We give them experiences so they can think about things and then take action. At the end of the day, thinking and doing is of more value than anything else. Knowing when violent images are part of the context of a story or completely unacceptable is something we need our children and young adults to ascertain for themselves, so they choose appropriate and rich pieces of literature to read.

Using a variety of literature that touches on violent events and situations as they arise to introduce a concept for deep discussion serves children in so many ways as they continue to navigate this world of violence in all of the mediums accessible to them. Whether it be in movies, TV, video games, or books, we know they are exposed. But using good literature to cultivate their consciousness so they themselves make good choices is an easy and tangible step teachers and parents can take.

REFLECTION QUESTIONS FOR THE TEACHER

1.   What are my views on violence in children's books?
2.   What television, media, video games, and popular images are available to my students?
3.   When would it be okay to include violence in children's books?
4.   How can I justify historical violence?
5.   How can I help my students cope with the violence they see around them?

[handwritten margin notes: Community setting should be appropriate, East Cobb elementary would not be an appropriate setting / students]

SAMPLE RESPONSE LESSON 6.1

Violence

Primary Grades: In the Classroom, by Parents, Tutors, and Librarians

Duration: 1 Day

Overview

The teacher will read *It Doesn't Have to Be This Way* (Grades 4–8), by Luis Rodriguez, about a young boy who reluctantly becomes more and more involved in the activities of a local gang, until a tragic event involving his cousin forces him to make a choice about the course of his life. For the younger children, the teacher will read *Cool Calvin's No Bandanas for Me: Staying Gang Free* (Grades 1–4), by Ralph Burgess, about a boy, Calvin, who convinces a schoolmate that gang life will only lead to a troubled life. After the read-aloud, the teacher will lead students through a discussion about what it means to be part of a gang or a clique and the consequences associated with both.

(Continued)

(Continued)

Materials

It Doesn't Have to Be This Way, by Luis Rodriguez, or *Cool Calvin's No Bandanas for Me: Staying Gang Free,* by Ralph Burgess, poster paper, paint, colored markers, colored pencils

Key Vocabulary

Gang, Clique

Anticipatory Set

1. *Focus:* Students will have several opportunities to discuss what they know about gangs or cliques and why to avoid being involved (i.e., violence, bullying, peer pressure, etc.).

2. *Objective:* By the end of the lesson, students will create antigang or clique posters vowing to avoid joining. For older students, they will also be required to write an essay about why it's important to avoid a gang or clique.

3. *Transfer:* As students experience the peer pressure of joining a gang or popular clique that engages in negative behavior, having these conversations early and sharing their realities and fears about this topic will give them schema for future reference when these kinds of situations arise.

Instruction

1. After the read-aloud, the teacher will lead students through a discussion about what it means to be part of a gang or a clique and the consequences associated with both. Begin by simply asking about the main idea of the story. Be open to discussion that ranges across the spectrum, depending on the real-life circumstances of your students. The teacher may want to gear the conversation toward "cliques" as opposed to "gangs" but keep the door open to rich and even unsettling discussions.

2. There are a series of questions the teacher might ask to elicit a deep conversation: (a) Why do people join gangs or associate with a particular group of kids (cliques)? (b) What if you don't want to join a gang or clique but your friends do? (c) What kind of activities do you think or know gangs or cliques are involved in? (d) Could any of you be pressured to join a gang or clique? (e) What do you recommend to those who are thinking about joining a gang or clique?

3. As students respond, the teacher can transcribe these responses on the board or chart paper as a means of reference for further use. Once this is done, students can break into small groups of four or five and have more informal discussions about what it means to join a gang, any experience they have with this topic, and how one might persuade friends or family members to avoid joining gangs. Clearly, the discussions will vary depending on the age of students. First graders might only go through the whole-group discussion, whereas fifth-grade students can guide their own discussion after the general whole-class conversation.

Independent and Group Practice

After discussion groups, students will work in pairs or small groups to create a nonviolence or antigang slogan and poster as a pledge against this type of activity. This can be followed up by a writing assignment that addresses the aforementioned questions, which can vary depending on the age group. The teacher will need to show two or three models of posters or slogans and carry out a guided experience in writing an essay about this topic so that students can then write their own. For younger students, the teacher might decide to create one slogan and poster where each child puts his or her handprint and name on the poster as a signature to pledge against joining gangs.

Closure

Have student volunteers share their posters and essays. Have a closing discussion about what they can do to help themselves, friends, or family members who are interested in joining a gang or being part of a negative clique walk away from such actions. Create a list of actions to post with their posters.

Evaluation

Using a 4-point rubric, teachers review students' posters and essays, if applicable, looking for their understanding of violence prevention or staying out of gangs or negative cliques.

Modifications: English Language Learners

ELLs will be paired with peers of higher ELD levels for translation to support student understanding and practice. In addition, if possible, use "big book" formats to ensure that all students can see the pictures, because the illustrations strongly depict the text.

SAMPLE RESPONSE LESSON 6.2
Violence

Secondary Grades: In the Classroom, by Parents, Tutors

Duration: 1 Day

Overview

The same lesson described for the primary students can be carried out in the secondary grades as well, although one might decide to teach this as a unit rather than as a lesson. This can be done with a book like *Always Running: La Vida Loca: Gang Days in L.A.*, by Rodriguez, which is a documentation of the author's youth as an East Los Angeles gang member, in an effort to discourage his teenage son away from the gang that he recently joined. Another choice might be *My Bloody Life: The Making of a Latin King*, by Sanchez, which depicts a disturbing portrayal of a Puerto Rican teenager who lost himself to violent gang activity. He eventually joined the "Latin Kings," and through this, we share in his journey as he witnessed gang member killings, interethnic hatred, and sexual abuse of gang-affiliated youngsters. Although both of these novels offer grueling, real, and even scary violence, they are also stories that will elicit incredible dialogue and offer a critical analysis of the reality of violence that takes place in such environments, as a way to get young adults to consider the consequences of such affiliations.

Materials

Always Running: La Vida Loca: Gang Days in L.A., by Luis Rodriguez, or *My Bloody Life: The Making of a Latin King*, by Reymundo Sanchez

Anticipatory Set

1. *Focus:* Students will keep a daily journal where they will summarize and reflect on the varying and difficult circumstances of the main character in the book.

2. *Objective:* By the end of the unit, students will use their written summaries, reflections, and class discussions to create plays about some of the issues the main character was dealing with in the book. This will be done in small groups.

3. *Transfer:* This experience is meant to give students a view into the lives of people their age who have endured the foster care system and succeeded no matter one's difficult circumstances.

Guided Practice

1. On day one, read aloud the first chapter together from whichever book is chosen. Form small groups of four or five where students discuss the chapter and come up with a summary, including a reflection on how the chapter and characters relate to their own lives. Have students also include a list of words that they would like defined, an illustration, and a prediction.

2. Come back as a whole group, after the small groups have had enough time to discuss the first chapter. The teacher then takes contributions from the class and transcribes the group's summaries, reflections, and predictions onto chart paper to be used as a reference point throughout the book, because vocabulary study will be required of them each night. As a whole group, go through the words to be defined and write those definitions, and have one of the small groups attach its illustration.

Instruction

1. As students read a chapter a night from the book, they will keep an entry journal where they will summarize the chapter, predict the next one, and then react to it as it relates to their own lives. Remember to tell them that although they may not be dealing with these experiences personally, they can relate through those they know who are dealing with such issues. They may only know from TV or the movies about such topics, so in their journal, they are to relate the chapters to what they have experienced, and they should tell how they have experienced this, leaving out any names. In addition, have students include a list of words that they did not understand and definitions for those words as well as an illustration for that chapter.

2. Each day, at the beginning of class, students will join their small group to share about the chapter and how they relate to it. They will compare words that needed defining, their illustration, and their prediction for the next chapter. They will add to their journal entry from the night before if anything new comes up that they'd like to include. This will continue until the book has been read in total. Journals will be turned in on Friday and returned on Monday so that the teacher can peruse them for evaluation purposes.

Independent Practice

Upon completing the book, students will then be instructed to join their small groups of four or five and create a play using scenes from the book. Each member should have a role and the play needs to be a scene of about 5 to 10 minutes. These will be delivered to the whole class, and it will be up to the audience to pinpoint the scene in the book.

(Continued)

(Continued)

Extension

what???

At the end of the novel, the teacher may want to invite to class former gang members from the community to discuss the reality of this violent existence to bring more authenticity to the novel.

Closure

Have a closing discussion about what students can do to help themselves, friends, or family members who are interested in joining a gang or being part of a negative clique to walk away from such actions. Create a list of actions to post for reference.

Evaluation

After all plays have been delivered, students will write a book report using their journal summaries and reflections to guide them. In addition, their plays will also be taken into account for telling a scene or story from beginning to end, with authenticity and seriousness.

SELECTED ANNOTATED BIBLIOGRAPHY

Bunting, E. (1994). *Smoky night*. San Diego, CA: Harcourt Brace.

When the Los Angeles riots break out in the streets of their neighborhood, Daniel and his mother are forced to leave their apartment for the safety of a shelter. They learn the values of getting along with others no matter what their background or nationality. The author addresses urban violence in this thought-provoking book inspired by the Los Angeles riots.

Bunting, E. (1996). *The blue and the gray*. New York: Scholastic.

One Black boy and one White boy explore the fields near the construction site of their new homes. In 1862, this was the same space that served as a Civil War battleground. One of the boys' fathers helps them remember the freedom that was won so long ago.

Burgess, H. (2008). *Cool Calvin's no bandanas for me: Staying gang free*. Minneapolis, MN: Burgess Publishing and Media.

Calvin convinces a schoolmate that gangs will only lead to a troubled life.

Dudley, W. (2006). *Hurricane Katrina*. Farmington Hills, MI: Gale Group.

This book includes discussions of the government's preparedness and response, when or if New Orleans ought to be rebuilt, various stories stemming from news reporting, as well as discussions of racism and global warming as factors in the disaster.

Garland, S. (1994). *I never knew your name*. Boston: Houghton Mifflin.

This story tells of a lone teen who commits suicide, as reflected on by a young boy. The young boy recalls the teen being left out on the basketball court, feeding a stray dog before it was hauled off to the pound, and being spurned by a girl who he had a crush on. The narrator's own lost opportunities to reach out provide a regretful counterpoint, echoed in others' shocked reactions to the death.

Gruwell, E. (2006). *The freedom writers diary: How a teacher and 150 teens used writing to change themselves and the world around them*. New York: Broadway Books.

In this book, readers witness Erin Gruwell's journey as a teacher at a high school rampant with hostility and racial intolerance. For many of the students she works with, substance abuse, gang activity, homelessness, and physical and sexual abuse are all very real day-to-day experiences for them. Erin Gruwell was the first person to treat these students with dignity, to believe in their potential and help them see it themselves.

Lamb, N. (1996). *One April morning: Children remember the Oklahoma City bombing*. New York: HarperCollins.

This book speaks to millions of children who watched or heard about the Oklahoma City disaster and others who have suffered trauma of their own. Fifty Oklahoma City children, ranging in age from 3 to 14, offer their memories of and feelings about the bombing of the Federal Building on that day.

Mann's Miracles: 4th Graders from Gulf Breeze Elementary School. (2005). *When the hurricane blew*. Gulf Breeze, FL: Clear Horizon Books.

Fourth graders who have personally experienced two major hurricanes as well as the resulting devastation to their Gulf Breeze, Florida, community, wrote this book. They know what it's like to be a kid, watch a hurricane approach, and then experience the aftereffects it can cause. It's meant to help kids understand what to expect as the storm approaches and in case of a direct hit, find comfort in knowing that their lives will move forward.

Rodriguez, L. (1993). *It doesn't have to be this way*. San Francisco: Children's Book Press.

This is a story about a young boy who reluctantly becomes more and more involved in the activities of a local gang, until a tragic event involving his cousin forces him to make a choice about the course of his life.

Rodriguez, L. (1998). *America is her name*. Willimantic, CT: Curbstone Press.

America is a young girl who is unhappy in school until a poet visits the class and inspires the students to express themselves creatively, in Spanish or English. This story deals realistically with the problems in urban neighborhoods and has an upbeat theme: You can succeed in spite of the odds against you.

Rodriguez, L. (2005). *Always running: La vida loca: Gang days in L.A.* New York: Touchstone.

Rodriguez documents his youth as an East Los Angeles gang member in an effort to discourage his teenage son away from the gang that he recently joined. A member of various Latino gangs based in and around the South San Gabriel Valley during the late 1960s, Rodriguez participated in random acts of violence and presents highly charged events, such as shootings, funerals, rapes, and arrests, as well as his experiences being imprisoned on several occasions for the crimes he committed.

Sanchez, R. (2000). *My bloody life: The making of a Latin King.* Chicago: Chicago Review Press.

This story portrays a disturbing description of a Puerto Rican teenager who lost himself to violent gang activity. Set in Chicago, we read of a place of territorial graffiti and racist cops, drugs, sex, and gunplay. The author discusses his family's arrival on Chicago's Northwest Side in the late 1970s, when he was a small boy. We learn of the beatings his stepfather doled out, which had much to do with Sanchez's interest in teenage gangs. He eventually joined the "Latin Kings." He shares his experiences in witnessing gang member killings, interethnic hatred, and sexual abuse of gang-affiliated youngsters. This book captures the dark, self-destructive experiences of urban teens.

Snicket, L. (2006). *The complete wreck: Books 1–13 (a series of unfortunate events).* New York: HarperCollins.

This is the "gloomy" series of unfortunate events books. You never know what will happen to those Baudelaire orphans except that whatever it is, it's going to be a head-shaking shambles.

Soto, G. (1997). *Chato's kitchen.* New York: Penguin Young Readers Group.

Chato, the coolest cat in East Los Angeles, is thrilled when a family of mice moves into the barrio. When Chato prepares a feast in honor of his new neighbors, he gets more than he can handle with the surprise guest the mice bring along.

Thoms, A. (2002). *With their eyes: September 11th—The view from a high school at ground zero.* New York: HarperCollins.

Ms. Thoms was an English teacher at Stuyvesant High School, located four blocks from the World Trade Center, on the day of September 11, 2001. Because of what happened within a few hours that Tuesday morning, and the experience of such an event that transformed all their lives completely, she took on a school production based on 10 students' recorded interviews about that day. The students transferred these stories into "poem-monologues," which they presented, and the text of which appears in this book.

REFERENCES

Anderson, K. (2002). *Violence in society.* Retrieved October 26, 2009, from http://www
.leaderu.com/orgs/probe/docs/violence.html

Boehm, S. (2006). Violence in video games. *Children's Voice: Child Welfare League of
America, 15*(1), 12–14.

Choudhury, S. (2003). *The enticement of the esoteric.* Retrieved October 26, 2009, from
http://www.hinduonnet.com/lr/2003/09/07/stories/2003090700040100.htm

Kiefer, B. (1995). The disturbing image in children's picture books: Fearful or fulfilling. In
S. Lehr (Ed.), *Battling dragons: Issues and controversy in children's literature* (pp. 51–60).
Portsmouth, NH: Heinemann.

Pasadena Child Care Provider. (2008). *Violence in children's literature.* Retrieved October
26, 2009, from http://www.pasadenachildcareprovider.com/wp-blog/featured/violence-
in-childrens-literature

Tomlinson, C. (1995). Justifying violence in children's literature. In S. Lehr (Ed.), *Battling
dragons: Issues and controversy in children's literature* (pp. 39–50). Portsmouth, NH:
Heinemann.

Vandergrift, K. (2008). *The culture of violence and picture books.* Retrieved October 26,
2009, from http://www.scils.rutgers.edu/~kvander/911/childwar.html

PART III

REALITIES IN LIFE AND MULTICULTURAL CHILDREN'S LITERATURE

Chapter 7

War, Terrorism, Justice, and Freedom

I know that you are smart and I know that you think
You're doing what is best for me.
But if Freedom is handled just your way
Then it's not my freedom or free.

—Refrain from *The Big Box*
Toni Morrison and Slade Morrison (1999)

these terms are subjective

I t appears that the four terms, *war, terrorism, justice,* and *freedom,* are linked, depending on the person's point of view. It can be argued that wars are fought to quell rebellion, to conquer (for freedom, power, and domination), or to mete out justice. Look at war through the eyes of a people whose entire families and communities have been erased, or through the eyes of women and children who have been killed, raped or maimed, and you find the same definitions for terrorism as war. Because, "however 'just' or 'humanitarian' may be the claims, at the irreducible core of all war is the slaughter of the innocent, organized by national leaders, accompanied by lies" (Zinn, 2001, p. 18). Ultimately, depending on which side of the border a person is on, one becomes a terrorist or one becomes a brave warrior.

Because of the emotionally charged and unpredictable nature of these terms, they may be called "alternate realities." And, as these are especially difficult topics to broach with children, creating an alternate world may help us facilitate empathy and understanding. In this chapter, these four terms, are explored as these terms may be both abstract as well as surreal, sometimes for children and adults alike. And yet these terms are at the core of each person's world, interlinked with the very existence and realities of today. Through a discussion of what these terms mean to teachers today, and through a review of several books, this chapter tries to understand and critically examine these difficult terms through rhetorical questions in the hope that we can at least begin to view these difficult terms critically and what they mean in our lives.

Making Meaning: A Historical Perspective

Wars have always been fought; history is peppered with all kinds of armed conflict. Similarly, so has terrorism been around for many decades, in the name of justice and freedom. However, while war is always given an optimistic connotation and soldiers in a war are considered justified in their killing and bombing, terrorism, on the other hand, is thought to be the work of madmen, fanatics who kill innocent people for no apparent reason. But a closer look at the connections between war and terrorism reveals many similarities: war kills people, and so does terrorism; war kills children, and so does terrorism; war maims innocent bystanders, old and young, and so does terrorism. Essentially one could say that war is no different than terrorism as war could be construed as sanctioned mass killing of innocent people under the guise of justice. As Zinn (2002) put it,

> The term "just war" contains an internal contradiction. . . . Because war is inevitably indiscriminate, innocent people are killed. In fact, the politicians admit it, they say, "Well yes, innocent people will be killed, but it is too bad." This is what the terrorists say. That's what Timothy McVeigh said. (p. 24)

One definition of terrorism is "the unlawful use or threatened use of force or violence against people or property to coerce or intimidate governments or societies, often to achieve political, religious, or ideological objectives" (GlobalSecurity .org, n.d.). From this definition of terrorism, it seems to be a natural progression from war. Further, with such a definition of war and terrorism, surely the Nazis and their atrocities would be considered terrorism? What about the Ku Klux Klan and its systematic killing, maiming, and lynching of African American people? In fact, it would not be a far cry to compare the actions of the Ku Klux Klan and the Nazis to the present Muslim *mujahideen groups* (those who struggle for freedom), who fight their *jihad* (holy war). Based on all of these groups' modus operandi, they may all be considered fundamentalists, supremacists, who appear to be regular citizens but do these acts under the guise of ridding the world of "dirty" or "unholy" people.

Although wars have been fought for various reasons, what is different now is that terrorism has become a form of war and we are living it. War and terrorism are undeniably connected; for example, the United States has been fighting a "war against terrorism" since 2001, first against Afghanistan's Taliban rulers and then in Iraq. On the other hand, the many Islamic fundamentalist groups are fighting a

"Jihadi War" or holy war through terrorism. For the laymen, while war and terrorism may be sacrilegious to compare, as one is supposed to be for a good cause whereas the other is not, the point here is that the end results of both are similar; both adversely affect all those who are involved.

MAKING MEANING: A CURRENT PERSPECTIVE

Until recently, for many of us fortunate ones, war and terrorism were things we read about in a history text or that happened to "other" people in faraway lands. However, the recent decades have given us a small taste of these, for better or worse. Unfortunately, this brings us to yet another aspect of these alternate realities in current times, the wrongly held belief that Muslims are terrorists and that Islam sanctions terrorism. While it is not in the scope of this chapter to go into the discussions of political aspects of these stereotypes, a basic explanation could be that this sort of extreme stereotype is perpetrated mainly by mass reactions to the September 11, 2001, attacks on the World Trade Center. The racial prejudice toward anyone who appears Muslim is affecting everyday life akin to what happened to Japanese Americans after the Pearl Harbor bombing. Of course, astute thinkers have realized that much before the 9/11 attacks, Timothy McVeigh, a White American citizen, bombed and killed 168 people in the Oklahoma City bombing. Ultimately, whether it is called "war" or "terrorism," for those affected by these events, it becomes merely a semantic distinction in the mass destruction and pain that these acts cause to millions of people.

This is how it is for Malaak, the 11-year-old protagonist of *A Stone in My Hand,* by Cathryn Clinton. Malaak, who only communicates through her adopted pigeon, describes how her family was shattered by the events of the *intifada* (literally, a shake-up or unrest) between Israel and Palestine. She describes how her father loses his job as Israeli soldiers close down his workplace and how he goes to Israel to look for a job. She describes how the bus in which he travels is bombed by a suicide bomber who claims to be a *mujahideen.* Malaak describes a dinnertime conversation where her brother, who is 15, wants to join the Islamic Jihad (an extremist group) to fight for justice. She describes how Israeli soldiers bang on the door in the middle of the night and do a search of the small, two-room apartment in which they live, merely because their electricity bills are not paid. She describes how her brother's friend, Nasser, is beaten to death by Israeli soldiers because he threw a ball that broke a window. To Malaak, her reality is the barbed wire that she sees everywhere, the bombed school building that she attends, the gun-toting soldiers who seem to be everywhere, and dinner conversations with her family that are about death, terrorism, and fear.

Making Meaning and Critical Connections

Characters such as Malaak still seem faraway to children who read about them. Further, such readings are difficult and confusing to mediate in a classroom unless, as teachers and educators, we make an effort to make sense of these terms for ourselves. With this in mind, a quick survey was conducted in a Southern California college classroom of 22 diverse teachers. They were asked to jot down answers to the following questions: What is freedom? What is justice? Why is there war? What is terrorism? Why is there terrorism? They were told that this was an anonymous survey and that they simply needed to write down the first thing that came to mind when they heard these terms. These teachers' answers revealed their confusion and struggle to comprehend these terms. In this diverse group, there were 19 women and three men, of whom four were White, two African American, five Asian, and the majority Latino(a), all from various socioeconomic backgrounds. Their answers ranged from personal beliefs to philosophical musings to media-generated ideas. Their answers are briefly cited here, according to the responses for each term.

Freedom

Most felt that freedom is to be able to do and say what one wants, speak your mind, choose and make decisions, and live without constraints in expression and thought. Some had a different opinion and said that freedom is abstract in that it is both physical and emotional, that it is a state of mind, which everyone is "entitled" to. Freedom is also an "ability" that is "given," that is "allowed," that does not need the "permission" of others and it is not controlled.

It was interesting to note the language used in the teachers' attempts to define freedom. Words like "allow," "permission," and "given" indicate that some of them believe that freedom cannot be taken for granted. It also indicated their uncertainty in being able to put into words their feelings about this term. One teacher rightly said that freedom is very personal in that it can be defined only by people for themselves. This teacher says that it is a state of mind, of being at peace.

Justice

Justice was defined in very broad terms, from single word answers to half a page; it was interesting to see teachers grappling with what they felt was a fit definition for justice. Some put it very simply as fairness, a God-given right, security, honesty, and so on. Others defined it in legal terms, as paying for negative actions, being punished for committing a felony, settling a case, and being held accountable for certain actions. Others were more generic and said that justice is rules, norms created by a society, and people using their authority in a positive manner. Some answers proved vague in that responses showed either that teachers had not put a lot of thought into answering or that they had a narrow definition of these terms. For example, some said that justice is "when right prevails over wrong" or that "when good is rewarded."

Some teachers' responses, however, were very thoughtful and analytical, like the person who said that "anything" is fair if a group of people decide so. In other words, this teacher realized that justice evolves through the agreed upon rules a society makes and is very subjective in that not everyone in the society may agree to the rules, but they all have to follow them for the larger good of the group. Two responded that this is an ambiguous question to answer, as "what is justice to one group may not be for another" and "justice can only result from knowledge and understanding of all viewpoints."

War and Terrorism

As to the reasons for war, power, control, domination over religion, government, hatred, and anger were the most commonly cited. Some went so far as to give oppression, cultural ignorance, and mistrust as valid reasons. One person simply said, "War exists to keep the ignorant busy . . . so does terrorism," which, while funny, is also disturbing. War was also justified by these teachers as reasons to prevent oppression and maintain justice, that "it is often necessary but never desired destruction." One teacher alluded to war as an ideological choice and said, "war is needed for ideas to be challenged; everyone in society has different perceptions of what they deem to be correct."

At least 10 out of the 22 teachers in this survey independently came to the conclusion that war and terrorism are the same or are similar. They cited power, domination, religion, beliefs, and opinions as reasons for forceful control through terrorism. They cited anger, hatred, and government as other reasons. Some said that they honestly do not know why there is terrorism, that perhaps it is anger or jealousy of freedom, and that terrorists are cowards who are coerced into doing certain acts to "challenge the world." At least five out of this group later revealed that they had either been refugees of war or currently had a family member at war in Iraq. War and terrorism were very close to these teachers.

USING CHILDREN'S BOOKS TO ADDRESS WAR, TERRORISM, JUSTICE, AND FREEDOM

As is clear from this short and quick survey, there is much confusion in terms of comprehending and understanding what these terms mean to us as teachers. How can we begin to teach about issues that we don't quite comprehend or understand? Although this is a tough question to answer, children's books give us unique angles from which to approach these topics. One of the most important things that these teachers showed in their responses to this short survey was honesty, their honesty in not knowing how to comprehend these terms, their honesty in being able to say "I don't know," and their willingness to go on this journey of mediating these tough and rather abstract notions with students. In the following paragraphs, many examples of excellent stories that talk about war, terrorism, justice, and freedom are described. Although it is difficult to describe how teachers should use these wonderful books in detail, as the context of each classroom is different, there are some basic principles that may be useful for teachers:

- *Show that it is real:* Impress upon students that the books that they are about to read are about real people, in real times, although the stories themselves may be fictionalized. Sometimes, violence and pictures of violence may simply titillate students, who may not have a context in which to place these situations. A discussion should be conducted before and after reading the books in an open, honest way and with passion by the teacher to show that these are difficult for her to mediate also. This will help to impress upon students that actual people were affected by the events depicted in the books.

- *Set the context, time period, situation:* Help students understand the larger context, what was happening in the real world to people at the time that this book is set. What was happening to children, especially those that are of the same age as the children in the class? How were the characters' lives different from the students in the class? Help students put themselves in the shoes of the characters by talking about brief and well thought-out analogies.

- *Allow students to react in any way:* Lehr (1995) said that students' responses to children's literature are untamed. What she means is that we cannot predict how students will react to a situation that they encounter in a book. They will respond honestly to whatever attracts them and interests them the most. Perhaps they may see pictures of Holocaust victims and notice only body parts that may be funny to them. Although this may seem heartless to the teacher, it is important to take their responses and use them to help them understand the consequences. In other words, no responses are silly or wrong. The teacher should be prepared to channel students' responses in the appropriate direction.

- *Allow for a variety of discussion tools:* Whenever there are topics that are hard to comprehend, allow enough time for discussion. Allow students to respond in writing, talking, in doing a skit, and so on. Sometimes, difficult topics are best understood and discussed days after the actual book or topic is introduced in the classroom. Help students find connections to discuss and let the topics continue for however long the students want them to continue.

- *Help students make intertextual connections:* Gather lots of resources that give students many points of view about difficult topics. These could be first-person accounts, movies, historical documents, artifacts, and so on. Reading and seeing other things connected to this event helps students comprehend the book that is being read.

- *Help students make narrative connections:* Have them do narrative connections—storytell about a situation in the book; let them place themselves in the characters' shoes and storytell what they would do. Booth and Barton (2000) say that telling stories helps us comprehend and shape our lives into meaningful events that we can accept. When discussing difficult topics such as war and terrorism, students can especially benefit from storytelling techniques that will help them comprehend these issues.

PAST DEPICTIONS

Historical perspectives of war are usually heroic, and depictions of war in children's books talk about the bravery and courage of either the refugees or the soldiers. Although the horrors of war and terrorism are depicted in some picture books and described in others, the focus, as it should be, is more on courage and bravery. For example, *Pink and Say,* by Patricia Polacco, is set during the Civil War and is about the interracial friendship between two teenage boys, Pink (Pinkus Aylee), who is Black, and Say (Sheldon Curtis), who is White. Pink saves Say's life, and the story is a moving historical account of how the war disrupts these two young lives. This powerful tale captures these 15-year-old soldiers' bravery and courage in the face of adverse conditions.

A historical perspective of war would give us a sense that wars are mainly fought for justice and freedom, such as the Colonial War, the Civil War, world wars, and so forth. However, although not characterized as such, there were many acts of terrorism during these wars, such as the Pearl Harbor bombing and the retaliation with the bombing of Hiroshima and Nagasaki, the thousands of people killed during the Holocaust, to name but a few. Children's books about these times are moving tales of heroism and resilience, usually told from the points of view of children. Authors who write these tales must have had the hardest job in trying to balance the horrors without putting off their readers while at the same time conveying the catastrophic consequences. For example, *Hiroshima No Pika,* by Toshi Maruki, tells the story of 7-year-old Mii and her experience during the "Flash," as the atomic bombing of Hiroshima and Nagasaki are known. This is a heartrending tale that affects the reader immensely as each page of the book is turned. Done in abstract splashes of color, with lots of line drawings, it conveys Mii's suffering through simple yet straightforward words and pictures. There is no agitation in the words, simply quiet sadness, as if we could actually hear Maruki telling us this story in a hushed voice, who, even after decades, still does not believe the horror of what happened on August 6 and August 9, 1945. Here is an excerpt:

> There were crowds of people fleeing the fire. Mii saw children with their clothes burned away, lips and eyelids swollen. They were like ghosts running away crying in weak voices. Some people, all their strength gone, fell face down on the ground and others fell on top of them. There were heaps of people everywhere. . . . Mii felt something moving past her feet. Hop . . . hop. . . . It was a swallow. Its wings were burned and it couldn't fly. Hop . . . hop . . . (pp. 7–10)

Maruki continues in the story and tells us how Mii and her mother survived. Mii, now an adult, still has the body of a 7-year-old, as the "Flash" arrested her growth.

Sadako and the Thousand Paper Cranes is another such tale, told by Eleanor Coerr and illustrated by Ed Young in two different books. This is the true story of Sadako Sasaki, an energetic preteen who lived in Hiroshima and developed leukemia when she was 12 years old in 1955. Upon knowing about her sickness, she decides to fold a thousand paper cranes, as legend says that doing this will make her better. A tragic true story, Sadako did not survive in spite of her not giving up. The memory of a 12-year-old girl, who wanted to get better and be a long-distance runner, is kept alive through statues and memorials in Hiroshima City and in Seattle, Washington (see http://www.sadako.org).

Sadako and the Thousand Paper Cranes is a classic example of the effects of war on children and their resilience in trying to control their destiny. Considering that there is evidence to suggest that the bombings of Hiroshima and Nagasaki were premeditated, especially considering that they occurred 4 years after the bombing of Pearl Harbor; considering that an atomic bomb was used for the first time for maximum damage, against the warnings of several scientists of its of long-term effects; and considering that they affected largely civilian populations, could one characterize these bombings as terrorism?

Another such tale is *Anne Frank: The Diary of a Young Girl* (1952/1993). Set in Amsterdam during the Nazi occupation, *Anne Frank* chronicles the life of 13-year-old

Anne and her family, who hid from the Nazis for 2 years. Anne was given a blank diary on her 13th birthday, and this diary was discovered after her death in 1945. Published for the first time in 1947, the diary is a unique chronicle of Nazi occupation during World War II. The diary format is kept throughout the book and the pages have the authentic feel of the young writer. Among the obviously terrifying moments of being in hiding, she reflects on her sometimes boring and claustrophobic life, has her first kiss, and grows from a teenager to an adult through the pages of the diary. This first-person account allows the reader to feel her pain and pleasure at each moment.

CURRENT DEPICTIONS

In recent times, the perspective of war has changed considerably. Especially in the United States, wars are being fought in the name of keepers of justice and democracy, what Giraldi (2003), a former CIA counterterrorism specialist, characterized as "pre-emptive war." The Vietnam War, the Gulf War, the war in Afghanistan, and the war against terrorism in Iraq were all started as the United States and the Western world took it upon themselves to be the supreme powers to help fight against oppression in the rest of the world. While there are many views on these wars and many justifications, the fact remains that all of these wars were started and fought under great disagreement, even among the leaders of the Western world and the international community. Although some thought these wars were not right, some others felt that it was the United States' duty, as it had the money and power to fight them. Still others question why only these wars were fought in the name of justice and democracy. Why weren't people in South Africa, Sudan, Somalia, or the Congo, protected and given monetary help when they needed it? Some cultural analysts are sure that these wars were fought with hidden agendas—as are all wars—in that the Western world was safeguarding its oil resources (Zinn, 2002). Although these are tough questions to answer without making value judgments and without taking sides, the bottom line is that war, terrorism, and violence are inexplicably connected. As teachers and educators, we are left to help our children comprehend these issues critically and sensitively.

Children's books about the recent wars tell poignant tales of refugees in the affected countries, like *The Whispering Cloth*, by Peggy Dietz Shea. Illustrated through eloquently embroidered panels of story cloths, little Mai recounts her life as a refugee in a Hmong refugee camp situated in Thailand, by learning how to stitch her own story cloth in the 1990s. Mai has known life only in the refugee camp and lives there with her grandmother and other older ladies who make *pa'ndau*, or embroidered story cloths to sell to local traders. Mai wants more than anything else to learn to stitch a cloth by herself and asks her grandmother for a story. Her grandmother, however, says, "If you do not have a story of your own, you are not ready to do a pa'ndau." Mai then begins to stitch her own life story, and through the beautiful embroidery, gains resolution for her troubled heart.

Children's books also tell heroic and moving tales of American soldiers and their families who lost their lives, like *The Wall*, by Eve Bunting. This story, told through a young boy and his father who have come to find their grandfather's name on the Vietnam War memorial, is so beautifully written that the words convey the utter sadness and solitude that the boy and his father feel when they find the grandfather's name. As they stand quietly for a moment before the memorial, the boy overhears another man and his grandchild talking and thinks to himself, "but I'd rather have my grandfather here."

More recent tales talk about the war in Afghanistan and the terror under which people there lived from 1994, when the Taliban came to power, until 2001. Particularly, Deborah Ellis wrote three very readable books about a young girl who disguises herself as a boy because there are no male members in her family who could earn money. These are *The Breadwinner, Parvana's Journey*, and *Mud-City*. Written in very simple language, these stories are told through the eyes of Parvana, a preteen girl, and another narrator. Parvana loses her father and then her family in Afghanistan. Escaping from soldiers, she runs into Asif, a 10-year-old with a tough exterior and one leg; Leila, a 7-year-old who is in denial that her grandmother is dead, having lived with the body for more than a month; and Hassan, a baby. With this new family, Parvana undertakes the dangerous journey of crossing the desert to reach a refugee camp along the Pakistan border.

READING AUTHENTIC ACCOUNTS

One of the biggest dilemmas of teaching about war and terrorism is how to convey the horrors of these without creating a picture of despondency, despite the fact that war and terrorism create utter desperation. How can we explain and justify the vagaries of sanctioned violence of war and terrorism and yet hope to teach tolerance and sensitivity? How can we hope to give our children security and trust when all that they see and hear around them are mass destruction, mass killing, and "bloody" messes (literally and figuratively)? How can we explain children who are maimed, women and children who are raped, soldiers who are themselves barely children, tortured beyond recognition, and yet have an optimistic and life affirming outcome? How can we expect understanding and empathy when it is hard for *us* as adults to comprehend this?

Certain genres of children's literature have particularly been developed to accommodate and serve the purpose of facilitating tough issues such as these. Historical fiction and real stories, such as autobiographies, biographies, and first-person accounts, are highly valuable tools in creating authentic literature for children about tough times. Some nonfiction books like memoirs, and what could be called "docu-books," teach invaluable lessons for children. The contents of these genres also matter in that who writes these and who these are written about make a huge difference in perception. For example, accounts of slavery; autobiographical, biographical, and fictionalized accounts of refugees; diaries, and sometimes even interviews, are very useful tools in beginning discussions and broaching difficult issues, as these are authentic literature.

Year of Impossible Goodbyes, by Sook Nyol Choi, is an autobiographical tale written through the eyes of Sookan, who is 10 years old when the Japanese army occupies her country, North Korea, in 1945. Left without any male support, as her father hides in Manchuria and her brothers are away in different Japanese labor camps, the women run a sock factory to support themselves during the end of World War II. Through heartrending prose, Choi recounts her experiences during the Japanese occupation and her escape from North Korea to free South Korea as the communist Russians occupy her country. Some of the most horrible and haunting chapters in the book talk about older members of the sock factory forced into becoming "comfort girls" for the Japanese soldiers, including some as young as 14 years old. A rarely touched upon by-product of war, the stories of these Korean girls and women forced into sexual servitude by the Japanese army, slaps readers into awareness. Written in simple yet vivid language, Choi tells such a compelling tale that it is impossible to put the book down until one is finished reading. Unfortunately, before we can thrust these appalling images away as something that happened during World War II, the testimonies and letters of women from the Congo in 2005 remind us that as long as human beings are at war, inhuman acts such as rape are possible.

A picture book that is sensitively portrayed is particularly useful for young children, as it helps facilitate deep responses from those children (Kiefer, 1995). A visual image goes much farther in eliciting reflective responses than any words could. Particularly, if these pictures are not realistic, their "lack of specificity, . . . may be what lends them their emotional punch" (Kiefer, 1995, p. 53). *Hiroshima No Pika, The Whispering Cloth,* and *The Wall* are all such stories. However, author Naomi Shihab Nye has managed to do the same with a surprise twist in her story, *Sitti's Secrets.*

This innocuous tale of a young girl, Mona, going to visit her grandmother in another country, is an unexpected break away from the regular war story in that it does not fit in any category that would characterize it as a book about war or terrorism. Mona has a wonderful time with her grandmother, whom she calls Sitti, in Palestine, helping her with everyday chores such as milking a cow, making flat bread, and picking olives and lemons from the trees in her grandmother's orchard. Mona does not speak the same language as her grandmother, yet she falls in love with the quiet, strong woman who has tattoos shaped like birds on her hands. On her return to the United States, Mona writes a letter to the President in reaction to news she hears on TV. It isn't until we read the letter that her worry is revealed. She says, "If the people of the United States could meet Sitti, they'd like her for sure. You'd like her too. . . . Mr. President, I wish you my good luck in your very hard job. I vote for peace. My grandmother votes with me." Mona's letter helps us put a name to a face. We see Sitti going about her daily business, and if not for the illustrations, there is hardly anything in the text that would particularly characterize it as a Middle Eastern or Palestinian story. Through this simple, heartwarming tale, Nye reveals that it is much harder to hate and hurt a known face or person than to do so with nameless "barbarians."

Another deviant picture book from the genre of picture books, although this is nonfiction, is *One Day We Had to Run!*, compiled by Sybella Wilkes in association with the UNHCR (United Nations High Commissioner for Refugees) and Save the Children foundations. In this book, refugee children from Somalia, Sudan, and Ethiopia draw and tell their own stories of survival during their stay at a refugee camp in Kenya. These children's firsthand testimonials of their experiences in the civil unrest in their countries, along with heartbreaking color drawings made by them, is a nonfiction book written in a documentary style. There is commentary by the author, historical facts, maps, actual photographs, and reproductions of children's art work accompanying their translated stories. This picture book is really unique in that it reads like a film, hence my term "docu-book."

FINDING RESILIENCE IN THE FACE OF ADVERSITY

If there is anything at all redeeming about war stories, it is in reading about the resilience, courage, emotional strength, and perseverance of human goodwill in the face of adverse conditions, the ability to find contentment in whatever is thrown their way, and the ability to get up and move on from dire circumstances. Books that relate such stories offer us glimpses of hope and redemption.

One such story is *Baseball Saved Us*, by Ken Mochizuki. In this story, a young boy's father decides that "people need something to do in camp," and he builds a baseball camp for the young children. The children, however, are not in a fun camp like a summer camp; rather, they are at a camp for Japanese Americans, interned during World War II. Even in the face of gross injustice, this father helps his son and their friends form a baseball team. The baseball games give these children a purpose in life at the camp. Set at a time when Japanese Americans faced dire racism and hatred, the book shows them playing this all-American game. With beautiful language and stirring pictures, this book symbolizes the freedom that these internees yearn for.

Other books about Japanese Americans and the hardships and injustices they faced during World War II are *The Bracelet* and *Journey to Topaz,* both by Yoshiko Uchida. *The Bracelet* is told from the point of view of 7-year-old Emi, who has to leave in 48 hours for an internment camp with her mother and big sister, with just two suitcases full of things. Earlier, we learn that her father had already been taken away for questioning and was incarcerated. Given a bracelet to remember her neighbor by, Emi is distraught when she loses the bracelet, but she later realizes that she does not need material things to hold onto her memories. *Journey to Topaz* is a semiautobiographical tale of Uchida when she was a little girl. Told through the eyes of Yuki, the 11-year-old protagonist, it talks about the shame and confusion of people when they are sent away to the camps. The sequel to this book is *Journey Home,* also by Uchida, which continues the story of Yuki, when she and her family are allowed to go back only to have to pick up their lives from scratch, as their livelihoods and freedom were taken away during the internment. In addition to these shorter vignettes from her life, which are semiautobiographical, Uchida has also published her autobiography, called *The Invisible Thread.*

Passage to Freedom: The Sugihara Story, by Ken Mochizuki, shows us a different kind of resilience in the face of adversity. Sugihara was the Japanese consul general in Lithuania during World War II. This story, told through the voice of his son, talks about how Sugihara single-handedly saved hundreds of Polish Jews from the Nazis and the horrors of the Holocaust by handwriting their visas to enable them to get out of the country. These "freedom papers" were written by Sugihara under great threat and danger to his own family and well-being. This is a beautifully told tale from a child's viewpoint, yet it is powerful in its impact, as Hiroki was only 5 years old when his father was consul.

Another powerful Holocaust story is *Fireflies in the Dark: The Story of Friedl Dicker-Brandeis and the Children of Terezin,* by Susan Goldman Rubin. Dicker-Brandeis was a teacher and an art therapist who, when told to pack and come away from her home in Prague, packed art supplies and began teaching children in the concentration camp at Terezin how to draw and paint. Hundreds of her students' artworks from those horrific years are still preserved today and reproduced in this book. The paintings and drawings are testimony to the horrors, but they also provided a wonderful outlet for many children. This nonfiction book is poignantly written by Rubin and pays homage to a true teacher whose thoughtfulness in carrying art supplies rather than personal items provided numerous children a ray of hope in despair.

A recent book about what our children feel about war and peace is *Lines in the Sand: New Writing on War and Peace,* by Mary Hoffman and Rhiannon Lassiter. In this book, 150 children from around the world write their stories about war and peace. There are memoirs, essays, artwork, stories, pictures, and poems all calling for peace. Although the book began as a resistance to the war in Iraq, the vignettes are about people who are caught up in the conflict of war and their cries for peace, which can be applied to any war at any time. Some of the vignettes are almost a slap in the face with their shocking words and stories. This is a book that is sure to generate a lot of questions that have no easy answers.

CONCLUSION

Every generation has its share of war and terrorism, and each deals with them in its own way. Intricately linked to issues of money and power, war, terrorism, justice, and freedom make different sense to different groups of people. Ask the many Native tribes who existed in the Americas about freedom and justice today and one would most likely hear that they still don't have freedom and justice. Ask the average American, and he or she may answer that we live in the most progressive country. Although this chapter has only scratched the surface in bringing up issues around these four terms, it is with the hope that teachers and educators will consider these important topics to discuss in schools. There are no easy answers to teaching and facilitating these issues except to raise critical questions and to give students the ability to scrutinize our cultural and political systems, if we are to prepare our youngsters for the future with a view to global awareness and sensitivity. At the heart of any war are control, power, and ideological issues, which also come into play in terrorism. As teachers and educators, we are left to pick up and make meaning of the carnage that is left behind by wars and terrorists. One hopes that exemplary books, like the ones mentioned in this chapter, make for easier facilitation.

REFLECTION QUESTIONS FOR THE TEACHER

1. What do the terms *war, terrorism, justice,* and *freedom* mean to me?

2. What steps can I take to help mediate these difficult terms in my classroom?

3. Is it okay to "water down" what really happened/happens in wars or terrorist acts to protect our children? When is it okay to do this and how far would I go?

4. What resources, such as videos, museum visits, guest speakers, songs, live shows, and so forth, can we find to connect history in the curriculum with current and past events?

war - the act of 2 entities at odds with one another, where there is either ① no evident solution or ② there is no compromise (whether not evident, or 1 or more parties is unwilling)

terrorism - when one group creates conflict to impose their personal feelings on another

justice - the solution (remedy) to an injustice

freedom - the ability to think for oneself w/o restrictions on one's rights   inalienable

SAMPLE RESPONSE LESSON 7.1
Exploring Issues of War Using Educational Drama

Elementary Grades (2nd–5th): In the Classroom, by Teachers, Parents, and Tutors

Duration: 1 Day or 1 Week (Preparation May Be 1 to 3 Weeks)

Overview

As mentioned in the chapter, these four terms are difficult to mediate with children and may become easier if an "alternate world" can be created to help students understand through imaginary scenarios. These imaginary scenarios are created based on the classroom curriculum. Often with historical events, **educational drama** encounters help put into perspective the attitudes and emotions that may have been felt by people living during the actual events. For students in today's classrooms, putting themselves into the shoes of people from history may make these events come alive for them.

The teacher may pick a historical event in which people struggled during a war, dealt with a conflict, and so on. For example, Ohio history has it that on August 3, 1795, over 1,100 chiefs and warriors from various native Indian tribes were forced to sign a treaty called the Treaty of Greenville, which required them to give up Indian lands amounting to all of present day Ohio and a good part of Indiana.

The teacher creates several artifacts about the incident, which may include real pictures of a war, chiefs who fought in the war, important parties that were affected, and so on. The teacher also tries to find a way that students can connect with the incident in their real lives such as creating banners, slogans, themes, or art. The teacher then gives enough information about the incident or conflict and asks the students if they would like to engage in imagining this incident in the classroom. With a carefully paced role-play students engage in talking about the incident and imagining themselves as people participating in the incident.

Materials

Various books, artifacts such as maps, pictures, authentic literature, and some authentic historical documents pertaining to the topic such as the original script of the treaty, butcher paper for writing in groups, banners or chart paper to make slogans, markers, and so on.

Key Vocabulary

Treaty, War, Forced, Signing a Treaty, Deal

(Continued)

(Continued)

Anticipatory Set

1. *Focus:* Students learn to view an incident from an insider's point of view. They react and talk from their hearts so that they may critically analyze what has happened.

2. *Objective:* To put historical incidents, which may be too abstract for students, into perspective by having them respond within a frame of reference as characters in the incident, such as one of the 1,100 chiefs and warriors who were forced to sign the treaty that they may not have even comprehended.

3. *Transfer:* As students react and respond as characters or chiefs from within the perspective, they begin to appreciate and empathize what people like themselves may have gone through. Students also learn to make connections to their lives today through their reactions and written responses.

Instructions

1. The teacher has already discussed the topic of Native tribes in Ohio for the last couple of weeks. The students have been doing research, writing in their journals, reading authentic literature, and so on. For this lesson, the teacher tells them that on August 3, 1795, the Treaty of Greenville was signed. She shows them drawings of that incident, authentic information such as maps of the area before the treaty and after the treaty, and a list of famous chiefs who appeared at the treaty and signed it.

2. Six major tribes that existed in the Ohio Valley before the treaty are chosen. The students are divided into six groups and asked to make a symbol that shows all of the qualities of each of the six tribes. As students have been learning about the tribes and what they stand for, they may enjoy this art activity, while also internalizing what they learned about each tribe. Students quickly share what they created. This could be the end of the first day's lesson.

3. Second day: With the help of an overhead color picture that depicts Chief Little Turtle of the Miami tribe handing over a wampum belt in agreement to the treaty, explain what happened in the treaty. The actual treaty is then read aloud to all the students. It is important to remember that the authentic treaty was read without translation. Although written in English, the archaic and technical language makes it virtually incomprehensible to students. After 5 minutes of uninterrupted reading, students are asked if they understand it, and the teacher offers that she doesn't understand it either. The idea is to show that many of the chiefs present that day also may not have understood what they were being forced to sign.

4. Abridged versions of the treaty that were translated into everyday English are then handed out so that students are not at a loss. The groups are asked to review the "treaties" to see if they are agreeable to the terms and conditions. They are asked to review the map and determine how it will change once the treaty is signed.

5. Students are engaged in a dialogue in role to see if they agree with the terms of the treaty. They should tell whether they agree and explain why or why not.

Independent Practice

Students are asked to rewrite the treaties so that they may become more agreeable to their tribes. The groups are asked to come back with their suggestions and rewrites to the whole group, and the teacher then mediates between the groups to find out if they agree. The teacher could be a United States Army official, whose only job is to make sure that the treaty is signed. This added pressure may bring up questions of existence and fairness when they have to fight for their groups' lands.

Closure

Rewrite the treaty to make it more agreeable, and find a way to accommodate all and work toward peace.

Extension

Visit a museum, invite a guest speaker, or watch a film from an opposite perspective.

Modifications: Secondary Grades

A similar lesson may be followed with an historical event that pertains to the respective class.

EXAMPLES OF RESPONSES TO LESSON 7.1

The lesson described earlier was conducted over a 3-day period in a fourth-grade classroom. The class had students of varying abilities in terms of writing and reading. It also had two special needs students who were being assisted by an aid. This educational drama lesson was planned and conducted in conjunction with the class unit plan for that week. The classroom teacher and I worked together to engage students in the lessons. The following are rewritten treaties that the students wrote in their groups at the end of the 3 days.

The Wyandot group wrote:

We are a peaceful tribe, we don't want any war, but we also don't want you to take away our lands. We can be friends and share this land. There will be no war and it will be peaceful because we just want to live in peace. We will also free your people so you can free our people. Please sign this treaty.

The Delaware group wrote:

We will make a deal with you, we want to divide the land half and half. We will keep our land and we will keep our hunting ground. We will not fine the people to use our hunting ground and we will not fight, we will keep our promise and you must keep yours.

The Miami group wrote:

For this treaty of Greenville, we would like to say that it is not fair. We think all of the land should be shared with everyone. We also think the rivers should be shared equally. We don't think you should have most of it.

The Seneca-Mingo group wrote:

It is not fair that we do not understand this treaty. We will not sign it unless you make it clear. We demand interpreters. We don't think this will make us happier as you say, you are just taking away our homes and our happiness.

The Shawnee group wrote:

We want a treaty that's an oath in peace. We want [to] make the line equal. We do not have an agreement until this is fair. We want more respect. Why can't we live together and be friends? We will not return your hostages until our orders are followed and you will return our hostages. We will kill them if you do not support this.

The Ottawa group wrote:

Split the land and let our tribes go and we'll let yours go. Not till you return our chief without harm, shall we return yours. We ask to meet up in the middle and free the people. We ask that you bring our people safely.

SELECTED ANNOTATED BIBLIOGRAPHY

Bunting, E. (1990). *The wall*. New York: Clarion Books.

A boy and his father visit the Vietnam War Memorial In Washington, D.C., to look for the boy's grandfather's name. Written from the boy's point of view, the book depicts sadness and yet pride of a family that has lost its loved one to the war. Recommended age 6 years and up.

Choi, S. N. (1993). *Year of impossible goodbyes*. New York: Yearling Books.

Although based on true events from the author's life, this book does not read like an autobiography; rather, it reads like a story told from the first person. It is the tale of 10-year-old Sookan, who lives in North Korea, which is occupied by the Japanese army in 1945. Through unimaginable tragedy and trouble, she and her family escape to South Korea. Written in a fast-paced adventure story style, this book cannot be put down. Recommended age 10 years and up.

Clinton, C. (2002). *A stone in my hand*. Cambridge, MA: Candlewick Press.

Eleven-year-old Malaak has just lost her father and lives in Gaza City in Palestine. All she has known in her life are gun-toting soldiers, barbed wire, and bombs. She is so traumatized by the events in her life that she talks only through her pet bird. The story is told through her voice and creates moments of fantasy and fright, like the night when Israeli soldiers bang on the door and ask about an unpaid utility bill, past midnight.

Coerr, E. (1977). *Sadako and the thousand paper cranes*. New York: Penguin Puffin Books.

It is 1954 and all that 10-year-old Sadako wants to do is to be a track runner. However, she gets leukemia, the "atomic bomb disease," and ends up in the hospital instead. She learns that an ancient Japanese saying says that if you fold a thousand paper cranes, your wish will come true. She bravely decides to do so but dies when she has more than 600 left to fold. Her classmates, inspired by her courage, continue folding paper cranes and also erect a peace statue in her name. Recommended age 7 years and up.

Ellis, D. (2000). *The breadwinner*. Toronto, Ontario, Canada: Groundwood Books.

This is the first in a series of three books about Afghanistan, just before and after the Taliban rule was overthrown by the American army. The first one introduces us to 10-year-old Parvana, who is forced to dress as a young boy and go out and earn a living, because under the Taliban rule, no women or girls are allowed to work outside the home, let alone even go out unescorted by a male relative. The offense of being caught with a male who is not a relative could be fatal. Recommended age 8 years and up.

Ellis, D. (2002). *Parvana's journey*. Toronto, Ontario, Canada: Groundwood Books.

This is the second in the series and talks about how Parvana loses her family and goes in search of them. She begins to walk across Afghanistan to the border, across the hardest and most difficult terrain. Along the way, she gathers a family of her own: 10-year-old Asif, a boy who has lost a leg to a land mine; 6-year-old Leila, who they find living with her grandmother's decomposing body; and a 10-month-old baby, who Parvana finds in an abandoned village. Recommended age 8 years and up.

Ellis, D. (2004). *Mud-City*. Toronto, Ontario, Canada: Groundwood Books.

This story, although not directly about Parvana, connects with the other two books as it is about Parvana's best friend, Shauzia, who is left behind in the refugee camp and dreams of going to Paris. Recommended age 8 years and up.

Frank, A. (1993). *Anne Frank: The diary of a young girl.* (Introduction by E. Roosevelt; B. M. Mooyaart, Trans.). New York: Bantam Books. (Original work published 1952)

This is the true story of Anne Frank, a 13-year old girl and her family who hid from the Nazis for 2 years. Written in the format of a personal diary, it tells her story as a first-person account.

Maruki, T. (1980). *Hiroshima no pika*. New York: Lothrop, Lee & Shepard Books.

This is the story of the atomic bomb dropped on Hiroshima, told from the point of view of Mii. The paintings are tragic and expansive, capturing the utter despair and dejection of the bombing. Recommended age 7 years and up.

Mochizuki, K. (1995). *Baseball saved us*. New York: Lee & Low Books.

During the Japanese internment in World War II, a young boy, "Shorty," and his friends at the camp, form a baseball team with the help of Shorty's father, to keep themselves engaged. The baseball games give them a purpose in life at the camp. Set at a time when Japanese Americans faced dire racism and hatred, the book shows them playing this all-American game. With beautiful language and stirring pictures, this book symbolizes the freedom that these internees yearn for. Recommended age 4 years and up.

Morrison, T., & Morrison, S. (1999). *The big box*. New York: Hyperion Books.

This is the story of three prototype children who "can't handle their freedom: and are hence locked up in a box, which only opens one way." It is a story where one can find one of the characteristics of these three in students in every classroom. Recommended age 7 years and up.

Nye, N. S. (1994). *Sitti's secrets*. New York: Aladdin Paperbacks

Young Mona travels to Palestine to visit her grandmother and upon her return is worried about events she sees on TV about the Israeli–Palestinian war. Recommended age 6 years and up.

Polacco, P. (1994). *Pink and Say*. New York: Philomel Books.

This is a Civil War story of a White boy and a Black boy who become friends, in spite of being on opposite sides of the war, when one saves the other. It is a very touching and tragic tale of friendship and redemption.

Shea, P. D. (1995). *The whispering cloth*. Honesdale, PA: Boyd Mills Press.

Young Mai is a Hmong refugee, living in the camp with her grandmother who earns a living stitching story cloths. Mai learns how to stitch from her and improves her craft so much that she is able to tell her own tragic story through the story cloth. This is a beautiful tale of liberation as Mai dreams of coming to America.

Wilkes, S. (1994). *One day we had to run!* Brookfield, CT: Millbrook Press.

These are actual accounts of three children, one each from Sudan, Somalia, and Ethiopia, and their journey by foot to Kenya over a period of a few months. It is a publication of the United Nations High Commissioner of Refugees. Recommended age 7 years and up.

REFERENCES

Booth, D., & Barton, B. (2000). *Story works: How teachers can use shared stories in the new curriculum*. Markham, Canada: Pembroke.

Giraldi, P. (2003, September 23). The jihadi war. *The American Conservative*.

GlobalSecurity.org. (n.d.). *Combat stress control in operations other than war*. Retrieved December 7, 2009, from http://www.globalsecurity.org/military/library/policy/army/fm/22–51/22–51_i.htm

Kiefer, B. (1995). The disturbing image in children's picture books: Fearful or fulfilling? In S. Lehr (Ed.), *Battling dragons: Issues and controversy in children's literature* (pp. 51–62). Portsmouth, NH: Heinemann.

Lehr, S. (Ed.). (1995). *Battling dragons: Issues and controversy in children's literature*. Portsmouth, NH: Heinemann.

Zinn, H. (2001). *Howard Zinn on war*. New York: Seven Stories Press.

Zinn, H. (2002). *Terrorism and war*. New York: Seven Stories Press.

Chapter 8

Prejudice, Bullying, Abuse, and Other Challenging Situations

Kimberly Persiani-Becker

Today's children and young adults are exposed to so much more than those from previous generations. Whether this is a result of perceptions of childhood or whether it is a result of children themselves being more mature, there is certainly a feeling that children nowadays lose their "childhood" a lot faster. Although it is true that children have always faced their share of social and challenging situations, such as poverty, abuse, divorce, abandonment, and so on, these situations have not been the focus of many children's books in the past. If there have been stories on these situations, these have been mostly fantasy tales that usually end on a hopeful note so that children find a happy ending. In fact, the popular traditional tales that were originally written as cautionary tales to scare or warn children into good behavior have been watered down to such an extent that their original message is usually lost. Traditionally, as these tales were "off the folk" (therefore called folktales), they may have had some element of social relevance and truth to their original versions, which are more than 1,000 years old in some cases and hard to trace. Therefore, although these stories talk about real situations that children may have been in, such as *Cinderella* (child labor, poverty), *Hansel and Gretel* or *Snow White* (abandonment, child abuse), and Little Red Riding Hood (bullying), these stories are not known for those situations today. In this chapter, real situations such as poverty, bullying, child abuse, child labor, abandonment, and so on, are discussed with a focus on contemporary multicultural literature that relates to these situations. These situations could be called "social realities" as they are a development of the current and past society, whose reality includes many of these situations and some recent ones, such as divorce. In short, this chapter focuses on books related to social realities and challenging situations occurring at home and at school.

DEFINING AND DISCUSSING CHALLENGING SITUATIONS

One of the objectives of educators and caring teachers has been to work effectively with students from diverse backgrounds in all grade levels. One way to do this is to become more familiar with some of the challenging situations that students confront in their worlds today. And while many of these struggles have been around forever, it's only recently that such situations have been brought to the forefront for discussion in the classroom, a place where most children feel safe and familiar. Some of these more apparent and relevant realities and challenges include, but are not limited to, bullying, poverty, abuse, and child labor. There are many others, such as divorce and abandonment, that are also faced by youngsters every day.

Although some might think that we should shelter children from these realities or challenging situations for as long as possible, others would argue that without giving children the opportunity to address these in safe environments such as classrooms, they will never have the means to deal with such experiences. Further, children today also show an earlier sophistication in regard to noticing and talking about situations taking place at school and at home, perhaps because of the access to information that they have on television, the Internet, and other mass media. Unfortunately, some educators simply don't know where to start and how involved they should become in opening discussions about such critical situations. For example, combating prejudices about those different than oneself is a behavior that needs to be addressed early in life so it does not spill into adulthood. More specifically, bullying is one of those behaviors that stems directly from having certain prejudices and ought to be taught in conjunction with one another. In order to eliminate such behavior, teachers and parents alike find themselves addressing these consistently throughout a school year. Introducing rich literature to children is one way to encourage dialogue and reflection as a means of combating such behaviors, including the development of prejudices.

In fact, one could go so far as to say that one of the objectives of children's authors in writing multicultural children's literature has been to reflect authentically the situations and challenges that the children and youth of today face on a daily basis. Teachers and educators, therefore, can use meaningful resources, such as multicultural and rich literature, to encourage discussions around bullying, poverty, abuse, divorce, abandonment, and child labor, and other situations plaguing our children at school and at home, as a means to help them make decisions about repeating negative behavior in the future. In the following sections of this chapter, each challenging situation is explored, offering exemplary literature that may help to discuss those with students.

PREJUDICE

Rather than focus on others' differences as a means to use them, "When teachers confront prejudice actively in [elementary school] settings, the classroom can be a place where children celebrate diversity" (Araujo & Strasser, 2003, p. 178). Knowing the diverse backgrounds of the students in our classrooms and using their unique circumstances to drive our teaching will not only introduce them to their many wonderful differences, but it will also shine a light on the abundance of similarities they share across ethnicities, gender, ability levels, and so on. Doing this not only creates a more cohesive space for everyone to be themselves but also opens the door to all students as they share their lives and experiences, which in turn will lend itself to combatting stereotyping and misunderstandings often associated with prejudice.

> Capitalizing on the diversity of our students will enhance our joy of teaching. The nation is enriched by the ethnic, cultural, and linguistic diversity among its citizens and within schools. Every year we will work with a group of different individuals, each with unique challenges and gifts, so each class we teach will be completely different. (Zarrillo, 2008, p. 27)

This means that each year, we will benefit best if we get to know our students and then develop an environment where general stereotyping, which can lead to prejudice, ridicule, and even bullying if not addressed, is less of an issue due to our immediate recognition of students' uniqueness, personal stories, and experiences. Oftentimes, bringing something unknown to the surface and talking about it is a way to dispel any myths about it. Taking away the power of something typically used as offensive helps to make it less of an issue.

Many of the characteristics that young people draw on when they consciously or unconsciously develop prejudices and then use them against one another might include the following: race and skin tone, gender, clothes and dress or economic privilege, ethnic names, children with special needs, size including height and weight, sports ability level, academic ability level, and many others. For example, it may be common for students to change their native given name to an "American name" because they don't want to face discrimination for having a different sounding name or a name that is difficult to pronounce. A story like *The Name Jar,* by Yangsook Choi, is a good choice in explaining why a child might want to change his or her name while also being respectful of it. In schools, there is often ridicule associated with having a "cultural" or "native" name that is hard to pronounce, and this can lead to being bullied.

Campbell - not really a lot of students have ethnic names - no one says anything

Another common point of prejudice or discrimination is when students, who may have just immigrated or migrated recently, are struggling with speaking English or connecting with the flow of their new school. Stories like *La Mariposa*, by Francisco Jimenez, for the younger kids, or *Esperanza Rising*, by Pam Muñoz Ryan, for older readers, can serve as excellent discussion starters and introductions to the rest of the students who might not understand what it means to move from one place to another, have difficulty with the language, and have to make friends with strangers, while dealing with the challenges of a new home and neighborhood.

One of the most noticeable differences are skin color and racial features, which may become topics of prejudice or discrimination, especially in an early childhood setting. If this has caused students to wonder why they are all different in this way or if there has been a kind of altercation between students, a teachable moment such as this could benefit from a story like *Blue and the Gray*, by Eve Bunting. In this picture book for older elementary children, two young friends, one Black and one White, explore the grassy fields near the construction site of their new homes. They learn that the area was a Civil War battleground, as the father of one of the boys talks about the freedom that was won so long ago, a freedom that allows them to be friends today. Another usable story by Eve Bunting, which addresses race, language, and culture, is *One Green Apple*. In this picture book for all ages, a young girl named Farah feels alone, even when people surround her. She listens and nods but doesn't speak. She has just arrived from another country and doesn't know the language. On a field trip to an apple orchard, Farah discovers that there are lots of things here that are similar to home. As she helps the class make apple cider, Farah connects with the other students and begins to feel that she belongs. This story is relevant to youngsters today in so many ways. And because racial differences tend to comprise much of the prejudices we deal with in classrooms today, having access to such quality literature as these two selections not only helps address the issue more successfully and relevantly, but it also offers a place for students to safely discuss traditionally taboo topics like race and culture.

In addition to stories about language, race, culture, immigration, and migration, other prejudices young people develop about others include topics like image-related issues, economic privilege, and more. *The Hundred Dresses*, by Eleanor Estes, is the perfect choice for chapter book readers. Although the text is not difficult to read, the topic of prejudice and understanding is something relatable to many age ranges. In this classic novel, Wanda faces mockery at school, both because of her "funny" last name, Petronski, and her claims that she has 100 dresses at home, even though she wears the same one to school each day. This heartfelt story is both endearing and tangible as it highlights the reality of discrimination that occurs because of how someone dresses or where one comes from. In addition to this book, *One Fat Summer*, by Robert Lipsyte, is one of those stories that makes one really consider his or her own biases about how people look. This is a good story about the pressures one boy faces due to his obesity, which is not unlike many of our youth today. The story gives older readers a good sense about what Bobby is thinking as he's being taunted and ridiculed by his peers. Similar stories for older elementary and early secondary grade students include more recent titles, such as *Fat Kid Rules the World*, by K. L. Going, and *Fat Girl*, by Marilyn Sachs. Both of these stories include experiences of boys and girls who feel inadequate and unaccepted due to their size while being made fun of and criticized by their peers.

Introducing these topics could also draw unwanted attention to those that suffer from obesity

BULLYING

Consider the following two scenarios:

> Ms. Mori was teaching fifth grade. Toward the end of the year, when two of her young ladies who identify as Muslim began covering their heads once they turned 12, some of the boys in the class began to bully them while on the playground. This went on for days. Ms. Mori did not know what to do. Another teacher told her about a book by Naomi Shihab Nye titled, *Sitti's Secrets*. She read aloud the story to her class and continued with a discussion about the tradition of head coverings. Once the boys understood what was happening, it took the power away from them. Oftentimes, people tease or torment others when they are unaware of the reason for a situation.

> Mr. Jackson began teaching in a class of third graders while he was finishing his teaching credential program. He was in a wheelchair and the children were quite taken aback upon his entry to their class. At recess, several of the students were making fun of Mr. Jackson, which a group of girls heard and relayed to him. Rather than get upset and lash out at the group who was making fun of him, Mr. Jackson decided it was the perfect opportunity to share the book, *Our Teacher's in a Wheelchair*, by Mary Powers. Although this book is hard to find today, there are many more just as wonderful to read aloud, like Mr. Jackson did, as a way to allow the children to talk openly about their concerns rather than tease him, because bullying is only a form of fear.

These two scenarios portray some of the types of bullying that occur in schools today. These scenes are not specific just toward children but also toward teachers, staff, administrators, parents, and others. Being bullied can easily result in the crushing of a person's spirit. Because teachers, parents, and administrators alike have worked hard to make schools safe and accepting of all people, they also have the power to fight against destructive behavior often associated with bullying. They can begin by gathering the children to introduce relevant books with a critical look at what bullying is, how it feels to be bullied, and how to avoid being bullied, such as stopping one's own conduct. In the cases of Ms. Mori and Mr. Jackson, the teachers chose to address bullying by using books to lead the topic and discussion. These two examples are the epitome of what is often referred to as a "teachable moment."

Bullying is an experience many of us can relate to. According to Lingren (1997), "about one in seven school children, that's about 5 million kids, has been either a bully or a victim." The sayings "boys will be boys" or "it's a common part of growing up" can no longer be tolerated in dismissing this serious behavior.

> It is an early form of aggressive and violent behavior that can be persistent over long periods of time. It is true that bullies tend to grow to be aggressive adults who stand a much higher chance than average of obtaining multiple criminal convictions. (Entenman, Murnen, & Hendricks, 2005, p. 352)

According to the *Webster's New World Dictionary* (1986), a *bully* is "a person who hurts, frightens, or tyrannizes over those who are smaller and weaker" It can be said that one who identifies this way consciously and willfully acts aggressively or manipulates one or more people against another person or people. This doesn't even include the potential of physical mistreatment as a sense of power to intimidate or dominate others. This can just as easily be accomplished through words as through physical harm.

Sadly, bullying can take many forms, like being teased; having homework, money, or school supplies stolen; or receiving insults, threats, or kicks. A child who endures this may become afraid, depressed, withdrawn, or angry. "A bullied child may avoid school, lose his or her appetite, have nightmares, or want to carry a protection item such as a knife" (Entenman et al., 2005, p. 253).

Because so much of bullying occurs at school, the role of the teacher in confronting this issue is critical. Although most teachers encounter instances of bullying between their students and even toward themselves, they aren't always equipped to deal with it, especially if they have little or no training in intervention. Others fear they may make the situation worse by getting involved. With this in mind, teachers can look for typical signs and be proactive in discontinuing this kind of aggression. In particular, teachers will benefit by having access to several of the books available that can be used to discourage bullying and aggressive behavior among students.

Choosing appropriate books to share with students to address bullying is essential in combating this problem. Anything too "cutesy" or "over the top" will take away from the issue, and anything too complex or too simplistic for older students can cause them to lose the concept altogether. So, when choosing appropriate books, use some of Jalongo's (1983, p. 32) guidelines, as described here:

- Can the children [and/or young adults] identify with the plot, setting, dialogue, and characters?
- Does the book use correct terminology, psychologically sound explanations, and portray events accurately?
- Are the origins of emotional reactions revealed and inspected?
- Does the book reflect an appreciation for the individual differences?
- Are good coping strategies modeled for the child?

Further, Entenman et al. (2005, p. 356) also added the following points:

- Does the book present crises in an optimistic, surmountable fashion?
- Does the story line avoid stereotypes?
- Does the plot appear realistic as opposed to the dramatic or implausible?

Because research supports the notion that bullying plays a big role in schools today, educators are often confronted with a range of incidents among students. In such situations, teachers must decide how best to address the problems associated with bullying. Children's literature is an appropriate tool and is effective in helping children and young adults resolve problems. Galda and Cullinan (2002) stated that "Literature prompts students to explore their own feelings. They gain insight into human experience and begin to understand themselves better" (p. 8). Bullying starts early. A story that is simple, colorful, and comprehensible for very young children in this regard might be *The Ant Bully*, by John Nickle. In this story, Lucas, who "wore funny glasses and a strange hat," is made fun of by Sid, the neighborhood bully. Unable to strike back, Lucas instead attacks the ants with his squirt gun and learns a hard lesson when they fight back. Eventually, he wins the trust of his new companions and returns home. Older children, such as those in the first through third grades, might relate to *King of the Playground*, by Phyllis Reynolds Naylor. In this story, the playground bully, Sammy, does not like to share his space, and he won't let Kevin use the swings or the slide or the monkey bars. Kevin finally stands up to Sammy and gets to use the playground. There are few children who wouldn't be able to relate to this story either as the victim or the perpetrator.

While bullying does start early, simple picture books like those mentioned offer understandable story lines. For upper elementary and middle school students, titles such as *Jake Drake, Bully Buster*, by Andrew Clements, and *The Bully*, by Paul Langan, as well as *The Chocolate War*, by Robert Cormier, for high school readers, are other examples that introduce us to characters who are being bullied and the ways in which they overcome the obstacles. These kinds of stories offer an outlet for those being bullied as well as insight for those who do the bullying. This is a serious issue taking place at schools, in neighborhoods, and in homes. Making time to dialogue about something like this allows for fears to be addressed, aggression to be noted, and potential problem solving to occur.

Is reading aloud a book about a teacher in a wheelchair going to cure the bullies of the world? Probably not. But if all teachers consistently include such books and critical discussion openly in their classrooms, especially in the early years as the children are molded and impressionable, chances are children and young adults will have a more clear consciousness about how they talk about and treat others. And although bullying is an issue that occurs way too often, which many young people have to contend with, there are other realities they are also dealing with, such as those who come from disadvantaged homes and impoverished communities.

There is also a risk of placing too much attention on negative behaviors, which in turn, encourages those behaviors

→ *especially at a middle school level*

POVERTY

For children, poverty can be a very difficult situation to handle, as usually there is extreme discrimination associated with poor or homeless people. Although schools and classrooms are supposed to be safe havens and a level playing field for children, they are reminded of poverty and class differences on a daily basis when they see other students with something they want, or when they are aware of their deficiencies in hygiene and nutrition, or when they are socially stigmatized, sometimes even by school authorities. Sometimes, they see adults in their lives also model discrimination against people who are homeless or poor. Although most of this can be explained away as the tough times we live in and safety issues around talking with strangers and so on, confusing messages are often passed on to children. Addressing these kinds of potential prejudices with literature consistently through their schooling years can be a natural and realistic way to bring these concerns to the forefront of thought as a way to dispel images and preconceived notions children might have. In fact, there may be valuable lessons that all students can gain by reading about some of the barriers and challenges that children in poverty face and overcome on a daily basis. Given some good titles, teachers can validate the realities of students living in poverty and the impact of it on learning and society.

Middle school books such as *Bud, Not Buddy,* by Christopher Paul Curtis, a story about a 10-year-old boy who lives in a bad foster home environment in Flint, Michigan, during the Great Depression, and escapes and sets out in search of the man he believes to be his father, is one every school and classroom library ought to have in its collection. Another serious story for this grade level can be found with

Gracie's Girl, by Ellen Wittlinger. At the start of sixth grade, Bess is on the path to "be cool." She knows she will get a lot of attention this year, at least more than she gets from her parents who overschedule themselves. Her mom is a teacher, her dad a lawyer, and both of them feel strongly about volunteering for a soup kitchen. Bess sometimes feels like she would have to eat out of a dumpster before they'd notice her. At one point, she meets an elderly woman named Gracie who actually does eat other people's tossed out food. Bess begins to realize there are real human faces belonging to the people her parents serve at the soup kitchen. Soon she and her best friend, Ethan, are involved in Gracie's life and help establish a shelter for homeless women. Bess manages to make new friends and make a difference. Because children of this age are in the midst of their search for identity, and they want to be recognized while being invisible, grown up while still being a kid, Bess's story is one that can serve as a realistic picture of how helping others less fortunate than us makes us feel better about ourselves. It helps us recognize our own privileges and the circumstances we might take for granted.

For younger children, the multicultural picture book, *Beatrice's Goat,* by Page McBrier, introduces us to Beatrice, who is very happy to accept her family's new fat, sleek goat when it arrives in her poor Ugandan village. She feels lucky because the goat bears two kids and provides enough milk to feed the family and be sold for profit. Until they brought the goat home, life was very hard for Beatrice and her five brothers and sisters. The family could not afford to send the children to school, and it was difficult to make ends meet. This one animal opens up a new world of wealth and prosperity. Before the year is out, Beatrice gets to go to school and her family moves to a sturdy new house. Again, a story like this offers a view into the life of a young girl who would be grateful for the chance to go to school while many of our own young learners today take such a thing for granted.

Another socially conscious picture book available is *A Castle on Viola Street,* by Dyanne DiSalvo, where we learn of the importance of community and home life. Andy lives with his parents and two younger sisters in a cramped apartment that is cold in winter. His father rises before dawn each day to go to work, believing that things will change eventually. His mother's positive outlook keeps them going too. Once Andy learns of an organization that helps people build homes, his family joins the effort to refurbish a nearby abandoned home. Because of this selfless effort, Andy's family ends up being able to move into the next house the group tackles. Although most students have their basic needs met, such as shelter, food, and clothing, not all do. Introducing characters and story lines where a person without much is willing to still give to others is the kind of example we want to set for today's youth.

In another important multicultural picture book, *A Shelter in Our Car,* by Monica Gunning, we meet 8-year-old Zettie, better known to other children as "Junk Car Zettie." After her father died, Zettie and her mother left Jamaica in search of education and a better life in America. They now live in an old car. This picture book brings close the harsh realities of being homeless, scavenging for food, washing in the park restroom, and being harassed by police. Zettie wakes up to blaring sirens and flashing lights, washing in cold water in a park restroom, being bullied by boys at school, and feeling hungry and unhappy. Spending time with a friend who is also homeless and having a reassuring encounter with a concerned policeman bring comfort at crucial moments, but the girl's life is not an easy one. Eventually, her mother spends a day helping at a health fair and not only becomes more hopeful for her children's future but also obtains a job, which leads to a bed and shower in a motel. Children will be moved by Zettie's story and relieved that there are people out there willing to offer a helping hand. This kind of story is important for those children who can relate but also for those more fortunate who can help. It's the kind of story teachers might use to create an opportunity for students to come together and adopt a family in need or pull together a collection of clothes and money to help those in the school community who are in need of a boost.

For high school students considering their future, *Nickel and Dimed,* by Barbara Ehrenreich, is a must read. She takes us on a journey through the workforce's bottom rung. She seeks answers to how anyone could make ends meet on $7 an hour. She gives up her middle-class life as a journalist, except for $1,000 in start-up funds, a car, and her laptop computer, as she sets out to live the life of a low-skilled worker for a month at a time. She worked as a waitress in Key West, Florida, as a cleaning woman and a nursing home aide in Portland, Maine, and as a clerk in a Wal-Mart in Minneapolis, Minnesota. She endures the telling experience of the application process, drug tests, and personality tests. Overwhelmed by transportation costs and high rents, she learns the tricks of the trade from those she works with, some of whom sleep in their cars, work even when their arthritis is in full gear, have back pain or worse. All the while they still manage small gestures of kindness. Despite the advantages of her race, education, and good health, and the fact that she had no children to provide for, her income barely covered her monthly expenses. This journey is humbling and real as she gives readers much to consider about those caught in the economy's undertow, even in good times. Her story will give high school students a clear picture of what faces them if they don't think about furthering their education.

Through the use of relevant picture books, nonfiction accounts, and multicultural literature, teachers can have a positive impact on the lives of students by validating their real-life circumstances in an effort to get them to read their surroundings so that they can become change agents for their own lives. It's also an opportunity for those children and young adults to help those in need, especially when they don't know what steps to take. It is, therefore, important for teachers to bring books like these into the classroom, as without them, it is hard for many students to even begin to fathom the serious struggles to get out of poverty. Reading such books in the classroom and then following through with real action may help young people not only empathize with the characters, but more specifically, they may begin to help others.

ABUSE

Beyond poverty, our children take on even more challenging situations in their young lives. Abuse is an issue that some children deal with on a daily basis. Administrators and teachers aren't even all that comfortable talking amongst themselves about it, much less addressing the topic in a classroom, but it is an issue that is very real and very serious. Though the educators in their lives might be uncomfortable, many youngsters not only endure physical and verbal abuse, but they also witness the abuse of drugs and alcohol within their own homes. Never having a chance to consider alternatives of dealing with stress in one's life outside of these kinds of abuses will only perpetuate these cycles as these children grow up.

How does a teacher delicately bring up the topic of abuse? Should it be discussed in the classroom? Should it be a social reality shared with one's peers? Should it be a specific lesson taught to the whole class? Is it an ongoing unit appropriate for the classroom? Or is there a simpler way to let those who are going through it know they are not alone? Books are often one of the most appropriate tools to use in putting such issues on the table. Whether it be reading aloud picture books or assigning chapter books for literature discussions, children and young adults will be more apt to dialogue about such an important concern when they know it isn't themselves they are discussing. This kind of reading and conversation allows for them to consider their options, be it as one who is living the reality or one who knows someone who is, by focusing on characters in a book, rather than themselves. After visiting the stories of others, children and young adults will then have more of an understanding with which to make decisions about their own circumstances or that of others as a means to avoid taking on the same behavior for themselves. Sadly, but thankfully, there are many books available to children and young adults that take this social reality to heart.

Physical and Emotional Abuse

Publishers Weekly ("Call Me Hope," 2007) reminds us that anyone who equates child abuse only with physical contact may reconsider such thoughts after reading a book like *Call Me Hope*, by Gretchen Olson. It's a heart-wrenching story of a sixth-grade girl tormented by her mother's hurtful words. Hope's father left when she was a baby. Her mother told her it was because Hope "cried all the time." Since then, she has been called stupid so often that she gets a "stinkin' stomachache" every time she hears the word. She can't seem to do anything to make her mother happy. Fortunately, Hope has some people in her corner. Hope's teacher, her school counselor, and her classmate Brody believe she does have worth. After making friends with two kind women who run a used clothing store and being greatly affected and inspired by Anne Frank's diary, Hope gradually begins to believe in herself. She does this even when her mother hands out her cruelest punishment by not allowing Hope to take part in the outdoor school program. This story is an example of where the protagonist's future will be considerably brighter than her past. Children who can identify with Hope's situation will find solace in this book as well as tips for survival, listed by Hope in the final chapter.

This name "Hope" itself speaks volumes, and in *A Child Called "It,"* by David Pelzer, and its sequel, *Lost Boy: A Foster Child's Search for the Love of a Family,* hope is all this child has as he crawls out of a desperate situation of abuse by his mother over a period of many years. Very powerful books like these must not be read without a teacher or parent for support, but they are both intelligent and poignant reads for older students and can be used for discussion about perseverance and courage.

Drug and Alcohol Abuse

Physical and emotional abuse are only a couple of ways that parents and caretakers affect children. Alcoholism and drug abuse also tend to create chaos in the home lives of young people. It can best be stated by the Phoenix House Center on Addiction and the Family (2008):

> In families where alcohol or other drugs are being abused, behavior is frequently unpredictable and communication is unclear. Family life is characterized by chaos and unpredictability. Behavior can range from loving to withdrawn to crazy. Structure and rules may be either nonexistent or inconsistent. Children, who may not understand that their parents' behavior and mood are determined by the amount of alcohol or other drugs in their bloodstream, can feel confused and insecure. They love their parents and worry about them, and yet feel angry and hurt that their parents do not love them enough to stop using.

These children suffer greatly and often blame themselves for their parents' substance abuse. Often their parents say they wouldn't drink or take drugs if the children didn't argue or kept the house clean or got better grades. Some children think that if they get good grades or keep the house clean or get along with their siblings, the parents will change. Others withdraw, in the hope that a quiet and calm home will keep their parents from drinking. Few realize that they cannot cause a parent to drink or use drugs, and they cannot cure a parent's substance problem. The feelings of fright, loneliness, and shame play a huge role in the lives of young people. Not only do they feel responsible in some ways, but they also feel alone.

A few titles that might be of great comfort for older readers to help them realize that they are not alone or the cause of their parents' substance abuse choices are *Jude*, by Kate Morgenroth, *Bottled Up*, by Jaye Murray, and *Lush*, by Natasha Friend. These three stories introduce readers to three teens going through many issues related to their parents' substance abuse. They feel guilty, neglected, and embarrassed, but in the end, they realize they can make it in the world without falling into step and becoming abusers themselves. They also realize that they are worthy of good things and good experiences. Their gripping stories are moving and horrifying as their lives include the quest for acceptance and their capacity for hope and resilience, which is a common desire for any young person going through this same thing.

This is a hard topic to broach with younger children because they may not have the maturity to distinguish between substance abuse and occasional use. For example, children may worry when they see their parents have a half a glass of red wine with dinner some nights. Yet when talking about the issue of drug and alcohol abuse, it's natural for children who don't have much context to perhaps assume their parents or caregivers fit into one of the substance abuse categories. A story such as *Dear Kids of Alcoholics*, by Lindsey Hall, is one that some children will be able to relate to. Although it is a bit dated, this story is about a young boy named Jason whose father is an alcoholic. Jason explains facts about alcoholism and his dad's sensitivity to alcohol, destructive behavior, and recovery process. Jason shows what it's like for children with a parent who drinks too much.

Another story that will make an impact on young people's lives, *Emmy's Question*, by Jeannine Auth, is about a 9-year-old girl whose mother is an alcoholic. Emmy has heard arguments at night through her parents' bedroom wall, and her mom doesn't act like other mothers, but Emmy doesn't want anyone to know. Then she finds a wine bottle hidden in her toy chest, but she doesn't tell her dad. Emmy tries to keep her mom's drinking a secret from her friends at school, but everybody finds out anyway. Emmy tries to pretend that everything is okay, but the kids tease her on the playground and some of the parents won't let them play with her anymore. She thinks that things can't get much worse until her parents decide to divorce. Emmy does end up getting counseling and realizes she is not alone. This kind of book reaches out to the 11 million children in America who live through this kind of situation every day. And although teachers may not always feel comfortable reading a story like this, these kinds of books are excellent tools for teaching about alcoholism and how it affects families. They can also be used to encourage readers to talk about their own feelings and experiences as children of alcoholics.

Abuse, whether it is physical, emotional, or entails the abuse of substances, is a real experience that our young people are living through. They may be dealing with this in secret or openly. No matter the circumstances, they need to feel protected and know that there are others out there going through this that are making it. And even though books are only one way to reach out to them, literature has a powerful influence in reader's lives and can help take away some of the burdens, especially if the connection to text unfolds into dialogue and a request for help.

DIVORCE

As stated in Jayson (2005), "Couples who once might have wed and then divorced now are not marrying at all [in order to avoid divorce], according to 'The State of Our Unions 2005,'" an annual report that analyzes census and other data. (See the 2009 report at http://www.virginia.edu/marriageproject/pdfs/Union_11_25_09.pdf) At a time in our nation when we are trying to set a moral example for our children, what does this say for what so many of our children are going through when their parents either divorce or don't find marriage of value? In addition, for every 1,000 married women, 17.7 of those women divorce, whereas marriage itself among women is down 50% since 1970 (Jayson, 2005). What does this say about the state of children being raised in homes across the country?

David Popenoe, coauthor of the "The State of Our Unions 2005" report, shows concern that cohabitation is on the upswing: "As society shifts from marriage to cohabitation—which is what's happening—you have an increase in family instability" (cited in Jayson, 2005). This is in light of the report's statistics, which show that "cohabiting couples have twice the breakup rate of married couples" and that "40% of those couples bring kids into these often-shaky live-in relationships" (Jayson, 2005). But at the same time, Popenoe also reminds us that "many European countries have higher cohabitation rates, divorce rates in those countries are lower, and more children grow up with both biological parents, even though the parents may not be married." Although this is seen as good news to many, we can't ignore the fact that "the United States has the lowest percentage among Western nations of children who grow up with both biological parents, 63%" (Jayson, 2005). According to Popenoe, "The United States has the weakest families in the Western world because we have the highest divorce rate and the highest rate of solo parenting." From this we know that more and more children are either being raised by one parent, by an extended family, or are sharing time between households. This kind of social reality contributes greatly to children's feelings of isolation, while going through the process of the parents' separation, and they need to know they are not alone and that it is not their fault that their parents are no longer together. They can benefit from hearing stories about other children going through similar situations. There are several available for a variety of ages, with a variety of characters with whom children and young adults can identify.

In *Was It the Chocolate Pudding? A Story for Little Kids About Divorce*, by Sandra Levins, a book meant for young children, the concept of divorce and joint custody is described in a child-friendly way. Two young brothers attempt to comprehend why their parents no longer live together and why the boys shuttle back and forth between them. Although this real-life circumstance affects many children today, parents often don't know how to talk to their own children about what is or has happened to their family. For concerned parents trying to help their own child understand divorce, this is a good choice for opening up such a conversation about the adjustment the family must make. Teachers and librarians might choose to put together a list of titles for this purpose if they know that children in their class or at their school are dealing with such an adult situation.

Another very special and very rich piece of literature that is less than obvious in its approach is *I Don't Want to Talk About It: A Story About Divorce for Young Children,* by Jeanie Franz and Kathryn Finney. The story helps children reflect on the full range of feelings they might experience when the family is confronting divorce, including anger, grief, fear, and loneliness. This book comes from a child's perspective as she confronts her basic concerns about the reasons for the divorce and about what life will be like afterward. The story draws from the welcoming images of animals that young children relate to. This story reassures children that it is normal to feel as fierce as a crocodile or want to roar as loud as a lion or fly away like a bird. Most importantly, it emphasizes that divorce does not change parents' love and commitment regarding their children. For any of us who have experienced such a difficult situation as divorce, it's easy to relate to the many emotions attached to it. Most scary for children might be the feeling that they are responsible for their parents' break-up. A story like this shows that is not true.

In another relevant and very serious book, one for older children, another child must endure big changes in her life because of her parents' divorce. In the *Divorce Express,* by Paula Danziger, readers are introduced to Phoebe, who has to leave her New York City apartment and friends, move to the country with her dad, and take the bus every weekend to visit her mom in the city. She has to attend ninth grade in a new school. She witnesses her father's dating. The biggest struggle is not feeling like she really belongs with the kids in either place. This story is one very similar to many children in today's world. Trying to find oneself while being pulled in many directions is not easy for any child. A book such as this gives readers a chance to know others are experiencing the same thing and that, given time, one will find a place to call home, even if it is a combination of two places.

For children in the upper to middle grades, a book like *It's Not the End of the World,* by Judy Blume, is a must-have on library and classroom bookshelves. It's a story about a young lady named Karen, a sixth grader who tries desperately to get her parents in the same room together in the hope of helping them reconcile their marriage. Once her father moves out and plans to go to Las Vegas for a divorce, Karen realizes she has only a few days to get the two of them together in the same room so they would just forget about the divorce. However, after some time, she realizes that sometimes people who shouldn't be apart are impossible together. This isn't an uncommon sentiment, but it is not often realized as easily by the children who are affected by their parents' separation.

There are too many children in our classrooms who experience this same thing. Divorce is part of every single child's life in one way or another, be it friends whose parents are divorced, a family member, their own parents. or their parents' friends. This issue is not going away and it is one that children need to know they can discuss. Books like these bring the topic to the forefront of thought and open the door for young people to talk about their feelings and their own reality in regard to divorce.

There seem to be no books on the market to show children how to go about bringing their parents back together successfully, as it is not their fault that their parents are separated or divorced, and it is not their place to initiate such a reconciliation. However, there are many books, as illustrated here, that do show these children that they are not alone and provide some advice on how to handle such enormous changes in their lives, through the actions of characters in the stories. Because divorce can be a frightening, embarrassing, and emotional topic to discuss, using these books to create a space for general conversation shows that it is okay to share experiences and talk about such tough issues.

Abandonment

Because divorce is such an ever-present topic in our lives today, it's no wonder that children fear being abandoned by one parent or the other. In a divorce, the children are the ones who usually suffer most and experience great confusion and hurt. More importantly, they have questions about who will take care of them, where they will live, if the parent they don't reside with will visit them, and they wonder, if life gets difficult again, will the parent they do live with leave them. Said children often take on a tremendous amount of stress to do the right thing, behave, go above and beyond the call of duty, and even become the caretaker for the parent they live with in hopes that he or she will not leave them. These are real concerns for children of divorce, and that sense of abandonment is lonely and terrifying. In several of the picture books discussed earlier, these questions are dealt with both subtly and obviously.

Besides children of divorce who fear being left alone, children who live with extended family, because their own parents are unable to care for them, are also affected. This can be due to financial reasons, crime, death, or choice. There are many children today living with aunts and uncles, grandparents, or in foster care who are constantly feeling that they have been abandoned and wish desperately for their parents to come for them. Developing a sense of "home" or consistency in their lives must be difficult.

No matter what the age of a child, there is a real possibility that these kids will never be reunited with their parents. And if so, there is even more pressure on them to be the "ideal child," so as not to be left again. Whether children are a product of divorce, left to be raised by someone other than a parent, or have had a parent walk out on the family for one reason or another, they feel alone, not just because they have been abandoned by a parent, but because they don't think anyone else is going through the same thing. Some may even hide their circumstances out of embarrassment. Knowing someone else is in your shoes and that that person has triumphed makes the situation more hopeful for the one living it. Reading books and stories about children just like themselves and who have found a way to survive is one way to make that fear of being alone or abandoned turn into hope.

The Decoding of Lana Morris, by Laura McNeal and Tom McNeal, is about a young woman of 16 who moves into a new foster home where four kids with special needs already reside. Unfortunately, she is living in a home where her new foster parents have a struggling marriage and a boy next door comes over with mean friends, while Lana tends to the other four kids in the house. One of her main issues is that she believes she is in love with her foster father. This story for older kids is not a pretty picture of foster care. And although it is also not a typical foster care situation, it is one that exists and speaks to those who can relate.

The Decoding of Lana Morris is ultimately hopeful, even though the story includes adult betrayal and humiliation, teen confusion and fear, and acts of cruelty and weakness. Because the writers explore difficult subjects, such as child abandonment, teen sexuality, and adult treachery, readers will be comforted that all these topics are dealt with sensitively and compassionately. For young adults who read this book, these issues should generate meaningful discussions and help them better understand such topics. Being able to talk about concepts like being abandoned, growing up in foster care, and having to find one's identity, is essential in offering a safe haven for these young adults to work through their problems and fears.

Another very poignant and real story is *Here Today,* by Ann Martin. This story for older elementary and middle school readers is about an 11-year-old girl in 1963, whose flamboyant mother abandons the family to pursue her dream of becoming an actress. Eleven-year-old Ellie takes charge of her younger siblings, while also trying to deal with her outcast status in school and frightening acts of prejudice toward the "misfits" that live on her street. Not only do many of our students relate to this situation of a parent leaving the family, but they can also relate to caring for younger siblings and hiding the fact that a parent has left the home to avoid ridicule. *Skate,* by Michael Harmon, is yet another very important story about a high school boy caring for his brother Sammy after his mother disappears on one of her drinking binges. Although both of these books are sad examples of young people being abandoned, the children still persevere, which makes them great stories that serve as a tool of triumph for others in the same situation.

Abandonment is such a serious issue for young people. The sense of loss and blame is truly a lonely place to be. So many children take on great responsibilities at very young ages when a parent leaves the home. Helping to care for their siblings, having to get part-time or full-time work to help pay the bills, having little or no private time or downtime are just a few of the repercussions these young people must deal with in such circumstances. And although most of these children are willing to help, sometimes going to school is the only time they have to escape it all. That being said, sharing stories with them about their real-life situations may not be the answer, but at least making stories like these available to them offers a mirror of hope into their lives.

CHILD LABOR

When one thinks of "child labor," the term may suggest sweatshops in countries afar, but many children's books of today tell stories of children at work who lead hard lives of poverty as they labor in country fields or city streets. These children are portrayed with a strong sense of "character, enterprising, hard-working and persevering, with a tremendous sense of responsibility to others, especially their families and younger siblings" (Lamme, 1998, p. 15).

Just like any other child, they have dreams of success later in life. Reading about similar characters in stories, cheering them on and wishing a better life for those they read about, can help them believe the same is possible for themselves.

Lamme (1998, p. 15) offered a handful of class activities that can be tailored to the appropriate grade level and might include the following:

Elementary Grades

- Ask students to write about their dreams, aspirations, and hopes for the future. What can they do now to make their dreams come true?
- Investigate the types of work or chores done by young girls and boys today. Are there gender differences in work opportunities? How about age? If so, why?

Elementary and Secondary Grades

- Explore the differences in work opportunities provided to people based on education. What types of education are needed for different careers?

Secondary Grades

- Invite students to explore the labor history of their own families, neighbors, and friends. What kinds of jobs did their grandparents have? At what ages did they enter the workforce? What were the working conditions like?
- Debate issues such as the age at which children should be permitted to work. Conduct inquiries into the problem of child labor today. Learn about activist organizations that protest child labor.
- Study the book illustrations. Then conduct a study of artwork in museums, books, or the Internet on the topic of child labor.

Child labor is nothing new. In some countries, it is a matter of a family's survival whereas in others, it is illegal, and in others, it is unspoken but very much a reality, as are the minimal pay and abusive working environments. That being said, child labor is not uncommon, and in some circumstances, it is a necessity if a family is to make it day-to-day. In *Sold,* by Patricia McCormick, we are introduced to Lakshmi, a 13-year-old girl who lives with her family in a small hut in a mountain village in Nepal. There is desperate poverty that threatens the lives of the villagers, and one day, Lakshmi's father brings her to a shopkeeper in town and tells Lakshmi that she is going to go work as a maid in India so that her wages can be sent home. This is a common occurrence in her hometown and many families prosper because of the opportunities afforded some of the girls; however, Lakshmi undertakes the long journey and arrives at "Happiness House" full of hope, only to discover the unthinkable truth: she has been sold into prostitution. We don't often see stories like this. Many of the stories we read are about families coming together to make ends meet, even if that means the children have to work. In this case, we do experience the danger in having children work, and this is a story that will hit the heart of many young adults as they take this journey with Lakshmi.

In other circumstances that are not much easier on the children, but certainly better situations, children find work to help their parents and families take care of the home. Ten-year-old Rebecca Putney, in *The Bobbin Girl,* by Emily McCully, works 12 hours a day in a factory mill, changing the bobbins on the sewing machines every hour. Rebecca comes from a single-parent family due to her father's death. Similarly, in *Peppe the Lamplighter,* by Elisa Bartone, Peppe has lost his mother, his dad is sick, and Peppe has seven sisters to consider. Peppe takes a job from a friend as a substitute street lamplighter to help the family financially. Another character, Mirette, who works for her mom, changing sheets and running errands in *Mirette on the High Wire,* by Emily McCully, decides to get up 2 hours earlier every morning so that she can practice her high-wire balancing skills and hopefully become a performer. These are just a few examples of stories that show children having to work to help their families while trying to better their own lives in the meantime.

Additionally, child laborers are not uncommon on American farms. Those who come from poverty often require that their children work in the fields as well so that the family can meet their needs financially. In fact, still in some parts of the world, school years begin late or end early so that the children in the family can help bring in money for the rest of the year. *Working Cotton* is a perfect example of this. Sherley Anne Williams exposes us to her own experience as a child in a migrant family and how she had to pick cotton all day long. The story tells of how the bus came early in the morning and picked up the cotton pickers at dark after a long day's work. Each member of the family worked side by side, taking care of the baby and earning a living (Lamme, 1998).

In many places around the world, children from poor communities don't always get the chance to earn an education. This is seen in *The Day of Ahmed's Secret* by Florence Parry and Judith Gilliland. Ahmed is a child vendor who drives a donkey-pulled cart and delivers heavy glass bottles of fuel to customers in present-day Cairo. Ahmed becomes the major money earner for his family. Throughout the story, we wait patiently to find out a secret Ahmed is keeping: He has learned how to write his name. This task is one taken for granted by many children in classrooms today, but it is such a critical lesson for these same children.

Rich literature about child labor can introduce children to problems of poverty and the unavoidable experience of child labor in some places. This literature can help humanize the poor and allow readers to develop empathy for people in those situations and create a sense of humility in them, thus making characters more real.

> Stories intrigue us, bind us to each other, give models of how to live and how not to live, and offer experiences we may never have in our lives . . . literature is not a miscellaneous pile of discrete works but a coherent structure in which works are related to each other like members of a large, extended family. (Baghban, 2002, p. 16)

It is clear that the social realities of today's children are greater and more complex than ever before. Although it is not in teachers' hands to fix all of the problems their students are confronting, we can create a classroom environment that offers a safe place for reading relevant and rich literature that is socially conscious and relatable to students, while opening the door for critical dialogue, so that no child feels alone or confused. Books pave the way for deeper understandings about the world we live in and are tools for helping young people see a way out by becoming change agents of their own reality. Literature has the power of bringing readers together for a common goal so that we can see the lives of others, share our own, and work with one another to make our lives just a little bit better. When teachers add lessons to their daily curriculum that include opportunities to respond to the literature, we are one step closer to all children having a voice and seeing alternative life choices through those of the characters in books.

REFLECTION QUESTIONS FOR THE TEACHER

1. What steps could I take to create a safe and healthy environment in my classroom for students to be able to discuss real and challenging issues and situations?

2. If I have students in my classroom who may be facing some of these real and challenging situations, what steps can I take to help them feel comfortable?

3. What "projects" could I start as a class to involve my students in facing and combating prejudice?

4. What "projects" or information could I give them to help connect to real situations?

5. What organizations can I take help from or contribute to as a class so that my students can become more sensitive and aware?

6. What support systems or help can I expect from my school, district, or city, and what can we do as a class to contribute?

SAMPLE RESPONSE LESSON 8.1

Poverty

Elementary Grades: (1st–5th): In the Classroom, by Parents, Tutors, and Librarians

Duration: 1 Day

Overview

The teacher or parent will read aloud *Sam and the Lucky Money,* by Karen Chinn. This story is about a boy named Sam who finally gets to spend his New Year's gift money any way he likes. He has trouble finding anything within his budget while shopping with his mom in the stores in Chinatown, so he eventually decides to go without a tasty treat or a new toy for himself and instead donates his money to a barefoot homeless man. This story is the perfect segue to a discussion about poverty and homelessness.

(Continued)

(Continued)

Materials

Two pieces of blank chart paper, markers, *Sam and the Lucky Money,* by Karen Chinn, photos of people less fortunate who may be receiving assistance from their community

Key Vocabulary

Poverty, Poor, Homeless, Less Fortunate

Anticipatory Set

1. *Focus:* Students will use class discussions to develop a letter requesting donations for the poor.

2. *Objective:* Students will analyze pictures and listen to a story about people of poverty and use these examples to take action to help those in need. By the end of the lesson, students will write a letter home asking their parents and family members to help with donations in assisting those less fortunate.

3. *Transfer:* This experience will get students to consider ways they can help those less fortunate than themselves, which will hopefully become a lifelong topic for them to consider and act upon.

Instruction

1. The teacher or parent will label chart paper with the word "Poverty." He or she will discuss the photos depicting people in need and then transcribe what is seen in one or two of the pictures.

2. On a second sheet of chart paper, he or she will label it "Things We Can Do" or "Action We Can Take." Under this, the teacher or parent will write "Donate outgrown clothes/uniforms to a church or community center." These charts will be used later as the children add to the charts.

Guided Practice

Once the read aloud is completed, open the floor for discussion about how students have come across people less fortunate then them. The teacher or parent will want to list these ideas on chart paper or the board (i.e., homelessness, children of war, etc.).

During the discussion, the teacher or parent can develop a list of ways the children can contribute to those less fortunate. This can be done by having children form small groups to come up with four or five ideas. Then, they will offer said ideas aloud while the teacher or parent lists them on chart paper. Once all groups have shared, the teacher or parent can ask the children to choose their top two favorite ideas. He or she may want to help guide their decision based on realistic goals. For instance, raising a million dollars by Christmas may not be realistic, but having every child donate a lightly used coat or jacket might be attainable.

Once the two choices have been decided on, have students vote by secret ballot for their choice. Then set the action into motion. If the children decide to each donate a dollar to prepare Thanksgiving baskets for families, they will then write a letter home explaining what they plan to do with that dollar so their parents understand clearly where this donation will be going. Even some of least fortunate students in class will be able to donate something, if nothing more than a dime. If that is not possible, students can always request canned goods to add to the food baskets that will be put together. Any way that children can contribute is essential in making them a part of the project.

Independent Practice

Depending on the two ideas voted on, students will write a letter to their parents about what is planned in order to help those less fortunate. The teacher or parent will model how to write such a letter and the children can create the same or similar document to send home. The class will do this for both ideas but allow time in between. For example, if you collect canned food in December, wait until March or April to collect money to make up Easter Baskets. If you are a parent doing this with your child, have him or her write the donation request letter, make copies of it on colorful paper, and hand them out to well-known neighbors.

Closure

Although many of the students in the classroom or at home are not as destitute as others, some might be close. In other classrooms where the children may come from privilege, their experience with the poor may be limited or even skewed. In order to include all students in the discussion, be careful not to single out anyone. Many of the children may have real experiences working with the poor, be it through their church, within their community, as volunteers throughout the year, and the like, regardless of their own circumstances. It's important to discuss with them as a whole group that no matter how much experience they have working with those experiencing poverty, a story such as this is real for many people and will hopefully get them to consider ways they can help others, even if it means giving up something of theirs, such as clothes or uniforms they've outgrown, lightly used toys, their time, and so on.

Extension

Although this response lesson is geared specifically for the elementary grades, there is no reason this activity can't be carried out in the later years as well. In fact, at K–12 campuses or elementary schools in near proximity to a middle or high school, students in the later years could adopt an elementary classroom to team up with and fulfill the goals. This doesn't just have to be a class project or a grade-level project; it can be schoolwide and filter into the local middle and high school.

Sample Response Lesson 8.2
Foster Care

Secondary Grades: (7th–12th): In the Classroom, by Teachers, Parents, and Tutors

Duration: Daily for About 2 Weeks

Overview

As a class, for homework over a 2-week period, students will read *The Decoding of Lana Morris,* by Laura McNeal and Tom McNeal. This story, about a young woman of 16 who moves into a new foster home, is optimistic, even though it includes some difficult realities teens have to deal with much too early in their lives. But being able to talk about concepts like being abandoned, growing up in foster care, and having to find one's identity is essential in offering a safe haven for these young adults to work through their problems and fears.

Materials

Class set of *The Decoding of Lana Morris,* by Laura and Tom McNeal, class set of reflection journals or composition books

Key Vocabulary

Foster Care

Anticipatory Set

1. *Focus:* Students will keep a daily journal where they will summarize and reflect on the varying and difficult circumstances of the main character in this book.

2. *Objective:* By the end of the unit, students will use their written summaries, reflections, and class discussions to create plays about some of the issues the main character was dealing with in the book. This will be done in small groups.

3. *Transfer:* This experience is meant to give students a view into the lives of people their age who have endured the foster care system and succeeded no matter the difficult circumstances.

Instruction

1. On Day 1, read aloud the first chapter together as a shared reading. Form small groups of four or five where students will discuss the chapter, come up with a summary, and then reflect on how the chapter and characters relate to their own lives.

2. Come back as a whole group, after the small groups have had enough time to discuss the first chapter. The teacher will take contributions from the class and transcribe the groups' summaries and reflections to create a class-constructed summary and reflection chart to be used as a reference point throughout the book, because this will be required of them each night.

3. As students read a chapter a night from the book, they will keep an entry journal where they will summarize the chapter and then react to it as it relates to their own lives. Remember to tell them that although they may not be dealing with these experiences personally in their own homes, they can relate through those they know who are dealing with such issues. They may know about such topics only from television or the movies, so in their journal, they are to relate the chapters to what they have experienced and should tell how, but they should leave out any names.

4. Each morning, at the beginning of class, students will join their small group to share about the chapter and how they relate to it. They will add to their journal entry from the night before if anything new comes up that they'd like to add. This will continue until the book has been read in total.

5. Upon completing the book, students will then be instructed to join their small groups of four or five and create a play using topics discussed in the book to guide their story. Each member should have a role and the play needs to be a scene of about 5 to 10 minutes. These will be delivered to the whole class, as well as followed by class discussion.

Evaluation

After all plays have been delivered, students will write a book report using their journal summaries and reflections to guide them. In addition, their plays will also be taken into account for authentically depicting a scene or story from beginning to end.

SELECTED ANNOTATED BIBLIOGRAPHY

Auth, J. (2007). *Emmy's question.* Ponte Vedra Beach, FL: Morningtide Press.

This is a powerful story of a young girl's struggle with parental alcoholism and the caring adults in her life who made a real difference.

Bartone, E. (1993). *Peppe the lamplighter.* New York: Lothrop, Lee & Shepard.

Peppe has lost his mother, his dad is sick, and he has seven sisters to consider. Peppe takes a job from a friend as a substitute street lamplighter to help the family financially.

Blume, J. (1986). *It's not the end of the world*. New York: Random House Children's Books.

Karen's parents get divorced while she is in sixth grade and she struggles to understand that they are simply unable to live together.

Bunting, E. (1991). *Blue and the gray*. New York: Scholastic.

As a Black boy and his White friend watch the construction of a house that will make them neighbors on the site of a Civil War battlefield, they agree that their homes are monuments to that war.

Bunting, E. (2006). *One green apple*. Boston: Houghton Mifflin.

Farah feels alone, even when surrounded by her classmates. She listens and nods but doesn't speak. She has just arrived from another country and doesn't know the language. On a field trip to an apple orchard, Farah discovers that there are lots of things that sound the same as they did at home, from dogs crunching their food to the ripple of friendly laughter. As she helps the class make apple cider, Farah connects with the other students and begins to feel that she belongs.

Chinn, K. (1997). *Sam and the lucky money*. New York: Lee & Low Books.

This story is about a boy named Sam who finally gets to spend his New Year's gift money any way he likes. He has trouble finding anything within his budget while shopping with his mom in the stores in Chinatown, so he eventually decides to go without a tasty treat or a new toy for himself and instead donates his money to a barefoot homeless man.

Choi, Y. (2003). *The name jar*. New York: Bantam Doubleday Dell Books for Young Readers.

Being the new kid in school is hard enough, but what about when nobody can pronounce your name? Having just moved from Korea, Unhei is anxious that American kids won't like her. So instead of introducing herself on the first day of school, she tells the class that she will choose a name by the following week. Her new classmates help out by filling a glass jar with names for her to pick from. But although Unhei practices American names, one of her classmates comes to her neighborhood and discovers her real name and its special meaning. On the day of her name choosing, the name jar disappears. Encouraged by her new friends, Unhei chooses her own Korean name and helps everyone pronounce it.

Clements, A. (2007). *Jake drake, bully buster*. New York: Simon & Schuster Children's Publishing.

Fourth-grader Jake Drake relates how he comes to terms with "SuperBully" Link Baxter, especially after they are assigned to be partners on a class project.

Cormier, R. (2004). *The chocolate war*. New York: Random House Children's Books.

A high school freshman discovers the devastating consequences of refusing to join in the school's annual fund-raising drive and arouses the wrath of the school bullies.

Danziger, P. (2007). *Divorce express*. New York: Penguin Group.

Phoebe moves from New York, leaving her friends to live with her dad in the country. She has to take the bus every weekend to visit her mom in the city and she has to go to a new school. She struggles with the many changes that occur because of this divorce and wonders if she'll ever be able to be part of both her parents' worlds.

Estes, E. (2004). *The hundred dresses*. Orlando, FL: Harcourt Children's Books.

A restored edition of a classic, this is an award-winning book about prejudice and understanding. In winning a medal she is no longer there to receive, a tight-lipped little Polish girl teaches her classmates a lesson.

Franz, J., & Finney, K. (2000). *I don't want to talk about it: A story about divorce for young children*. Washington, DC: American Psychological Association.

When a child's parents tell her they are divorcing, the last thing she wants to do is talk about it. Instead, she wants to roar as loud as a lion so she can't hear them, or turn into a fish and hide her tears in the sea, or become a turtle and hide in her shell. But her mother and father show her that although some things will change, many other things will stay the same. Most importantly, she realizes that although her parents may not agree on everything, one thing they do agree on is that they both love her very much and will always be her mom and dad.

Friend, N. (2007). *Lush*. New York: Scholastic.

Samantha is a 13-year-old girl whose father is a drunk. The story shows how this adds an extra layer to everything, such as your family's reactions to things, the people you're willing to bring home, and the way you see yourself and the world. For Samantha, this is something that's been going on for so long that she's almost used to it.

Going, K. L. (2004). *Fat kid rules the world*. New York: Penguin Young Readers Group.

Troy Billings is 17, 296 pounds, friendless, miserable, and considering suicide. He meets Curt, an emaciated, semihomeless, high school dropout who plays the guitar. Even though Troy's dad thinks Curt is a drug addict and Troy's brother thinks Troy is a loser, Curt recruits Troy as his new drummer. Together, Curt and Troy change the world of punk, and Troy's own life, forever.

Hall, L. (1993). *Dear kids of alcoholics*. Carlsbad, CA: Gurze Books.

This is an honest, hopeful book for children of an alcoholic parent. Its main character, a boy named Jason, explains facts about alcoholism with touching stories about his dad's sensitivity to alcohol, destructive behavior, and recovery process.

Harmon, M. (2006). *Skate*. New York: Random House Children's Books.

There's not much keeping Ian McDermott in Spokane, but at least it's home. He's been raising Sammy, his brother, practically on his own ever since their mom disappeared on one of her binges. They get by, finding just enough to eat and plenty of time to skateboard. After some trouble at school, Ian grabs Sammy and heads out of town in search for the one relative they can think of. Ian and Sammy head across the entire state of Washington, requiring Ian to protect Sammy, letting no one split up their family of two.

Jimenez, F. (1998). *La mariposa.* Boston: Houghton Mifflin.

Because he can speak only Spanish, Francisco, son of a migrant worker, has trouble when he begins first grade, but his fascination with the caterpillar in the classroom helps him begin to fit in.

Langan, P. (2007). *The bully.* New York: Scholastic.

A new life, a new school, a new bully. That's what Darrell Mercer faces when he and his mother move from Philadelphia to California. After spending months living in fear, Darrell is faced with a big decision. He can either keep running from this bully, or find some way to fight back.

Levins, S., & Langdo, B. (2006). *Was it the chocolate pudding? A story for little kids about divorce.* Washington, DC: American Psychological Association.

This story follows a 6-year-old and his little brother as they try to understand why their parents no longer live together and why the boys shuttle back and forth between them.

Lipsyte, R. (1991). *One fat summer.* New York: HarperCollins.

An overweight 14-year-old boy experiences a turning-point summer in which he learns to stand up for himself.

Martin, A. (2004). *Here today.* New York: Scholastic.

In 1963, when her mother abandons the family to pursue her dream of becoming an actress, 11-year-old Ellie Dingman takes charge of her younger siblings, while also trying to deal with her outcast status in school and frightening acts of prejudice toward the "misfits" that live on her street.

McCormick, P. (2006). *Sold.* New York: Hyperion Books for Children.

Lakshmi is a 13-year-old girl who lives with her family in a small hut in a mountain village in Nepal. There is desperate poverty that threatens the lives of the villagers. One day, Lakshmi's father brings her to a shopkeeper in town and tells Lakshmi that she is going to go work as a maid in India so that her wages can be sent home. Glad to help support her family, Lakshmi undertakes the long journey and arrives at "Happiness House" full of hope. But she soon discovers the unthinkable truth: She has been sold into prostitution.

McCully, E. (1992). *Mirette on the high wire.* New York: G. P. Putnam's Sons.

Mirette, who works for her mom, changing sheets and running errands, decides to get up 2 hours earlier every morning so that she can practice her high-wire balancing skills and hopefully become a performer.

McCully, E. (1996). *The bobbin girl*. New York: Dial.

Ten-year-old Rebecca Putney works 12 hours a day in a factory mill, changing the bobbins on the sewing machines every hour. Rebecca comes from a single-parent family due to her father's death.

McNeal, L., & McNeal, T. (2007). *The decoding of Lana Morris*. New York: Knopf Books for Young Readers.

This is a hopeful story about 16-year-old Lana Morris who wishes her life were different. Her foster mother wants her gone and she has to take care of the other kids in the house. When Lana meets Miss Hekkity at her shop, she begins to realize that she might actually have the power to change things and make some of her wishes come true.

Morgenroth, K. (2006). *Jude*. New York: Simon & Schuster Children's Books.

After Jude watches his drug-dealer father get shot down at the kitchen table, he's taken from their dangerous neighborhood to a comfortable home, a private school, and a mother he doesn't know. At 15, Jude is under suspicion for his father's murder, but to save his own life, he can't tell the police what he knows.

Muñoz Ryan, P. (2002). *Esperanza rising*. New York: Scholastic.

Esperanza and her mother are forced to leave their life of wealth and privilege in Mexico to go work in the labor camps of Southern California, where they must adapt to the harsh circumstances facing Mexican farm workers on the eve of the Great Depression.

Murray, J. (2004). *Bottled up*. New York: Penguin Young Readers Group.

A high school boy comes to terms with his drug addiction, life with an alcoholic father, and a younger brother who looks up to him.

Naylor, P. (1994). *King of the playground*. New York: Simon & Schuster Children's Books.

With his dad's help, Kevin overcomes his fear of the "King of the Playground," who has threatened to tie him to the slide, put him in a deep hole, or put him in a cage with bears.

Nickle, J. (2006). *The ant bully*. New York: Scholastic.

It all begins when Lucas, who "wore funny glasses and a strange hat," is hosed down by Sid, the neighborhood "meanie." Unable to strike back at him, Lucas instead attacks the ants with his squirt gun, and he learns a hard lesson when he is forced into the ant colony, diminished in size, tried for his crimes, and sentenced to hard labor. Eventually, he wins the trust of his new companions and returns home.

Nye, N. (1997). *Sitti's secrets*. New York: Simon & Schuster Children's Books.

Sitti is an American girl who goes to visit her grandmother in a Middle Eastern village on the other side of the world, where they don't need words to understand each other's heart. They learn to read one another in many other ways.

Olson, G. (2007). *Call me Hope*. Boston: Little, Brown.

Hope is an 11-year-old girl struggling to live under the verbal abuse of her mother. Instead of running away, Hope chooses resilience instead, and she creates survival strategies for herself.

Parry F., & Heide, J. (1990). *The day of Ahmed's secret*. New York: Lothrop, Lee & Shepard.

Ahmed is a child vendor who drives a donkey-pulled cart and delivers heavy glass bottles of fuel to customers in present-day Cairo. Ahmed becomes the major money earner for his family. Throughout the story, we wait patiently to find out a secret Ahmed is keeping: He has learned how to write his name.

Pelzer, D. (1995). *A child called "It."* Deerfield Beach, FL: Health Communications Inc.

Dave Pelzer shares his story of the many abuses he suffered at the hands of his alcoholic mother and the averted eyes of his neglectful father. Someone with no one to turn to, his dreams barely kept him alive. Through each of his struggles, readers will find themselves enduring his pain, comforting his loneliness, and fighting for his will to survive.

Pelzer, D. (1997). *Lost boy: A foster child's search for the love of a family*. Deerfield Beach, FL: Health Communications Inc.

Now considered an "F-Child" (Foster Child), Dave is moved in and out of five different homes. He suffers shame and experiences resentment from those who feel that all foster kids are trouble and unworthy of being loved just because they are not part of a "real" family.

Powers, M. (1986). *Our teacher's in a wheelchair*. Morton Grove, IL: Albert Whitman & Company.

Brian is a male teacher of young children. He is open with his students about his disability and he does not allow it to get in the way of his working with them. This story provides an example of a way to show children that it is okay to ask for nurturing when they need it.

Sachs, M. (2007). *Fat girl*. Woodbury, MN: Llewellyn Worldwide.

Jeff Lyons can't stand Ellen de Luca, the fat girl in his ceramics class. She's huge, clumsy, and stares at him all the time. But he's a "nice guy" and feels terrible when Ellen overhears his hurtful remarks about her. He ends up giving her advice on weight loss, college, clothes, and hair, and, to everyone's surprise, Jeff actually starts dating the fat girl. He ends up confusing his recreation of Ellen with love. But as her pounds melt away, Jeff resents the happy, independent young woman she becomes.

Williams, S. (1992). *Working cotton*. San Diego, CA: Harcourt Brace Jovanovich.

The story tells a biographical tale of cotton pickers and how the bus came early in the morning and picked them up at dark after a long day's work. Each member of the family worked side by side taking care of the baby in the family and earning a living.

REFERENCES

Araujo, L., & Strasser, J. (2003). Confronting prejudice in the early childhood classroom. *Kappa Delta Pi, 39*, 178–182.

Baghban, M. (2002). Stories shape our lives: An interview with Glenna Sloan. *Journal of Children's Literature, 28*(1), 16–21.

Call me Hope. (2007). *Publishers Weekly, 17*, 51–52.

Entenman, J., Murnen, T., & Hendricks, C. (2005). Victims, bullies, and bystanders in K–3 literature. *The Reading Teacher, 59*, 352–364.

Galda, L., & Cullinan, B. (2002). *Literature and the child*. Belmont, CA: Wadsworth.

Jalongo, M. (1983). Using crisis-oriented books with young children. *Young Children, 38*, 29–36.

Jayson, S. (2005, July, 18). *Divorce declining, but so is marriage*. Retrieved November 25, 2009, from http://www.usatoday.com/news/nation/2005–07–18-cohabit-divorce_x.htm

Lamme, L. (1998). Child laborers in children's literature. *Middle Level Learning: Teaching and Learning Social Studies in the Middle Grades, 1*, 15–16.

Lingren, H. G. (1997). *Bullying–How to stop it!* Lincoln: University of Nebraska Cooperative Extension. Retrieved March 13, 2003, from http://www.ianr.unl.edu/pubs/family/nf309.htm

Phoenix House Center on Addiction and the Family. (2008). *Effects of parental substance abuse on children and families*. Retrieved October 30, 2009, from http://www.coaf.org/professionals/effects%20.htm

Webster's new world dictionary. (1986). New York: Simon & Schuster.

Zarrillo, J. (2008). *Teaching elementary social studies: Principles and applications*. Upper Saddle River, NJ: Pearson Merrill Prentice Hall.

Chapter 9

Disabilities and the Special Child

Kimberly Persiani-Becker

"What does it mean to be different than everyone else?" (Iaquinta & Hipsky, 2006, p. 209). This is a good question, and most likely, it's one we all have had to face at one point but may not have really had experience answering. It is possible that we have asked this question of ourselves or some have been asked it because of apparent differences that are very noticeable. No matter if you are able-bodied, intelligent, funny, active, interesting, and so on, each of us is very different from our family members, friends, and peers. Some of us are more obviously different by the way we look, act, or learn, but we are all different. Tapping into those differences is essential in teaching children how to accept one another.

At a time when the demands of mainstreaming and inclusion of students with special needs is so prevalent, teachers are left with the new challenge of making this transition work in the regular education classroom. Increasing numbers of children with various learning needs are now integrated into general education classrooms, though most of the teachers maintain a teaching credential that did not prepare them for the large variety of circumstances the children bring with them. The spectrum of these needs vary from mild to demanding and often out of the realm of expertise of the classroom teacher.

In the area of children's books, also, this is a new focus, with children's authors writing about children with various kinds of disabilities and special needs. In terms of multicultural children's literature, this is a necessary area to recognize and represent. In this chapter, we review various books that show characters who themselves either have a disability or special need or have a family member who has a disability that is affecting the entire family.

The Need for Representing Disabilities and Special Needs in Classrooms

Unfortunately, even in the 21st century, with great gains in available rich literature for children and young adults, texts tend to speak very little of disabilities and the special child. However, this is an issue that is important and relevant to those children who lead such lives. Disabilities and special needs are lived realities that change the lifestyles forever of all those who are involved, including, but not limited to, parents, siblings, teachers, classmates, and so on. However, these circumstances can be made more comfortable with the understanding and acceptance of these diverse children. Just like ethnic and cultural groups, people with disabilities and all those involved form a culture that is unique to them. Their diversity is written about in only a handful of children's books, but it is an important topic to bring to the fore. Health impairment and chronic illness are other topics that many children either experience or encounter with their peers at school or siblings at home. The topics mentioned here ought to be considered more often in schools and classrooms, as a means to encourage hope for those who may be facing them and to emphasize the reality of the situation for others.

The fact that this area should be recognized within the realm of multicultural children's literature is testimony that these groups of people also be recognized and represented as part of the multicultural world in which we live. Obviously, the success of mainstreaming and inclusion depends on the role that administrators and teachers take on. Their attitudes are critical in setting the tone of acceptance and patience that is necessary for children with special needs, as teachers and general education students readjust their thinking and develop these interactions. If the regular classroom teachers embrace the new addition of children with special needs into the classroom, then it is more likely that their regular education peers will also develop positive attitudes and understanding of certain needs.

[handwritten margin note: not in the real world]

In order for this to happen, not only do teachers need to show this acceptance, but their stories also need to be a part of the curriculum. "Books about individuals with disabilities can promote positive attitudes and can teach students about individual differences" (Salend, 2004, p. 169). These books are not only necessary for use in the classroom where children with special needs and disabilities attend, but also in classrooms where little or no exposure to such circumstances exists. It is just as important for children who don't have experience with those who have special needs and disabilities to have exposure to important books that depict positive portrayals of youngsters and people who have disabilities or special needs. Similar to any other multicultural or diverse group, all students need to be introduced to this real-life issue so that regular education students are more accepting, knowledgeable, and sensitive when the time comes for such interactions. Literature about people with disabilities or special needs and their families can provide a way for students to discuss and work through problems that the characters endure in the book and then apply the same strategies for problem solving to their own lives or those they know, who experience similar issues.

This is also important in keeping abreast of advancements in technology and access for people with disabilities. Books of this nature have changed from the earlier days of *Lisa and Her Soundless World*, by Edna Levine, where the concept of a hearing aid is described in more technical terms to the child reader. In this book children are shown the more daunting visual image of the older hearing aids that appear to look more like small backpacks rather than the small and more sophisticated instruments available today. Books that are more child-friendly have been on the shelves more and more in the last decade and serve their purpose well. From listening to and responding to current and relevant children's literature and young adult books, students will learn that all characters share universal experiences such as embarrassing moments, goals, challenges, and accomplishments, no matter if one is able bodied or not, healthy or not, learning disabled or not.

Through guided and whole group dialogues about characters' special needs or behaviors portrayed in literature, children and young adults can converse about the issue and realize they are not alone and that other people experience the same types of problems. "This type of conversation helps [children] as they develop insight into the character's difficulty and discuss the merits and shortcomings of any solutions" (Iaquinta & Hipsky, 2006, p. 210). Afterward children can come up with possible solutions to their own needs by using this new insight. Some possible solutions might be developing understanding and compassion, overcoming physical and intellectual hurdles, or simply being introduced to new people who have real-life struggles but still lead productive and meaningful lives.

In the last decade or two, teachers and parents have had more access to children's literature and young adult books that address real-life circumstances of today's youth. The focus of this literature includes, but is not limited to, children with special needs, learning disabilities, and behavior issues, as well as concerns like teasing and bullying. Because children identify with characters in literature when they can relate to them, they will begin to understand that not only do others experience the same challenges but also that several problem-solving strategies are possible. "In addition, children with and without disabilities may be more willing to engage in open discussion about their feelings with the book as a focal point" (Iaquinta & Hipsky, 2006, p. 211), rather than focusing on themselves. The fear of the unknown greatly exists for those with special needs when they are with regular education students because they are often considered "the special child."

THE SPECIAL CHILD

Who is the special child? Is it the child who is deaf? Is it the child who has behavior issues? Is it the child who has visual impairments? Is it the child who is physically disabled? Is it the child who has a learning disability? No matter the label, most children want to be treated equally. Stephanie Stuve-Bodeen, author of *We'll Paint the Octopus Red,* reminds us that sometimes people say that children with special needs or disabilities are "special" because they need extra time and help to learn and get around. But they are also special in the same ways that other kids are special. It's important to be careful when labeling children as "special," because too often this can easily perpetuate stereotypes. It is important to have the family and the child involved in the identification process so when the term "special child" is used, it is applied across the board with all our children who may require extra attention due to an established need.

In the story, *We'll Paint the Octopus Red,* a lovely 6-year-old girl named Emma spends time coming up with things she and her new sibling will do together. On the day her father tells her that her new baby brother has Down syndrome, she is concerned that he won't be able to share in all the fun events she has planned for them. After a little discussion, her father explains to her that her brother will be able to do all the things she has planned, but it will just take a little more time and patience for him to learn. This is an uplifting story that portrays the concept of Down syndrome in a way that shows how people with the syndrome lead meaningful and fulfilling lives.

People in current times have become more knowledgeable, understanding, and accepting of individuals with disabilities than in past decades. Today, individuals with disabilities experience increased access to education, buildings, programs, activities, transportation, communication tools, and employment (Dyches, Prater, & Cramer, 2001). Being introduced to the special child and all that we can learn from him or her is a step in the right direction. These positive representations of those with special needs in books should be considered in regard to Dyches et al.'s (2001) guidelines for characterizations in contemporary literature that achieve the following:

- Envision high expectations for the character with disabilities
- Enhance positive contributions
- Build on strengths
- Show the person acting on choices
- Depict expanding reciprocal relationships with others
- Ensure that the character with disabilities is afforded the same citizenship rights of others

These are the stories and people who ought to be considered when choosing books for children and young adults. Quality literature should include characters classified as credible, consistent, multidimensional, and ever growing (Dyches et al., 2001, p. 230).

In fact, books such as *Russ and the Firehouse,* by Janet Elizabeth Rickert, and *All Kinds of Friends, Even Green!* by Ellen Senisi, are perfect examples of real children being shown as having fun, fulfilling, and meaningful lives, making good friends and enjoying their world as they see and live in it. These two boys, Russ, with Down syndrome, and Moses, who uses a wheelchair, offer inspiring stories about how they get around and engage in activities every child enjoys. These types of representations of children with disabilities and other special needs are universal and take the often marginalized and stereotyped conceptualization of such children to a more positive and comprehensive level of understanding, showing that they are productive and happy people.

Lived Realities

As administrators, teachers, parents, and children are all too aware, disabilities and special needs are lived realities that change the lifestyles forever of all those who care for children, whether it be their health or academic well-being. At times, there can be a great deal of pressure put on those who tend to the needs of these children. Although adults are better equipped to seek out answers to assist, children such as siblings and peers aren't always sure how to approach a child who seems "different."

People related to or associated with children with disabilities have added challenges in their lives. Besides the additional responsibilities parents and adult caregivers take on in meeting the needs of these children, siblings and peers also experience extra roles and obstacles in spending time together, playing with one another, assisting with school and at home, and even in finding time alone, away from the children in question. Sometimes, siblings have even greater responsibilities in helping the family tend to a child's needs, whether or not the able child is ready to take on such tasks. This can result in anger, resentment, embarrassment, and confusion. In addition, the sibling child might find that he or she avoids others because the sibling looks or acts a certain way, which might be ridiculed by his or her peers. However, along with the mixed, negative feelings healthy children have toward their sibling with a disability, there tends to also be strong feelings of loyalty, love, and responsibility to stand up for their brother or sister in an effort to protect him or her from judgment. Because so many kids go through a period of deep embarrassment, usually in middle school and high school, this sense of protection can mean the difference for children with special needs to be accepted by their peers and teachers. One book that discusses this is *Ian's Walk,* by Laurie Lears. In this book, Julie looks forward to going to the park with her big sister. Her brother Ian, who has autism, wants to go too, but because he does things so differently for no apparent reason, Julie tends to shy away from spending time with him. He is a big responsibility, and sometimes Julie doesn't want to have to be in charge of him. Although Ian sees and hears things Julie doesn't understand, they walk to the park. Only when Ian goes missing does she realize how important it is to try to think the way Ian does, which leads Julie to her brother. It's a moment when she realizes she does understand him.

This story gets across the lesson that even under difficult circumstances, a healthy sibling will do what's right and ultimately find commonalities with the sibling who has special needs. Using stories to sensitize listeners and readers to these dynamics offers valuable and real experiences for all of us to learn from. This is not just a story about an older sibling watching over a sibling with special needs; it is one all children who have younger brothers and sisters can relate to. More importantly for those who tend to the needs of siblings with special needs, this story shows them that they aren't alone and they are needed and appreciated.

The difficulties of comprehending disorders and of handling the unpredictable behaviors accompanying some of them makes the sibling relationships and friendship relationships very challenging. Because of this, it is crucial that parents and adults acknowledge the negative feelings of brothers, sisters, friends, and peers of children with disabilities. This is also a good time for parents and adults to stress their appreciation for all the help the siblings, friends, and peers provide. They might want to discuss how a strong bond can be formed when they work together and the importance of the healthy child's right to have time alone and to spend time with other able bodied friends. The healthy sibling often finds himself or herself in a position of feeling like his or her efforts are ignored. The sibling may also feel that he or she can't escape his or her brother with special needs or disabilities. The healthy child needs an outlet to share his or her frustrations without fear that he or she will be taken literally, rather than just "blowing off steam."

The Sibling Slam Book: What It's Really Like to Have a Brother or Sister With Special Needs, by Don Meyer, is a great book choice for healthy siblings to know they are not alone in their frustrations. This book is intended for older siblings, Grade 6 and up. It is full of comments by 81 young people who display the theme of optimism and hope and their love for their sibling with special needs or disabilities. The book also recognizes the hard work, dedication, resentment, and fierce protection of these young people toward their siblings. A typical slam-book question such as, "Has your sib ever embarrassed you?" is also intertwined with a chapter like, "Ever Feel Invisible?" Reflections to many questions and relevant chapters provide insightful material so that all readers are sure to relate to some of the thoughtful or heartfelt responses shared by these brave individuals.

Children who have a sibling, friend, or peer with a disability experience a tremendous opportunity for growth. Such traits as compassion, responsibility, and acceptance of people's differences are all important qualities to obtain and can be learned when being a part of the lives of others who have disabilities. These children also learn that even though their sibling, friend, or peer is not perfect, he or she can still accomplish many things and lead a very "normal" childhood. And today, in more recent times, literature for children and young adults does a better of job of showing this by positively portraying characters with disabilities. Such books are used to promote awareness, understanding, and acceptance of those with disabilities. Because many of these books' characters are depicted with physical, sensory, or cognitive disabilities (Prater, Dyches, & Johnstun, 2006), they reflect many of the experiences peers and siblings come into contact with on a daily basis. More importantly, those children who have little or no experience with others their own age with disabilities now have the chance to learn about such children, which will help them be more aware of positive aspects when the time comes to meet a child with a disability.

Although there are several books available for young children, there is still a great need for nonfiction books that explore the feelings of the brother or sister of a child with a disability, especially for older children in upper elementary and middle school years. In *Views From Our Shoes: Growing Up With a Brother or Sister With Special Needs,* by Meyer (1997), readers are exposed to down-to-earth, sincere stories, ranging from mental retardation through a number of rare syndromes, contributed by 45 children ranging in age from 4 to 18. In talking about their siblings and their feelings, we are exposed to children's embarrassment by their siblings and their anger and jealousy. However, we also see how protective and loving they are when it comes to getting along in a family that is different. This book is the perfect complement for siblings who need to know they are not alone in having a brother or sister with special needs or disabilities.

Oftentimes, the healthy children in the family feel that they are treated unfairly and that their siblings can get away with things that they cannot. In some cases, these same children speak out against those who make fun of or misunderstand the youngsters who are different. In essence, we need more books that concentrate on what children with special needs can do rather than what they cannot. They need to be regarded in inclusive ways while also being recognized for what makes them so wonderfully different.

DISABILITIES AS A "MULTICULTURAL" GROUP

Just like ethnic and cultural groups, people with disabilities and all those involved find it comforting if they can find a group that has formed a culture that is unique to them. Because those people are quite isolated, being with others similar to them can make a huge difference in how they view themselves and their ability to succeed. Their diversity is written about in only a handful of children's books, but it is an important topic to bring to the fore. Literature for children and young adults is the perfect tool for doing just that. Children typically connect best with books that include characters who look or act like them. Whether the characters are carrying a book bag, wearing trendy clothes, or pushing a walker, they enjoy reading stories about themselves or at least characters like them. Children begin to notice similarities and differences, either in themselves or the people around them, at a young age. This means that children notice unfamiliar characteristics early on. Because children may be unsure about these differences, it is important that they have opportunities to talk about them and express their concerns and get questions answered (Blaska, Inkster, & Williams, 2005). Dialogues before, during, and after reading good books, where characters with special needs and disabilities are depicted realistically, open the door for honest communication, which can dispel myths, highlight struggles and triumphs, as well as assist in developing a better understanding of those who live with special needs and disabilities and those who are indirectly affected.

Children can easily be drawn into believing stereotypes as they are introduced to them, intentionally or unintentionally. Because of this, it is critical that young people receive accurate and positive information to help limit bias in their thinking and understanding of images and stories about people with disabilities and their connection to them. Reading books about people with disabilities and health impairments opens the door for them to ask questions, conquer fears, and eliminate stereotyping through discussions about these similarities and differences portrayed by characters in stories, fiction and nonfiction. In *My Friend Isabelle,* by Eliza Woloson, we meet Charlie and Isabelle. Charlie is what most people refer to as "normal," whereas Isabelle is a bit "different." The story takes the reader through some very practical yet simple descriptions of the similarities and differences between the two children without ever making them seem "normal" or "different" than one another. This easy reader is a useful tool in showing how a child with Down syndrome can just as easily enjoy the same things as an able bodied, healthy child, but he or she might need just a little more time and patience. Books like this can begin to build a foundation for acceptance for people who may look or act differently, which is not unlike what has been accomplished for many years in regard to race culture in children's books and young adult literature.

The deaf and blind cultures are two other groups who often find companionship and support in one another no matter the level of their hearing or sight ability. They serve to support each other in getting through everyday routines and learning to live in a sighted and hearing world. Many children and young adults spend much time without exposure to these groups and really don't have enough information or experience to feel confident in befriending a person who is deaf or blind. Having access to books that show people with said disabilities in a way that readers can view them living quality lives allows for them to dispel their prejudices and collapse their stereotypes of these groups of people.

For those in the upper elementary and middle school years, *Nobody's Perfect,* by Marlee Matlin, offers readers an experience with a deaf girl whose speech-reading and signing skills allow her to thrive in the hearing world. Megan and a new girl, Alexis, get paired up for a science project and end up learning a lot about one another. More importantly, readers get introduced to Alexis's brother with autism, who learns some basic sign language from Megan, resulting in Alexis being able to communicate better with her brother. It opens up communication with both him and Alexis. Readers unfamiliar with deafness will be intrigued by the descriptions of how Megan studies and her interactions with an American Sign Language interpreter during class time. It's a simple story that allows those with and without disabilities a glimpse of the nonhearing world.

Not only are books like these positive experiences for youngsters, but they serve as learning tools for the teacher and parent as well, as they read along with the students. For the most part, It takes only one or two required courses to obtain a teaching credential. Clearly such classes are useful, but because so much has to be covered, only the most basic information is learned. One of the most powerful things a teacher and his or her students can experience is learning together. Books like those mentioned earlier are just as powerful for the adult educator as for the student. So in addition to providing a variety of picture books and novels to the students, teachers might also ask students to bring in titles they might already have access to at home. For those who identify with the deaf or blind culture, they may be more helpful in finding books that they feel strongly about in portraying themselves to the rest of the population of learners.

CHILDREN WHO ARE HEALTH IMPAIRED

Acute and chronic illness is another underrepresented topic that many children either experience or encounter with their peers at school or siblings at home. Some of these ailments to consider might include human immunodeficiency virus (HIV) and acquired immune deficiency syndrome (AIDS), seizure disorders (epilepsy), diabetes, cystic fibrosis, and sickle-cell anemia. It ought to be included in the curriculum and discussions more often as a means to encourage hope, as a way to begin a dialogue for those who are afraid, and to bring an unspoken reality to the situation. Such discussions are also important so that teachers and parents can bring an awareness that allows us to avoid overgeneralizing and portraying pitying attitudes about those who experience such health conditions on a regular basis. At the end of the day, children want to be treated like everyone else, whether or not they are ill. With that said, a platform for discussion for children and adults is critical in making sure the kinds of assumptions made about children with health impairments aren't perpetuated.

Young people today have a difficult time wrapping their heads around their own mortality. They think they are invincible. How do they react when they hear of a young person being diagnosed with cancer or HIV or AIDS? It's terrifying, no matter what age, but especially in those who are young. How do they talk to their ill friend about this? Are children and young adults equipped to have such conversations if they have never been exposed or been a part of such discussions? Wouldn't a young friend want to know how to inquire about their friend's health after doctor visits or another round of chemotherapy? Would a youngster want to visit his or her friend in the hospital if that friend was on the verge of dying? Wouldn't denial seem to be a better option than facing the friend's health head on? And what if children and young adults never learn how to support a friend in need during such a difficult health crisis? Would it be okay for a child to say he didn't need to be there for a friend because of all the other people in that friend's life who were there and being supportive? Thinking one is not needed might even be a relief, especially for someone so young. Because of these questions that children and young adults might have in such circumstances, it's especially important that we expose them to books that discuss the realities of illness as well as how to cope and how to support one another. Kids come to school with a variety of health impairments, and knowing how to approach a topic is important not only for the healthy child but also for the kids in class who could use the support and understanding from their peers. This not only offers a safe environment for the child with health impairments, but it also teaches the healthy child about compassion and support skills for future situations with his or her own family.

We wouldn't want youngsters to act badly when they grow up and find themselves caring for their parents and grandparents. They need to learn to ask the right questions and be sensitive to the ailments of these family members. If one grows up and illness, deficits, learning disabilities, and the like are never discussed, then what will happen when that person is put in a place where he or she must face this kind of circumstance for the first time? If one's family doesn't talk about things that are "different" or "uncomfortable," books are a great place to start. If young people are exposed to those with disabilities and, more importantly, acute and chronic illnesses, they will be less anxious and more prepared when the time arrives that they have to support a friend who is recovering from cancer and will more likely visit one's grandparents in the hospital as their illness takes them from the world. If not, there is no schema to depend on when one is afraid. This is where children's picture books and young adult novels can be the perfect vehicle in introducing young people to positive portrayals and positive outcomes for those with health impairments. It's better to have some background and knowledge about young people surviving major illnesses and learning to live with recurring illness. We have much more access to books of this caliber today than we had 20 or 30 years ago. Today, we can introduce them in the classroom and at home as a way to encourage discussion and make a scary situation not so terrifying.

Health disorders affect many children today. Disabling features such as limited stamina, vitality, or alertness due to chronic or acute problems are hampering said children and can be just as obvious to peers and siblings as they can be to the child who has these characteristics due to his or her health condition. The illnesses and disorders mentioned earlier are just a handful of the conditions children are dealing with on a day-to-day basis. It is important for teachers not only to address the fears within the child who has acquired them, but also to have an understanding of these health impairments. It is also important for the teacher to make sure that these children's peers understand that the child who carries the illness is just like them in regard to the desire to do well academically and athletically.

Stories like *My Sister Rose Has Diabetes,* by Monica Beatty, and *My Heart Is Full of Wishes,* by Joshua Grishaw, are two examples of children who deal with the frustrations and ailments associated with diabetes and cystic fibrosis. Although the characters in these stories are highlighted as people who have dreams and hopes and try to lead as normal lives as possible, it is not always the case for every child afflicted with illnesses of this sort. However, bringing such stories to the forefront provides those with chronic illnesses or those who have friends or siblings with chronic illnesses knowledge about the conditions, and it helps them see these children thriving and living as "normal" a life as possible. It takes away the scariness of such terms as "diabetes," "cystic fibrosis," "sickle-cell anemia," and the like. Reading stories about children who deal with these issues but live relatively "normal" lives allows for a platform of discussion and a sense that not all children with these illnesses are bound to a bed or don't think about the future. They have the same dreams of a future as an astronaut, an artist, a doctor, a lawyer, or a teacher, and they have families that love them and support them, just like their healthy counterparts.

Reading and dialoguing about books that portray children with such impairments fulfilling their dreams and desires is one step toward helping all children realize that those with serious health issues can still live viable and productive lives. This is also very important for those who have little or no experience with children or young adults who have acute or chronic illnesses. A book like *It Happened to Nancy: A True Story From the Diary of a Teenager,* written by an anonymous teenager, would have been one, had I known about it, that all my friends would have needed and wanted to read while in middle school and high school. Knowing that a young girl, age 14, with all the hopes and dreams of so many teenagers, could fall in love only to contract HIV and eventually AIDS from a boy she trusted and cared for, would have been a story none of us would have forgotten. Looking back, it would have prevented so many of us from partaking in mature activities we weren't ready to handle. Knowing we could be so easily duped, and in turn, infected with such a long, debilitating disease, ending in death at such a young age, might have made us think twice before engaging in mature situations we weren't knowledgeable enough about.

On another note, it is often easier for children to recognize those with physical disabilities as opposed to those with chronic illness. Those with cerebral palsy, spina bifida, spinal cord injury, muscular dystrophy, a loss of limbs, or those in wheelchairs or walkers, who have more obvious signs of a disability, are often marginalized and stigmatized in our society, even in the 21st century. It is up to teachers, parents, and peers to model acceptance and treat their counterparts who are physically disabled with respect, patience, and understanding. There are many books available today that do just that in a way that shows said people with physical disabilities in productive and meaningful lives, without there being a sense of pity for them. In addition, teens who are embarrassed to ask real questions of adults and doctors have more books to choose from today to help them.

Geared toward students in high school, *Easy for You to Say: Q and As for Teens Living With Chronic Illness or Disabilities,* by Dr. Miriam Kaufman, concentrates on teens who are disabled or who have a chronic illness, and it focuses on their individual needs. This book is an opportunity for readers to view real, courageous questions asked of a physician who works with adolescents and teens with varied medical conditions, from spina bifida to cystic fibrosis to kidney disease. Some of the more important sections concern medical issues and sexuality. The answers that this physician provided in the book are especially for disabled teens who may be embarrassed to ask for information about safe and responsible sex and other similar situations. Another popular and beautiful story available for older kids is *Kira-Kira,* by Cynthia Kadohata. Two Japanese sisters, as close as ever, find themselves dealing with an illness that neither of them expected. Although this is no real account of how to get through such a tough experience, it is certainly a story to be read by those with siblings in the same situation.

More and more books written for and about children and young adults with special needs are being taken seriously and published. Whether children in class are diagnosed with a disability, know someone with a disability, or have never even met anyone with a disability, bringing this type of literature into the class, be it fiction or nonfiction, offers opportunities for all children and young adults to become familiar with these issues and see people with disabilities as productive members of their school, home, community, and society. Breaking the stereotypes about those who have a disability brings us a step closer to beating discrimination about people who are waking up each day and taking on the challenges that life has to offer, just like everyone else.

[handwritten marginalia: Out of my mind, Freak the Mighty of Rice + Men, Wonder]

REFLECTION QUESTIONS FOR THE TEACHER

1. What books on disabilities and special needs characters do I already have in my multicultural library?

2. What issues are important to concentrate on when choosing books for inclusion into a multicultural library that depict characters with special needs or disabilities?

3. What criteria can I use to evaluate books with characters with special needs, disabilities, or behavior issues so that I can resist stereotyping?

4. What information will be most useful to my general education class that can help students understand this group as a multicultural group?

5. What training or information must I obtain to sensitively and knowledgably discuss issues of special needs, disabilities, and behavior problems?

SAMPLE RESPONSE LESSON 9.1

Children With Special Needs

Primary Grades: In the Classroom, by Parents and Teachers

Duration: 1 to 5 Days

Overview

Over a period of about 4 days, read aloud and discuss the following stories: *My Friend Isabelle,* by Eliza Woloson, *Ian's Walk,* by Laurie Lears, *We'll Paint the Octopus Red,* by Stephanie Stuve-Bodeen, and *Special Olympics,* by Mike Kennedy . The teacher or parent will need to contact a representative from the Special Olympics about finding ways to introduce the students to children who have participated, to see if any of the athletes would be willing to become pen pals for the class. Students will begin a pen pal exchange with children or teens who have competed or are going to compete in the Special Olympics.

Materials

My Friend Isabelle, Ian's Walk, We'll Paint the Octopus Red, and *Special Olympics.*

(Continued)

(Continued)

Key Vocabulary

Special Olympics

Anticipatory Set

1. *Focus:* Students will become more aware of how hard people and children with disabilities have to work to achieve the same kinds of goals and dreams they may have.

2. *Objective:* By the end of the lesson, students will have a strong understanding of the significance of the Special Olympics by developing a pen pal relationship with one of its athletes. In order to do this, students will develop a list of relevant questions to use in acquiring information about their pen pal. They will also write a short narrative and include a photo of themselves to be introduced to their pen pal.

3. *Transfer:* This experience will not only give them a chance to see those with special needs excel at difficult, physical tasks and reach their goals, but it will also encourage them to not be afraid of the unknown and to befriend others no matter their physical, academic, or emotional development.

Instruction

1. For 4 days, after recess or lunch, the teacher will read aloud one of the stories, *My Friend Isabelle, Ian's Walk, We'll Paint the Octopus Red,* or *Special Olympic.*

2. After each read-aloud, the teacher will guide the students through a discussion about the similarities and differences addressed in regard to the characters in the stories, how others saw them, and how they all got along well together. On labeled chart paper by book titles, the teacher will keep an ongoing list of these thoughts to be used later in developing pen pal questions.

Guided Practice

As a class, develop a list of relevant questions to use in writing to students' pen pals, in order to request photos and brief biographies about the lives of the athletes. Use the previously transcribed students' thoughts from the read-alouds to help with this. Some of these questions might be, but are not limited to, the following: (a) What is your favorite sport? (b) How did you get involved in the Special Olympics? (c) What is your favorite event to compete in? (d) How often do you have to train? (e) Other than being an athlete, what else do you like to do in your free time?

On chart paper or an overhead projector, the teacher will model how to write a narrative as an introduction to his or her pen pal. He or she will include the class-developed list of questions and a photo of himself or herself.

Independent Practice

Using the teacher's letter as a model and the class-developed list of questions, children will write their own narrative to their pen pal.

Extension

If possible, invite a few of the pen pals to come to class and speak with the students. Although this activity seems obvious, it's important that able-bodied children and those in good health meet children with special needs and disabilities who go about living "normal" lives and excel at activities important to every child. They will have the chance to see that children with special needs and disabilities live just as fulfilled lives as anyone else. Parents and their children can get involved in the Special Olympics, either as volunteers or participants.

SAMPLE RESPONSE LESSON 9.2

Children With Special Needs

Secondary Grades: In the Classroom, by Parents and Teachers

Duration: 1 Day

Overview

After hearing excerpts from *The Sibling Slam Book: What It's Really Like to Have a Brother or Sister With Special Needs,* by Don Meyer, and *Easy for You to Say: Q and As for Teens Living With Chronic Illness or Disabilities,* by Dr. Miriam Kaufman, students will develop questions about both topics to refer to upon a visit from the school nurse or a teacher who specializes in youngsters with disabilities. This question-and-answer experience will offer great insight to those with difficult questions and emotions in regard to this topic.

Materials

Copies of the books *The Sibling Slam Book: What It's Really Like to Have a Brother or Sister With Special Needs* and *Easy for You to Say: Q and As for Teens Living With Chronic Illness or Disabilities*

Key Vocabulary

Slam

(Continued)

(Continued)

Anticipatory Set

1. *Focus:* Students will identify their thoughts and experiences with youngsters with special needs and how they can go about befriending one another or dealing with their experiences as a sibling of a child with special needs.

2. *Objective:* By the end of the lesson, students will have created two relevant lists of questions and will write an essay about what they learned from the school nurse or teacher who specializes in children with special needs.

3. *Transfer:* Students will use this information as a foundation for having a clearer knowledge base about this topic as it relates to being a sibling of a child with special needs, being the sibling who has a special need, and simply, being more cognizant of those in need of understanding and friendship as well as having their myths dispelled about those who have special needs.

Instructions

1. After the teacher reads entries from *The Sibling Slam Book: What It's Really Like to Have a Brother or Sister With Special Needs,* he or she will lead a discussion about the reality of siblings who have a brother or sister with special needs or disabilities.

2. Next, the teacher will have students work in small groups to develop a list of questions they might have if they are a sibling with special needs and disabilities or a sibling of a child with special needs and disabilities.

3. As a whole class, the teacher will help the students develop a list of questions they would have for a doctor after reading excerpts from *Easy for You to Say: Q and As for Teens Living With Chronic Illness or Disabilities.* Although some of these questions can be embarrassing, students will submit them anonymously on index cards and the teacher will read them aloud and transcribe them onto chart paper. It is advised that the teacher has support from resource personal such as a school nurse or special education teacher. Parents can also do these two activities at home with their own children with or without special needs or disabilities as a way to open up dialogue about this issue.

Independent Practice

1. During the question-and-answer session with the nurse or special education teacher, students will refer to the questions on the charts and take notes to be used later.

2. After the nurse or special education teacher visits, students will write an essay about what they learned, using their notes to guide their essay.

Closure

As a whole group, the teacher will review the class-developed list of questions and ask students to answer them based on the information obtained from the visits from the nurse and special education teacher, which they can use to write or add to their essay.

SELECTED ANNOTATED BIBLIOGRAPHY

Beatty, M. (1997). *My sister Rose has diabetes.* Albuquerque, NM: Health Press.

So many children in the United States are affected by diabetes. Rose is one of those children. This story discusses the issues of those who don't have diabetes but feel forgotten in a family engrossed with this chronic condition. This book introduces us to Rose and her brother James. We learn about how the family handles Rose's diabetes. Readers find that even though diabetes is a chronic illness, it is also manageable. This story takes the sting out of the name "diabetes" and shows how children with this ailment are able to live normal lives.

Grishaw, J. (1995). *My heart is full of wishes.* Orlando, FL: Raintree Steck-Vaughn.

This very lively, optimistic book appeals to the heart of every child with cystic fibrosis as it lets them know they are not alone. The main character, Joshua, is a smart child. He writes about being a superhero during the day, at the same time as he deals with his fears about his illness during the night.

Kadohata, J. (2004). *Kira-Kira.* New York: Simon & Schuster Children's Publishing.

Kira-Kira captures the family ties among two sisters, their parents, and their brother in post-WWII Georgia. The story shows the despair when one sister becomes terminally ill. When her sister Lynn falls sick, young Katie deals with many responsibilities that she never had before. As the family begins to fall apart, Katie finds ways to remind them that there is always something to look forward to in the future.

Kaufman, M. (2005). *Easy for you to say: Q and As for teens living with chronic illness or disabilities.* Buffalo, NY: Firefly Books.

This book is an opportunity for readers to view real, courageous questions asked of a physician who works with adolescents and teens with varied medical conditions, from spina bifida to cystic fibrosis to kidney disease. Some of the more important sections concern medical issues and sexuality. This physician is known to be frank and careful to remind teens to act safely and responsibly, especially in terms of sex, and he offers information to disabled teens who might be too embarrassed to ask questions.

Kennedy, M., Wessling, K., & Vargus, N. (2003). *Special Olympics* (A True Book). New York: Scholastic Library.

This is a nonfiction account of the Special Olympics, the many people who take part in making it happen, and the participants who compete.

Levine, E. (1974). *Lisa and her soundless world*. New York: Human Sciences Press.

Lisa's parents are worried about her growing up in a hearing world until they experience and understand the many successes available to her through a hearing aid. This book describes the use of a hearing aid in more technical terms than more current books. In fact, the more daunting visual image of the older hearing aids that appear to look more like small backpacks rather than small earpieces, like today's more sophisticated instruments, can be a bit telling. However, the story itself is uplifting. Although cochlear implants have changed everything, this book is worth reading.

Matlin, M. (2006). *Nobody's perfect*. New York: Simon & Schuster Children's Publishing.

This chapter book offers readers an experience with a deaf girl whose speech-reading and signing skills allow her to thrive in the hearing world. Megan and a new girl, Alexis, get paired up for a science project and end up learning a lot about one another. More importantly, readers get introduced to Alexis's brother with autism who learns some basic sign language from Megan, resulting in Alexis being able to communicate better with her brother. It opens up communication with both him and Alexis. Readers unfamiliar with deafness will be intrigued by the descriptions of how Megan studies and her interactions with an American Sign Language interpreter during class time. It's a simple story that allows those with and without disabilities a glimpse at the Deaf or nonhearing (Deaf—capital D makes it a cultural reference) world.

Meyer, D. (1997). *Views from our shoes: Growing up with a brother or sister with special needs*. Bethesda, MD: Woodbine House.

Readers are exposed to down-to-earth, sincere stories, ranging from mental retardation through a number of rare syndromes, contributed by 45 children ranging in age from 4 to 18. In talking about their siblings and their feelings, we are exposed to children's embarrassment of their siblings and their anger and jealousy. However, we also see how protective and loving they are when it comes to getting along in a family that is different. This book is the perfect complement for siblings who need to know they are not alone in having a brother or sister with special needs or disabilities.

Meyer, D. (2005). *The sibling slam book: What it's really like to have a brother or sister with special needs*. Bethesda, MD: Woodbine House.

This book is full of comments by 81 young people who display the theme of optimism and hope while recognizing their hard work, dedication, resentment, and fierce protection regarding their love for their sibling with special needs or disabilities. A typical slam-book question such as, "Has your sib ever embarrassed you?" is also intertwined with a chapter like, "Ever Feel Invisible?" Reflections to many questions and relevant chapters provide insightful material so that all readers are sure to relate to some of the thoughtful or heartfelt responses shared by these brave individuals.

Rickert, J. (2000). *Russ and the firehouse.* Bethesda, MD: Woodbine House.

Russ, a young boy with Down syndrome, is lucky enough to get to spend the day at a local firehouse. In real-life pictures, we get to see him help inspect and clean the equipment and the firehouse dog. It's a wonderful portrayal of a boy with Down syndrome enjoying the same experience any child would like to have.

Senisi, E. (2002). *All kinds of friends, even green!* Bethesda, MD: Woodbine House.

Moses has to do a writing assignment for school. He has to choose one friend to write about but he can't decide on which of his many friends to choose. Moses, who uses a wheelchair, remembers that he and his neighbor's iguana, Zaki, have missing toes and share many of the same obstacles in moving around throughout the day. So he decides to write about him.

Sparks, B. (1994). *It happened to Nancy: A true story from the diary of a teenager.* New York: HarperCollins.

This story is based on a real girl, age 14, named Nancy. She comes from divorced though loving parents and has a good Catholic upbringing. She has lots of friends and a future full of great things. She meets Collin at a concert and falls in love. He rapes her and then disappears. Her mother supports her as she recovers from this attack and tries to get on with her life. Eventually, she finds herself ill, infected with the HIV virus. She waits to tell her friends her situation. Throughout hospital visits and the eventual breakdown of her immune system as well as the pain and loss of control, she enters these experiences in diary form so that they can be shared with other teens upon her death. Nancy dies at age 16. Her accounts are followed by a question-and-answer section on HIV and AIDS, which ought not be skipped.

Stuve-Bodeen, S. (1998). *We'll paint the octopus red.* Bethesda, MD: Woodbine House.

A 6-year-old girl, Emma, finds that her new baby brother, who has Down syndrome, won't be as quick to learn the things she wants to share with him as she had thought. However, this story for young children is reassuring for those siblings who have the same fears. It shows them that they just need to be a bit more patient and keep introducing their sibling to fun, learning activities.

Woloson, E. (2003). *My friend Isabelle.* Bethesda, MD: Woodbine House.

In this story, we meet Charlie and Isabelle. Charlie is what most people refer to as "normal," whereas Isabelle is a bit "different." The story takes the reader through some very practical yet simple descriptions of the similarities and differences between the two children without ever making them seem "normal" or "different" from one another. This easy reader is a useful tool in showing how a child with Down syndrome can just as easily enjoy the same things as an able-bodied, healthy child, but he or she might need just a little more time and patience.

REFERENCES

Blaska, J., Inkster, C., & Williams, S. (2005). The Joan K. Blaska collection of children's literature featuring characters with disabilities or chronic illnesses. *Journal of Children's Literature, 31,* 71–80.

Dyches, T., Prater, M., & Cramer, S. (2001). Characterization of mental retardation and autism in children's books. *Education and Training in Mental Retardation and Developmental Disabilities, 36*(3), 230–243.

Iaquinta, A., & Hipsky, S. (2006). Practical bibliotherapy strategies for the inclusive elementary classroom. *Early Childhood Education Journal, 34*(3), 209–213.

Prater, M., Dyches, T., & Johnstun, M. (2006). Teaching students about learning disabilities through children's literature. *Intervention in School and Clinic, 42,* 14–24.

Salend, S. (2004). *Creating inclusive classrooms: Effective and reflective practices for all students.* Saddle River, NJ: Pearson Education.

Chapter 10 Influences of a Digital World

Kimberly Persiani-Becker

Is there anything better than getting lost in a story with quality characters who you wish were your friends in real life? How about all those settings we have been introduced to that we would never get a chance to encounter in our everyday lives? What about the thickening plots, scary events we'd never be brave enough to endure, interesting people we may never get a chance to meet? When and why have children and young adults decided they would rather play games on the Internet, their video player, or listen to their iPods in place of a good book? If what ABC reported in the news on Sunday, December 2, 2007, that only 52% of today's youth is choosing to read books on their own accord for pleasure, then we ought to be concerned. How are books supposed to compete with the availability of technology and media-related material for kids today? With that said, computer software, Internet games, and video games introduce children to technology, which is a critical factor in becoming computer literate in the 21st century. In addition, these activities teach kids to follow directions, and they help them obtain problem-solving skills and develop logic and critical thinking abilities. For younger kids, these practices with technology help develop fine motor and spatial skills. And of course, these activities are entertaining and fun. But aren't books entertaining and fun?

It wasn't too long ago, maybe just 20 or 30 years, when it wasn't uncommon to find homes without computers, cable television, cell phones, or even VCR players. Today, it's uncommon not to find most or all of these things and more. Back in the day of Speak and Spell, Hooked on Phonics, and a small amount of books on tape, children were intrigued by this simple technology. Today, it goes without saying. Children and young adults run circles around their elders when it comes to the variety of technology media available. Getting them to pick up a book for entertainment and fun when there is so much more to keep them engaged is something all parents, teachers, librarians, and the like, must contend with.

THE INTERNET, TELEVISION, AND THE VIDEO INDUSTRY

With access to the Internet, hundreds of channels on television, and the video industry today, little independent thought or creativity is even existent in the choices of childhood activities. Hearing a good story and visualizing the setting and the characters and relating the plot to one's own life fills this creative void, doesn't it? But again, how does the book industry make itself appealing to youngsters today? What is it about the wired world that keeps children from picking up a good book, asking to be read to, or passing on novels to their friends in order to share a wonderful experience depicted in the pages of a book?

Children enjoy the Internet, television, video games, and the like, because they (a) are enjoyable and take little or no physical activity, (b) allow children to feel in control, (c) are a great way to relieve school and home stress, (d) fill in for boredom, and (e) offer a sense of accomplishment when mastering skills. Can't books and stories do the same?

Unfortunately, there are still many questions about the effect that video games, computers, and television have on children's overall creativity, time spent reading books, and in particular, their academic achievement. If it is true that children spend more time watching television than any activity other than sleeping, and then you add video games and the Internet into the mix, not to mention cell phone use and listening to music, when is time made for books outside of classroom texts? This problem is even more compounded when the likes of the popular Wii Fit ask children and young adults to simply turn on their video game machine in order to participate in activities like strength training, aerobics, yoga, and balance games. If children don't even have to put down their handheld video devices to go to the park or backyard to exercise anymore, what makes us think we can get them to pick up a good book?

DIGITAL AGE LITERATURE

We know that successful readers read often and children obtain reading skills early if they have experience with books and other print media. This is especially true if they were read to at an early age by their parents or caregivers and were exposed to libraries and storytelling when they were young. In addition, reading fluency takes practice, which in turn leads to reading becoming a pleasurable experience.

But when television, the Internet, cell phones, iPods, and video games take the place of reading or being read to, one can easily miss the timeframe of acquiring solid reading skills, thus resulting in children and young adults not finding pleasure in books. The key is combining good books with child-identified enjoyable activities. One such Web site is http://www.tumblebooks.com.

TumbleBooks

TumbleBooks are created by taking existing picture books and adding animation, sound, music, and narration to produce an electronic picture book that children can read or have read to them.

Through the TumbleBook Library, children are introduced to a variety of multicultural themes, such as in the book, *Si, Se Puede! Yes, We Can!* by Diana Cohn. The library offers many books that raise awareness of different cultures. Also, it contains several books that relate to social issues children face on a daily basis. One favorite among kids today is *Enemy Pie,* by Derek Munson. Readers will find books on topics such as civic efficacy, the elderly, and cultural tolerance. The library also contains books that are biographical as well as additional nonfiction books. Books with bilingual titles celebrate stories in two languages. Silly books, like *Boy Soup,* by Loris Lesynski, are perfectly suited for those who want to just read for pleasure without being concerned about the typical "moral of the story." This Web site is a source of enrichment for children who read fluently, but it also provides reading support for those who need some skill building, while providing an interactive experience via technology for all children.

After reading one of the many wonderful books on this Web site, children are encouraged to engage in one of the interactive activities that go along with the book they just read. TumblePuzzles allow readers to complete an online puzzle using a picture from the book. TumbleGames allow readers to complete spelling games and "fill-in-the blank" games, reinforcing concepts from the book. TumbleQuizzes ask readers to answer five multiple-choice questions in order to gauge children's reading comprehension.

Although it appears that TumbleBooks is geared for young readers, this couldn't be further from the truth. Besides the fact that picture books are just as exciting to older readers as to younger ones, many of these picture books are rich in many cultural, social, and life skill issues that pertain to all of us. With that said, TumbleBooks provides plenty of books to keep the older reader busy, including some of the classics, such as *Anne of Green Gables,* by Lucy Montgomery, *Black Beauty,* by Anna Sewell, *The Legend of Sleepy Hollow,* by Washington Irving, and *The Wind in the Willows,* by Kenneth Grahame. In addition, books meant for older readers can even be found in languages other than English, such as the classic, *Madame Bovary*, written in French by Gustave Flaubert. The same kind of follow-up activities used for the picture books also exist for the chapter books. TumbleBooks is a place for all readers to go. Everyone can find something of interest to read at this one-stop reading network.

Although there are many kids who want to spend more time with technology in their classrooms, there are also committed educators who want to integrate more computer use into the curriculum. In a relevant *Book Links* (Mangelson & Castek, 2007) column (American Library Association), the authors focused on Web sites that get students involved with narratives. These Web sites included TumbleBooks, as previously mentioned, as well as several others, including International Children's Digital Library (ICDL) (http://en.childrenslibrary.org), Light Up Your Brain (http://lightup yourbrain.com/audio-stories-for-children.html), and Starfall (http://www.starfall.com).

The Light Up Your Brain Web site allows participants to download audio versions of well-known fairy tales and storybooks. Because these stories can be downloaded to MP3 players, they can be used in the classroom, computer lab, or in a classroom listening center. Stories such as Cinderella, Jack and the Beanstalk, and The Little Mermaid are just a handful of fun examples available for children to read. The stories on this Web site are comparable to books on tape, but at no cost. Once on this site, many other Web sites with similar features are introduced.

Starfall is also free and is a program created to help children learn to read. Many levels of readers can access this Web site and find books at the lower, intermediate, and higher levels. The stories include books for emergent and early readers where individual letters, vowel sounds, and letter combinations are highlighted. This is a great tool for second language learners and also for visual learners. Voice assistance is available if a reader does not understand a word in the text. The more advanced the reader, the more advanced the texts that are available, including myths, fables, plays, fiction, and nonfiction titles (Mangelson & Castek, 2007). What better way to get children of today excited about reading than through the Internet? If educators are going to have to compete with all the technology available to the youth of the 21st century, then we ought to have tools such as these to arm ourselves with.

Television, video games, computers, iPods, and cell phones dictate media advertising that is geared mostly toward the younger crowd, children and young adults especially. How often do we see commercials promoting good books, fun visits to the library for storytelling, trips to the bookstore, or children being read to? Rarely. And usually, these advertisements are influenced by a political candidate running for office or by a well-known actor hoping to make a difference. Commercials on television, advertisements in magazines, ads on billboards, announcements on radio, and so on, cater to the population that will buy the products; so instead of only focusing on the technology and media culture of it all, why not infuse endorsements for library visits, bookstore promotions, and the simple excitement of reading a good book? The *Harry Potter* books created a worldwide buzz; so why not others? Does a movie have to be made for kids to even consider reading the book before or after they see it? And what is the responsibility of advertisers in including literature in their planning for spots on television, billboards, and the like?

Consumers are inundated and caught in the middle of this media frenzy where children and young adults are the targets for the most part. The children of the 21st century are constantly introduced to more electronic media than one can keep up with. They are curious and can be easily influenced. It doesn't help that television networks and video game publishers target them. If we can't count on these executives to step up and take on this challenge, especially in light of the fact that children and young adults are so easily influenced, it is imperative that more book publishers offer stories and rich literature to children via the Internet and computer software that can be used at home, at school, or at the library. This is most important for those readers who do a good job of organizing their time between technology and reading. It is also important for those who speak more than one language and are socially and culturally conscious. As we know, technology, television, music, the Internet, and so forth, are known experiences all over the world. With this in mind, Web sites such as the ICDL, mentioned earlier, are places for today's savvy young people to meet others across the world through books.

ICDL Books

The ICDL Foundation has developed a collection that represents rich and meaningful historical and modern-day books from all over the world. These books are available for children who identify immediately with the culture in question and also for those with little or no experience with said culture. In a letter to all the visitors of ICDL, Tim Browne, the executive director of the ICDL foundation, wrote this:

> Every day the news media report misunderstandings, intolerance and outright aggression between people from different cultures. Age-old disputes over land, water, religious and cultural practices fuel intolerance. Children absorb the culture and attitudes of their community. Consequently, cycles of intolerance pass from generation to generation. But there is some hope for change: research has shown that sharing personal experiences can change attitudes. Change can happen when children read children's books from other cultures. (Browne, n.d.)

No matter if the child comes from another continent, country, state, or city, rural areas, urban areas, or suburban areas, teachers continue to contend with students whose first language is not English. No matter that we live in the 21st century where languages, cultures, and familial backgrounds are more celebrated than ever; the first language of families often gets left behind. Wherever their new home is, it may be difficult to find children's books from their cultures and in their native language. Families do a good job of oral storytelling, but having a book with pictures to depict such stories makes it more realistic and tangible. It may be hard for parents to find cultural stories from their homeland to share with their children. A Web site like ICDL offers a place for parents, along with teachers and librarians, to find books and stories in other languages that authentically represent a culture and its origin. The ICDL collection includes books from a variety of sources around the globe with the goal of reflecting as many of the world's cultures as possible. Libraries, publishers, authors, and illustrators work diligently to ensure that the ICDL collection is as diverse as possible. In addition, because it has to be viewed on the Internet, this makes said reading that much more enjoyable to the reader, given that technology plays such a big role in the lives of today's kids.

At the ICDL Web site, children, young adults, parents, teachers, and librarians can meet characters like 12-year-old Aliou, who lives at the edge of his city like so many poor children all around the world, in *Aliou et Jean* (Fourth World Editions). One can read about a lively family who finds pride in the father who makes a walking doll and becomes famous in the classic, *A Lively Family,* by Elye Kahan. And who wouldn't enjoy Francisco X. Alarcón's wonderful and humorous stories and poems? In a series of four books set in each of the four seasons, Alarcon's tales of Mexico and Southern California are about his boyhood and family. Readers should enjoy Titoy's magical chair as it turns into a car, an airplane, or a train. In this story, you travel with the chair and find out how a boy overcame his disability with the help of his imagination in *Titoy's Magical Chair,* by Russell Molina. Don't forget the classic, *Heidi,* by Johanna Spyri, about a Swiss orphan who leaves her family and home to go to school and take care of an invalid girl in the city. ICDL is not only for child readers; there is plenty for young adults too.

Introducing children to Web sites like the ICDL allows them to have better access to life in an ethnically and culturally diverse world through children's literature. Not to mention that those who identify with the culture, stories, language, and characters in the stories presented are much more apt to want to read, as they can see themselves and their own life circumstances in the books.

Although the Web site appears to be geared more toward teachers and librarians, it can also be used by older students (ages 9 and up). Younger students, with the guidance of a teacher or parent, should be able to navigate the Web site quite easily. Once students learn how to navigate the site, they ought to be able to select the stories on their own. Students will likely relish the opportunity to have access to books from different countries. The Web site can be used at home to allow students to explore at their leisure, but it is probably best used with the guidance of a teacher. It can be a great tool to use in the classroom as a unit to teach multiculturalism by exposing students to books from other cultures. By "reading" these books, students will not only notice the obvious differences between other cultures and America, but they will also notice the similarities between stories told in other countries and our stories here. Another way to use the Web site in the classroom is by teaching students about the power of art, how pictures can tell their own stories. They will learn that words are not necessary to tell a tale. Perhaps using this Web site may also make students empathize with those who are learning English as their second language.

COMPUTER BOOKS AND PROGRAMS

In 2000, the Media Awareness Network (MNet, 2005) initiated a research project that tracked and investigated the behaviors, attitudes, and opinions of Canadian children and young adults with respect to their use of the Internet. There were two phases that took place for this project: (1) In 2000 to 2001, the research consisted of interviews with parents, focus groups with parents and children, and a national school-based survey of 5,682 students in Grades 4 to 11; and (2) in 2003 to 2005, the research included a national school-based survey of 5,272 children and young adults in Grades 4 to 11 and findings from focus groups with parents and young people ages 11 to 17. The study found that young Canadians are being exposed to and connecting with the Internet at a very early age. In addition, it revealed that 94% of young people access the Internet from home. That's a huge number. According to the study, the following list shows some of the main activities children and young adults use the Internet for in Canada:

- Reading and sending e-mail
- Playing games online
- Using instant messaging
- Visiting chat rooms
- Downloading and listening to music, TV shows, and movies
- Writing an online diary or Weblog

If 94% of Canadian kids are using the Internet for most of their socializing and media entertainment, when does book reading get included? Are kids reading only at school these days? Are they at least finding books on tape and downloading them to their iPods as a way to hear a good book? Are they visiting Web sites geared for student reading? Are they utilizing software dedicated to stories of fiction and nonfiction? Is it enough to have children and young adults read only at school or for assigned homework? How can we get them to read on their own? Again, we need to combine technology and books.

Accelerated Reader

One of the many programs that has been around for quite a while is known as Accelerated Reader. And though it has been steeped in its own controversy over the years, it is one more way we can get children and young adults to get excited about reading while combining the use of technology to do so. It is much more assessment driven than one expects when just reading a book for pleasure, but for those Type A personality kids who like to have their story followed up with a quiz, comprehension questions, or a score of some sort, this is a place for that to happen. Accelerated Reader achieves the following:

- Facilitates detailed assessment
- Provides immediate feedback for the reader
- Develops metacognitive awareness
- Increases motivation to read more difficult books
- Provides feedback to the educator about the reader's abilities
- Promotes effective reading practice

The reader selects a book from thousands of available titles, each of which is assigned a point value based on its difficulty. He or she reads the book at his or her own pace. After reading, the reader visits the computer and takes a multiple-choice comprehension test. Then, the computer scores the test, awards the reader points, and maintains a record. It's best if the student can maintain an average of 85%.

Accelerated Reader is often used in a variety of ways. Proper training and consistency of its use are obviously important in making the program desirable and practical. This is a school-based software program, which can be made available in class, after school, and in the computer lab, just to name a few. It isn't a favorite among all educators, however. According to Krashen (2002), the most beneficial things about Accelerated Reader are that the program provides access to books and encourages more reading. That being said, the tests and rewards are not evidenced to make this program as beneficial as educators might hope. Whether or not one agrees with the benefits outlined by Accelerated Reader itself, if the books children are reading from this program are quality and rich in content and the students enjoy them, shouldn't it be used in the classroom? Isn't the whole point to get kids excited to read? Just make sure that if the program is used, there is sufficient time and access to the books via the program so that the readers have real opportunities to engage in the literature.

The Magic School Bus

One of the most popular book series for early childhood and elementary age students is *The Magic School Bus*. Talk about a title that gets the attention of kids. This is one of those themes that most kids can recognize and look forward to. Ms. Frizzle and her students take journeys through outer space, into the dinosaur era, through hurricanes, and more. This group of books is science related and child friendly. Not only are the books colorful and factual, but children love to read them. In addition, DVDs and videos associated with many of the titles are readily available to share with children after the book has been introduced. On top of that, students can go to *The Magic School Bus* Web site (http://www.scholastic.com/magicschoolbus) and spend time taking quizzes about science topics presented in the books; they can also play games related to the stories and learn more about science topics associated with Ms. Frizzle and her gang. It's also a great Web site for teachers to find lesson plans and field trip ideas. Not only can students read these books, they can follow up with a variety of activities without having to leave the computer.

Games such as mazes, habitat match-ups, pop quizzes, and coloring books can be found to enhance the reader's learning experience. Also, guided tours pertaining to insects, space, the human body, dinosaurs, and more can be found at this site. Themes like animals, motion and forces, different science strands, and the like, are available for perusal and very easy to access for students, parents, and teachers. In fact, parents and teachers have their own section where they can take museum tours, download science activities, and travel on Ms. Frizzle's bus of adventures. Lastly, there are clips and movies shown on this Web site that go directly with the books. It's fun, interactive, colorful, and more importantly, accurate, as it relates to science. Children and adults alike will find this site useful and it will keep the kids coming back for more. It's one that ought to be emulated by other book series that are popular with children today. Teachers might even choose to keep a log of all the titles, games, quizzes, and the like, that their students have completed and offer incentives for completing a certain number of them. An incentive such as a free book, extra computer time, first choice of books to check out at the next library visit, and so forth, are simple and easy in-class programs that can be used to encourage more and more reading. And for those older students struggling with reading, science, or both, Ms. Frizzle is a delight to them as well.

Dr. Seuss

In addition to *The Magic School Bus* series, the Dr. Seuss books are another very popular and well-known series. These books have been around for ages. All of us, no matter which country we are from, have most likely encountered them ("Dr. Seuss" is the pen name for author Theodor Seuss Geisel). Some of us learned to read and rhyme from his books like *The Cat in the Hat,* whereas others of us learned how to get along well with our peers and those of different cultural backgrounds by reading *The Sneetches,* a title useful for young and older students. These are only two titles of many that have been favorites of ours for a long time. Just saying "Dr. Seuss" usually makes people smile as they spout off their favorite titles or deliver lines from pages they know by heart. Today's children do not need to be deprived of this amazing author. The Web site associated with these books (http://www.seussville.com) is another interactive site devoted to Dr. Seuss stories and games. Children can read about the author, discover all the books available, and play fun, bright, energizing puzzles and games to go along with the characters they discover in the books. It's free and can be used in the classroom, the library, or at home. In addition, parents who visit this site with their children are able to purchase directly from the site should they so choose.

AUDIOBOOKS

It isn't easy growing up and being a part of a media- and technology-frenzied world. It's even more difficult for those of us who remember what it was like to spend a rainy day with a good book or an engaging board game. We don't have to lose hope. Although it's difficult for teachers, authors, parents, and librarians to understand when a child says, "I don't like to read," but he or she can run circles around them on the computer; it's also heartening to know that Web sites like those mentioned are available for our children to still read and play games on a blustery day. With this in mind, it's critical that we find ways to encourage reading, including the use of technology to do so. It's our hope that children will continue to choose books in hard copy form, but because we are competing with electronic media in such full force, we also have to embrace it and find ways to connect children and young adults to books, literature, and stories through a medium with which they are most familiar. Audiobooks are yet one more way that we can get our young people to hear good stories or even learn to read as they follow along in their own text.

Many of the mandated language arts reading programs in schools today include CDs to accompany the anthologies and excerpts of chapter books. Considering that this is something included into the classroom curriculum and usually enjoyed by students, young and older, it's also important to seek interesting audiobooks that they will find appealing and choose to listen to on their own. Parents can be a big help in this by popping an audiobook into the car CD player rather than listening to the radio or music CDs. Family members listening to the Harry Potter series on the way to school, the grocery store, soccer practice, and the like, are spending their time in a much more useful way than watching DVDs on the car player or tolerating the music no one in the car can agree upon. Seeing as Harry Potter is loved by all ages, including adults, this would be the perfect opportunity to get kids interested in this medium for exciting books. For the younger kids, the ever-popular *Frog and Toad* series is one they can relate to, as these stories were read to them throughout their youngest years.

In addition to listening to audiobooks for the pure joy of it, one might consider making assigned homework reading a car-related activity as well. Titles like *The Outsiders,* by S. E. Hinton, and *The Giver,* by L. Lowry, and classics such as *The Adventures of Huckleberry Finn,* by M. Twain, for older children, and *Charlotte's Web,* by E. B. White, for the younger readers, are good examples of audiobooks that would go along with books being read for school, as a way to get children engaged in the story and also serve as a model to follow the words as the stories are read aloud to them. In addition, having these audiobooks running in the car, downloaded to an iPod, playing on the bedroom CD player, and the like, will surely get them to complete their homework assignments and most likely, want to hear what happens next.

REFLECTION QUESTIONS FOR THE TEACHER

1. What are the pros and cons of children reading with books and reading on the Internet?

2. As a teacher, am I aware of all that my students are reading on the Internet and in books?

3. What are some of the latest programs or software games and Internet books that are available for my students?

4. What training or information do I need to use these resources effectively and to their maximum potential?

SAMPLE RESPONSE LESSON 10.1

http://www.tumblebooks.com

Primary Grades: In the Classroom, With Parents, Tutors, or Computer Lab

Duration: 1 to 2 Hours

Note to Teacher/Parent/Tutor: TumbleBooks is an enjoyable, meaningful, and productive interactive Web site for children to read stories, play games, and get excited about returning to in order to select another book. Although many of the books are designated for younger students through about 5th or 6th grade, there are also wonderful and stimulating books available for older students in the secondary grades. And isn't the goal during this time of media-infused culture to still get children to read good, rich stories? What better way is there to do this than by including this tool in your classroom or at home? The children will love this site and you will find them wanting to go back for more time and again. This makes a great classroom center, computer lab activity, Independent Work Time assignment, homework assignment, or just a fun reading activity when children have down time.

Overview

Once the teacher or parent has registered at http://www.tumblebooks.com, children should be introduced to the functions available on this Web site. If the teacher is planning to introduce TumbleBooks to his or her students, one way to do this easily is in the computer lab. If a parent is introducing this at home, sit with the child and do the same. Written reflections and illustrations of students' favorite scenes will accompany each independent practice. In addition, the children will complete a teacher-designed critique sheet on each story and puzzle, game, or quiz completed to be used as a reference for other students as they choose stories to complete on their own. The same kind of activities can be completed with *The Magic School Bus* Web site, the Seusville Web site, and the Accelerated Reader program.

Materials

Registration with http://www.tumblebooks.com, reflection journals, and critique sheets

Anticipatory Set

1. *Focus:* Students will read a variety of books and complete corresponding games, quizzes, and puzzles to show their comprehension of the stories read.

2. *Objective:* By the end of the lesson, students will read, complete quizzes, games, and puzzles, illustrate their favorite scene from chosen books, and critique books for others' use.

3. *Transfer:* Students will use this information as a way to distinguish meaningful literature from pieces less interesting to the peers and consider book choices when selecting titles on their own.

Instruction

1. If you are in the classroom or computer lab, choose a book that the majority of students will like. At home, allow your child to choose a book from a short list you offer after having perused appropriate selections yourself first.

2. Next, take the child through the read-aloud function for this book. This will be familiar to those who have had experience with phonics media games or karaoke. As the story is read aloud, the words being read are lit up just like songs when people sing karaoke. It's fun, manageable, and the children connect to the words.

3. Following the read-aloud, engage the children in a discussion about what the story was about, as a reminder, and then discuss the characters. When children connect immediately to the characters of a story, it becomes more of a personal discussion about their friends, thus making the dialogue more enthusiastic and enjoyable.

4. After the discussion, offer the children a few options for follow-up games, quizzes, or puzzles for the story. Then lead them through the option of choice.

Independent Practice

1. The children will be given time to read an additional story on their own or with a partner. If doing this at home, continue working with the child or allow him or her to read another story and complete another activity with your guidance, until the child feels comfortable with the variety of activities.

2. After the story has been read to them at the site, the children will write a summary of the story and illustrate their favorite scene in their reflection journal.

3. Upon completion of an accompanying game, quiz, or puzzle, the reader will critique the story and activity, then add this sheet in ABC order by book title in the classmade or homemade "TumbleBooks Critique Journal." If done in the classroom, students must sign their mane to their critique. The teacher or parent can assign points for each reflection and critique that is completed, which can then be used as incentives or extra credit.

(Continued)

(Continued)

Closure

Make sure students compile their critiques in the "TumbleBooks Critique Journal." Also, remind them to check the journal before choosing a book on their own to see what their peers think about the book. Keep in mind that some of the children will still complete a story if it is already in the book. These critiques can also be added to the journal as an alternative critique or to support their peers. Remember, the same kind of activities can be completed with *The Magic School Bus* site, the Seusville site, and the Accelerated Reader program.

Modifications: English Language Learners

ELLs can be paired with native speaking peers to help them navigate the stories in English. If any stories are offered in the child's native language, the story and activities can be completed in their first language.

Sample Response Lesson 10.2

http://www.en.childrenslibrary.org

Secondary Grades: Technical Class, Foreign Language Class, Language Arts Class, or at Home

Duration: 1 Day and Opportunities to Use All Year

Note to the Teacher/Parent: One of the most important characteristics of a good multicultural book is authenticity. This Web site is where students can find books written by and about cultural groups with which they identify or want to know more about.

Overview

In the computer lab, at a designated classroom center, or at home, have children navigate through this Web site, visiting other continents and countries in search of books in languages other than English. Because many of these books are not available in the United States, encourage them to find stories that they would never see otherwise. In addition, if they speak and read in another language, encourage them to seek books written in their native language. Written reflections and critiques will be used for evaluation purposes.

Materials

Computer and Internet access, reflection journals, and critique sheets

Key Vocabulary

Multicultural

Anticipatory Set

1. *Focus:* Students will read a variety of multicultural stories, some in their native language and some in other languages, if only through the illustrations.

2. *Objective:* Students will summarize stories they have read and will critique them for authenticity in languages they are familiar with or for interest in those books written in languages other than those they are familiar with.

3. *Transfer:* Critiquing books in this way offers readers an opportunity to write their own stories in their native language, illustrate their own pictures, and get in touch with cultural groups within and outside their own culture.

Instruction

1. If you are in the classroom or computer lab, choose a book that the majority of students will like. At home, allow your child to choose a book from a short list you offer after having perused appropriate selections yourself first. This can be very important if you are using this site to teach your child to read in your native language, as you will want the text to be comprehensible and appropriate.

2. Next, read a book aloud together either as a shared reading, choral reading, or guided reading. As the story is read aloud, remind children to view the illustrations, especially if it is being read in a language they are unfamiliar with, as the illustrations can be very helpful in understanding the story.

3. Following the reading, engage the children in a discussion about what the story was about. Discuss the characters, the language, and the illustrations.

Guided Practice

After the discussion, have the children help you write a summary of the story or chapter (you may be using a chapter book with the older students), a reflection, and a critique, as they will be doing this on their own for evaluation purposes.

(Continued)

(Continued)

Independent Practice

1. Students will select a book and read a story, using the illustrations for help if necessary.

2. Following this, the reader will write a summary and reflection of the book and then a critique of the book using the following questions: Is the story something they have heard about at home, at school, or within their cultural group? Have they just read a book in another language they are studying and were they able to follow the story line without the use of the English summary or illustrations? Did they learn something about the cultural group depicted in the story? What did the illustrations say about the story? If they followed the pictures of the story rather than the text because it is in a language other than one they can read, what story did they come up with through the drawings?

Closure

Encourage students to write to the Web site designer about ways to improve access and user friendliness of the site while also contributing book title ideas of stories they may have read or have had read to them in their home country, if applicable.

Evaluation

Students will have peers review their written reflection, summary, and critique, have them signed off, and then turn them in to the teacher for evaluation or to their parent for discussion purposes. Parents may want to use this Web site as an incentive for something their child is trying to earn. For example, for every book critiqued, for a total of five, their child will earn a new book or more computer time at home. Teachers may want to use this as incentive for earning extra credit that can be completed at school or at home.

Modifications: English Language Learners

ELLs will be paired with peers of higher ELD levels for translation in order to support student understanding and practice.

SELECTED ANNOTATED BIBLIOGRAPHY

TumbleBooks

Cohn, D. (2002). *Si, se puede! Yes, we can! Janitor strike in L.A.* El Paso, TX: Cinco Puntos Press.

Carlitos' mother is a janitor. Every night while he sleeps, his mother cleans in one of the skyscrapers in downtown Los Angeles. One night, his mamá explains that she can't make enough money to support him and his abuelita the way she needs to unless she makes more money as a janitor. She and the other janitors have decided to go on strike. Will he support her and help her all he can? Of course, Carlitos wants to help, but he cannot think of a way until he sees his mother on television making a speech in support of the strike. Finally, Carlitos knows how he can show his mamá how proud he is of her. He and the other children in his class make posters and Carlitos joins the marchers with a very special sign for his mom! (In both Spanish and English)

Collodi, C. (2007). *The adventures of Pinocchio*. Radford, VA. (Originally published in 1883)

Pinocchio is a wooden puppet who comes to life and has the most amazing adventures. He becomes a naughty, mischievous boy who is full of good intentions but tends to be greedy and lets nothing stand in his way. His maker, Gepetto, loves him like a son, but Pinocchio just can't stay out of trouble. (In Spanish).

Flaubert, G. (2008). *Madame Bovary: Provincial manners* (M. Mauldon, Trans.) New York: Oxford University Press. (Originally published in 1857)

This is a bold story of adultery and suicide in Normandy, France, a subject that was not usually written about in literature at the time it was published. (In French)

Grahame, K. (1908). *The wind in the willows*. New York: Charles Scribner's Sons.

The classic story of Rat, Mole, Badger, Toad, and their life by the river became an established part of children's literature.

Lesynski, L. (2008). *Boy soup*. Toronto, Canada: Annick Press.

When Giant wakes up with a big hurting head and a sore raspy throat, he finds that the cure is a bowl of Boy Soup! Giant captures five boys and Kate, who all protest his plan. But Kate soon comes up with her own remedy and convinces the Giant that the soup should be made, not of boys, but by boys.

Montgomery, L. (2008). *Anne of Green Gables*. New York: G. P. Putnam's Sons. (Originally published in 1925)

This is a lovely story about an aging brother and sister, Mathew and Marilla Cuthbert, who decide to adopt a boy to help with chores around their farm. To their surprise, the boy turns out to be none other than Anne, who is a bit feisty and energetic while being charming as well as stubborn. Not sure what to do with Anne, we begin to read about these three lives as they grow together in the Avonlea. Anne makes friends, including her best friend Diana, and her admirer, Gilbert Blythe, who often find themselves a part of Anne's escapades.

Munson, D. (2000). *Enemy pie*. San Francisco: Chronicle Books.

It began as the perfect summer, until Jeremy Ross moves into the house down the street and becomes the neighborhood enemy. But Dad knows what to do: Make Enemy Pie! Strangely, part of the recipe involves spending an entire day playing with the enemy. This boy learns an effective recipe for turning your best enemy into your best friend.

Sewell, A. (1877). *Black Beauty.* New York: F. Watts.

Another favorite among young children and older youngsters alike, Black Beauty is a magnificent horse that tells of his experiences with both good and bad masters.

Washington, I. (2007). *The legend of Sleepy Hollow.* New York: Atheneum Books for Young Readers. (Originally published in 1820)

Ichabod Crane is the new schoolmaster of Sleepy Hollow and soon adjusts to local ways. He visits the prosperous farmers of the area, eats their food, and spends time listening to local lore and legends while sitting by the fire. We all know that Ichabod hopes to marry Katrina Van Tassel and acquire her father's land and money, except for Brom Bones, known as the town hero, who also wants to marry Katrina, causing the rivalry between Ichabod and Brom to take on hilarious twists and turns.

ICDL Books

Alarcón, F. (1997). *Laughing tomatoes and other spring poems [Jitomates risueños y otros poemas de primavera]* (Maya Gonzalez, Ill.). San Francisco: Children's Book Press.

This is a bilingual collection of humorous and serious poems about family, nature, and celebrations by a renowned Mexican American poet.

Alarcón, F. (1998). *From the bellybutton of the moon and other summer poems [Del ombligo de la luna y otros poemas de verano].* (Maya Gonzalez, Ill.). San Francisco: Children's Book Press.

Alarcón tells the story of the creation of Mexico and ties it to the "Bellybutton of the Moon." Rainbows, trees, his family, and his pet cow, "Mariposa," make up his happy childhood world.

Alarcón, F. (1999). *Angels ride bikes and other fall poems [Los ángeles andan en bicicletay otros poemas de otoño].* (Maya Gonzalez, Ill.). San Francisco: Children's Book Press.

This is the story of a colorful journey to the writer's childhood in Southern California. He wants you to use all your senses and enjoy life in Los Angeles as much as he does.

Alarcón, F. (2001). *Iguanas in the snow and other winter poems [Iguanas en la nieve y otros poemas de invierno].* (Maya Gonzalez, Ill.). San Francisco: Children's Book Press.

The magical cycle of the seasons comes full circle with this tribute to winter through a collection of bilingual poems.

Fourth World Editions. (1990). *Aliou et Jean (enfants du Sénégal)* (Bassene, L. E., Ill.). Paris, France: Author.

"With books, you can travel all over the world and meet all kinds of people," says 12-year-old Aliou. So, follow Aliou and his friends who live at the edge of the city like so many poor children all around the world. The market, the school, the family, the soccer field, the festival, and the *rue* become stages for this surprising voyage to the country of hope.

Kahan, E. (1937). *A lively family*. Ukraine: Children's Publishing House at the Central Committee of the Leninist Young Communist League.

In the first of stories, "A Lively Family," a father who works in a toy factory is trying to invent a walking doll. He thinks about it day and night. His wife and children are very unhappy because he thinks too much about his work and doesn't take care of the family. Eventually, the father manages to make a walking doll and becomes very famous. The whole family is very proud of him.

Molina, R. (2002). *Titoy's magical chair [Ang madyik silya ni Titoy]*. Quezon City, Philippines: Adarna House.

Here comes Titoy's Magical Chair! Watch it turn into a car, an airplane, or a train. Travel with it and find out how a boy overcame his disability with the help of his playful imagination.

Spyri, J. (1919). *Heidi*. Philadelphia: J. B. Lippincott Company.

A Swiss orphan is heartbroken when she must leave her beloved grandfather and their happy home in the mountains to go to school and care for an invalid girl in the city.

Books on Tape

Hinton, S. E. (2000). *The outsiders*. Santa Ana, CA: Books on Tape.

Three brothers struggle to stay together after their parents' death, as they search for an identity among the conflicting values of their adolescent society in which they find themselves "outsiders."

Lobel, A. (2004). *Frog and Toad audio collection*. New York: HarperCollins.

The stories *Frog and Toad Are Friends, Frog and Toad All Year, Frog and Toad Together,* and *Days With Frog and Toad* are available in this collection. Frog and Toad are pals whose every adventure is filled with the magic of true friendship, whether they're telling ghost stories, searching for a lost button, or eating too many cookies.

Lowry, L. (2000). *The giver*. Santa Ana, CA: Books on Tape, Inc.

Given his lifetime assignment at the Ceremony of Twelve, Jonas becomes the receiver of memories shared by only one other in his community and discovers the terrible truth about the society in which he lives. This 12-year-old boy ends up with a gradual disillusionment with an outwardly utopian futuristic society.

Rowling, J. K. (2007). *Harry Potter CD collection.* New York: Random House Audio Publishing Group.

Harry Potter, a young wizard, and his eager companions, Hermione Granger and Ron Weasley, engage in this fantastic world of wizards and muggles, ghosts and trolls, and good and evil.

Twain, M. (1977). *Adventures of Huckleberry Finn.* Santa Ana, CA: Books on Tape.

This novel is about the adventures of a boy and a runaway slave as they travel down the Mississippi River on a raft.

White, E. B. (2002). *Charlotte's web.* New York: Random House Audio Publishing Group.

This is the timeless story of the pig named Wilbur and the wise spider named Charlotte who saved him.

REFERENCES

Browne, T. (n.d.) *Letter from the director.* Retrieved December 7, 2009, from http://en.childrens library.org/about/letter.shtml

Krashen, S. (2002). Accelerated reader: Does it work? If so, why? *School Libraries in Canada, 22,* 24–26.

Mangelson, J., & Castek, J. (2007). *Thinking outside the book: Online resources that make reading fun.* American Library Association. Retrieved December 9, 2009, from http://docs.google.com/viewer?a=v&q=cache:1zrz9zVdulwJ:www.pla.org/ala/aboutala/ offices/publishing/booklinks/resources/thinkingoutsidethebook.pdf+Book+Links+Mang elson+%26+Castek,+2007&hl=en&gl=us&sig=AHIEtbTKnbIKzVU40rUO-P3u YmK_LxTP6Q

Media Awareness Network. (2005). *Young Canadians in a wired world.* Retrieved November 3, 2009, from http://www.media-awareness.ca/english/research/YCWW/ index.cfm

Glossary

Anti-Bias Education/Curriculum: This grew out of the basic philosophy of multicultural education, although its scope includes any forms of bias, stereotyping, and misrepresentation. Anti-bias education is said to go further than simply race and ethnicity studies and includes gender, language, religious diversity, sexual orientation, physical and mental abilities, and economic class. Anti-bias education takes a critical literacy approach, which is an active, problem-solving approach that is integrated into all aspects of an existing curriculum and a school's environment. An anti-bias curriculum promotes an understanding of social problems and provides students with strategies for improving social conditions (Derman-Sparks and the A.B.C. Task Force, 1989).

Children's Literature: Specific books that are written for children as the main target audience. Deals with issues that children may face, can relate to, and identify with, and it reflects children's experiences. Usually has characters that are children, but it may also have animals, inanimate objects, fantastical creatures, and adults. These come in a variety of genres, like picture books, poetry, traditional tales, historical fiction, realistic fiction, science fiction, and so on, the most popular of which are picture books.

Critical Literacy: The process of becoming "literate" about a society or group through questioning, through seeing things from various viewpoints, through uncovering biases and reading "between the lines," through critically analyzing the workings of that society historically and culturally, in order to thrive in it. Although there are several ways to define critical literacy depending on the approach one takes or the field in which it is used, the theoretical basis for this term is founded on Paulo Freire's pedagogy. In the United States, the term is embedded in critical pedagogy and can be traced back to Freire's *Pedagogy of the Oppressed* (1970), in which he calls for a pedagogy that empowers people to take action against oppression mainly by larger entities such as politics, government, and society. The term has also evolved to include the ways in which language is a social construct that is used culturally to control, manipulate, and limit. One has to critically analyze the texts (in their broadest sense) produced through language in order to comprehend and understand these in their contexts.

Culturally Conscious: The critical awareness of one's own culture, cultural identities, cultural positions, and the role these play in the everyday actions and behaviors that one engages in, including interactions in the classroom.

Culturally Responsive Pedagogy/Approach: Grounded in the ideological foundations of multicultural education in general, and effective classroom practices in particular, culturally responsive pedagogy is a broad approach to successful and democratic teaching and learning practices with students. It draws its theoretical bases from multicultural education based on the concepts of equity in education as explained by Banks and Banks (1995a, 1995b) and Banks (1999). One study (Nel, 1995) attributes Erickson's (1986) "cultural difference theory" as directly having given rise to this term, whereas others, like those of Wlodkowski and Ginsberg (1995), Nawang (1998), Leavell, Cowart, and Wilhelm (1999), Gay (2000), Hollins and Oliver (1999), and Irvine and Armento (2001), use this term as a broad concept of reflective, democratic practices in teaching and learning, especially with, but not exclusively for, students who come from culturally diverse backgrounds. In fact, Irvine and Armento (2001) make no distinction between multicultural pedagogy and culturally *responsive* pedagogy (p. 4). Viewed in this way, culturally *responsive* teaching is, they write, "*responding to* or reacting appropriately to or being sensitive to culturally diverse students" (Irvine & Armento, 2001, p. 4; emphasis in original) so that teaching "uses the cultural knowledge, prior experiences, frames of reference and performance styles of ethnically diverse students" (Gay, 2000, p. 29).

Cultural Pluralism: When many distinct but smaller cultural groups coexist within a larger society and maintain their unique identities. After the civil rights movement, rather than a universal view of "we are all the same," that the United States is a "melting pot" of different cultures, came the view that, in fact, the different cultures need not lose their distinctness and can coexist together, a "salad bowl" metaphor. Cultural pluralism grew out of this view.

Cultural Relevance/Culturally Relevant Teaching: This is also grounded in multicultural education; however, it branches out specifically from excellent and successful practices of teaching and learning, particularly with African American students, and it is termed culturally *relevant* teaching. Popularized by Ladson-Billings (1990, 1992, 1994, 1995a, 1995b), this term has been used in relation to mainly African American students and teachers who use this pedagogy for successful teaching and learning practices *for* African American students. Ladson-Billings (1994, 1995b) especially mentions that this view is invested in "Afrocentric feminist epistemology" following Patricia Hill Collins's work. Foster (1995, 1997) and Byrd, Lundeberg, Hoffland, Couillard, and Lee (1996) also use this term specifically in terms of African American students and teachers who practice successful methods. Ladson-Billings (1992, 1994, 1995a, 1995b) explains that there are three main points that culturally *relevant* teaching emphasizes. These are academic achievement for all students, cultural competence, and critical consciousness or social political consciousness. In my review of studies that use either the term "culturally *relevant*" or "culturally *responsive*," I found that they emphasize many similar principles, although they *focus* on different philosophical aspects. Studies that use the term *relevant* are based on successful teachers and teaching of African American students and emphasize the importance of making teaching culturally relevant *for* students; however, they do not identify it as *exclusively* for African Americans. Studies that use the term *responsive* emphasize care and sensitivity *to* students' cultural difference and diversity.

Educational Drama: An inquiry method through which any topic may be learned and understood by putting ourselves "in the shoes" of the person, perspective, or event (Heathcote & Bolton, 1995). This approach is very different from improvisation, role-play, or creative dramatics, as there are no formal or informal presentations, performances, or practice. Rather it uses teaching principles that encourage students to think from within a situation.

Historical Fiction: Very similar to realistic fiction, except that it is set in an actual time period before the present time. As it is set in an actual past time period, the story must adhere to what happened historically during that time. However, the characters and situations could be fictional. Extensive research into the accurate portrayal of the time period is essential to this genre. This genre was specifically generated as a means to teach children history and historical facts in an interesting and engaging manner. Therefore, most protagonists are children and the stories are told from a child's perspective. Historical fiction is sometimes controversial in that it may bring up issues that were previously ignored or glossed over for children. The Newbery award may also be given for historical fiction.

Modern Fantasy: Children's books that have a few fantastical elements but the characters, time period, setting, and story are contemporary and realistic. Modern fantasy can further be divided into high fantasy and low fantasy depending on the amount of fantastical elements the story uses. High fantasy takes place in a secondary created world whereas low fantasy takes place in the recognizable world of every day but with some quirky differences.

Multicultural Children's Literature: Books that represent the sociocultural experiences of previously underrepresented groups of people. Books whose themes, language, characters, illustrations, and content validate these groups' experiences, including those experiences occurring because of differences in language, race, gender, class, ethnicity, identity, religion, and sexual orientation. There are two common approaches to Multicultural Children's Literature: the race and ethnicity approach and the sociocultural experiences approach. In this book, we take the sociocultural experiences approach. Some experts also include international literature under this category.

Picture Books: Often considered the main genre of children's books, over the years these have evolved into complex art works that sometimes may stand alone as pieces of art. Although it is rather hard to define a picture book, a simple explanation could be any book that has pictures and may have text in which the pictures and text contribute to the comprehension of the story. Neither the pictures nor the text alone could tell the story; rather they must blend together to form meaning. The unique thing about this genre is that the content could be of any other genre, that is, it could be realistic, historical, biographical, informational, or traditional, or it may be poetry, a fantasy tale, or even a graphic book (a throwback to the comic books of old times, except it is done through graphics). The Caldecott award is given each year to an exemplary illustrator of children's books.

Poetry: Any verse that is written with an emotional touch to it. It may include rhyme, rhythm, vivid imagery, differences in perspectives, insights, and so on. Over the years, poetry for children has evolved from simple rhymes to deep symbolic phrases that include music, art, and drama. Since 1977, the National Council for Teachers of English gives the Award for Excellence in Poetry for Children, an award to a children's author who writes poetry for children. Currently, these awards are given every other year.

Reader-Response Theories: The branch of literary theory that concentrates primarily on readers and their experiences rather than the text, the author, or the content of the work. Rosenblatt (1938) is credited with being one of the first to say that the meaning a text has depends primarily on the reader and the transaction that the reader has with the text, and not on the author or on the text. This was a radical view, because for the first time the reader was an active agent who imparted meaning to the text. This meant that the meaning of a text was not fixed by the author's intention or the words in the text; rather it can change with each reader. Over the course of the 20th century, especially in the latter decades, reader-response theories concentrated on various aspects of the readers' experiences as they played out in terms of readers' life experiences and their stances, including sociocultural aspects such as gender, race, class, and so on. Over the last several decades, reader-response techniques have become very useful in helping teachers create constructive classrooms. Reader responses allow teachers to help students become part of the dynamic process of experiencing reading through connections, hypothesizing, explorations, and so on. Most importantly, reader response allows students to become active learners, bringing their own cultural interpretations to the reading and thereby helping them understand other cultural positions in the readings.

Realistic Fiction: Books that are written about real issues, real people, and their dilemmas, conflicts, and resolutions. The setting and plot are also realistic, recognizable as if it could happen or is happening in a current time period. There are no exaggerations, fantasy, animal talk, or anything that is out of the ordinary or outside the realm of reality. This genre is different from biographies in that the stories are fictional. Each year, since 1922, the Newbery award is given to an author who writes exemplary realistic fiction.

Science Fiction: This is a subcategory of fantasy; however, the major distinction is that it is inspired by the possible theoretical and scientific concepts that are not practically possible today but may be possible in the future.

Traditional Tales or Traditional Literature: This is the body of stories and poems that came to us by oral transmission and whose authors are unknown. Traditional stories and poems had to have clear structures, plots, rhymes, or rhythms to be remembered and invite participation. With no system of recording but the human memory, traditional literature had to be memorable, so it relied on catchy patterns of plot and language. Folktales and fairy tales are the best known forms of traditional tales, although there are others such as legends, myths, fables, epics, and so on.

REFERENCES

Banks, J. A. (1999). *An introduction to multicultural education.* Needham Heights, MA: Allyn & Bacon.

Banks, J. A., & Banks, C. M. (1995a). Equity pedagogy: An essential component of multicultural education. *Theory Into Practice, 34*(3), 153–165.

Banks, J. A., & Banks, C. M. (1995b). *Handbook of research on multicultural education.* New York: Macmillan.

Byrd, J., Lundeberg, M. A., Hoffland, S. C., Couillard, E. L., & Lee, M. S. (1996). Caring, cognition, and cultural pluralism: Case studies of urban teachers. *Urban Education, 31*(4), 432–452.

Derman-Sparks, L., & the A.B.C. Task Force. (1989). *Anti-bias curriculum: Tools for empowering young children.* Washington, DC: National Association for the Education of Young Children.

Erickson, F. (1986). Qualitative methods in research on teaching. In M. C. Wittrock (Ed.), *Handbook of research on teaching* (pp. 119–161). New York: Macmillan.

Foster, M. (1995). African American teachers and culturally relevant pedagogy. In J. A. Banks & C. M. Banks (Eds.), *Handbook of research on multicultural education* (pp. 570–581). New York: Macmillan.

Foster, M. (1997). (Ed.). *Black teachers on teaching.* New York: The New Press.

Freire, P. (1970). *Pedagogy of the oppressed.* New York: Continuum Publishing.

Gay, G. (2000). *Culturally responsive teaching: Theory, research & practice.* New York: Teachers College Press.

Heathcote, D., & Bolton, G. (1995). *Drama for learning.* Portsmouth, NH: Heinemann.

Hollins, E. R., & Oliver, E. I. (Eds.). (1999). *Pathways to success in school: Culturally responsive teaching.* Mahwah, NJ: Lawrence Erlbaum.

Irvine, J. J., & Armento, B. J. (2001). *Culturally responsive teaching: Lesson planning for elementary and middle grades.* New York: McGraw-Hill.

Ladson-Billings, G. (1990). Like lightning in a bottle: Attempting to capture the pedagogical excellence of successful teachers of Black students. *International Journal of Qualitative Studies in Education, 3,* 335–344.

Ladson-Billings, G. (1992). Culturally relevant teaching: The key to making multicultural education work. In C. A. Grant (Ed.), *Research and multicultural education* (pp. 106–121). London: Falmer Press.

Ladson-Billings, G. (1994). *The dreamkeepers: Successful teachers of African American children.* San Francisco: Jossey-Bass.

Ladson-Billings, G. (1995a). But that's just good teaching! The case for culturally relevant pedagogy. *Theory Into Practice, 34*(3), 159–165.

Ladson-Billings, G. (1995b). Toward a theory of culturally relevant pedagogy. *American Educational Research Journal, 32*(3), 465–491.

Ladson-Billings, G. (2001). *Teaching and cultural competence: What does it take to be successful in a diverse classroom?* Retrieved November 3, 2009, from http://www.rethinkingschools.org

Leavell, A. G., Cowart, M., & Wilhelm, R. W. (1999). Strategies for preparing culturally responsive teachers. *Equity & Excellence in Education, 32*(1), 64–71.

Nawang, P. (1998, April 13–17). *The magic of culturally responsive pedagogy: In search of the genie's lamp in multicultural education.* Paper presented at the meeting of the AERA, San Diego, CA.

Nel, J. (1995). From theory to practice: Ogbu and Erickson in the multicultural education curriculum. *Action in Teacher Education, 27*(1), 60–69.

Rosenblatt, L. (1938). *Literature as exploration.* New York: Appleton-Century.

Villegas, A. M. (1991). *Culturally responsive pedagogies for the 1990s and beyond* (Trends and Issues Paper No. 6). Washington, DC: American Association of Colleges for Teacher Education.

Wlodkowski, R. J., & Ginsberg, M. B. (1995). *Diversity and motivation: Culturally responsive teaching.* San Francisco: Jossey-Bass.

Index

About the Author

Ambika Gopalakrishnan is an associate professor in the Division of Curriculum and Instruction at the Charter College of Education at California State University, Los Angeles (CSULA). Gopal, as she is called at CSULA, received her PhD in Educational Studies from Ohio State University, specializing in educational drama and children's literature. On joining CSULA, she rejuvenated two programs in the College of Education to include storytelling, children's literature, and educational drama. She has designed and regularly teaches courses on storytelling for teachers, and she also teaches an introductory class on multicultural children's literature. Gopal redesigned a graduate seminar on trends and issues in the use of children's literature, and this book is based on this unique course, which is a requirement in many graduate programs at the Charter College of Education. She has published articles on storytelling, educational drama, and children's literature, and presented at national and international conferences. Currently, she coordinates and advises in the program that she designed: Master's in Education, with an option in Creative Literacies and Literature.

About the Contributing Author

Kimberly Persiani-Becker, EdD, is an Associate Professor at CSULA in Curriculum and Instruction and the author of *The Organizd Teacher, The Creative Teacher, The Festive Teache,* and *The Master Teacher.* She is dedicated to teacher education and preparing teacher candidates for a career in urban school environments. Kimberly teaches courses in Multicultural Children's Literature, Classroom Management and Discipline, as well as English Language Acquisition. She enjoys attending conferences related to children and young adult fiction, and teacher-education-related workshops. Her current area of interest is learning about and working with children with special needs and the gifted.

Supporting researchers for more than 40 years

Research methods have always been at the core of SAGE's publishing program. Founder Sara Miller McCune published SAGE's first methods book, *Public Policy Evaluation*, in 1970. Soon after, she launched the *Quantitative Applications in the Social Sciences* series—affectionately known as the "little green books."

Always at the forefront of developing and supporting new approaches in methods, SAGE published early groundbreaking texts and journals in the fields of qualitative methods and evaluation.

Today, more than 40 years and two million little green books later, SAGE continues to push the boundaries with a growing list of more than 1,200 research methods books, journals, and reference works across the social, behavioral, and health sciences. Its imprints—Pine Forge Press, home of innovative textbooks in sociology, and Corwin, publisher of PreK–12 resources for teachers and administrators—broaden SAGE's range of offerings in methods. SAGE further extended its impact in 2008 when it acquired CQ Press and its best-selling and highly respected political science research methods list.

From qualitative, quantitative, and mixed methods to evaluation, SAGE is the essential resource for academics and practitioners looking for the latest methods by leading scholars.

For more information, visit **www.sagepub.com**.

Printed in the USA
CPSIA information can be obtained
at www.ICGtesting.com
CBHW061208030124
2918CB00012B/2